Praise for *The Book of J:*

"Like Shakespeare, Bloom's J is a pioneer who is uniquely aware of her characters' psychological complexity, and whose genius is not bound by the genres available in her culture. She welds together all the available genres to make a prose poem, neither epic nor romance nor tragedy nor comedy yet all these at once. She stands at the beginning of the Hebrew narrative tradition, but like Homer she is greater than all who come after her. . . . *The Book of J* should be read by students of general literature and of the Bible alike."

—John Barton, *The New York Review of Books*

"David Rosenberg's bold new translation of *The Book of J* . . . .is especially alert to the abundant wordplay and the elliptical nature of the text. . . . Rosenberg's innovative translation struggles to re-create J's distinctive voice, a tone of modulated ironic grandeur . . . words echoing within words." —Edward Hirsch, *The New Yorker*

"With the publication and surprising best-sellerhood of *The Book of J*, in which he argues that the original author of the Old Testament was a woman, Bloom argues a lot of other things, too, but that's the part that landed him on *Good Morning America*. It's an ironic fate for a man who . . . is the source of new thought in criticism and in literature itself." —Louise Kennedy, *The Boston Globe*

"Rosenberg's translation, which is clear, lean, skillful, and earthy, is the kind of translation that both honors the character of Hebrew rhetoric and serves Bloom's purposes well. . . . On the close reading, Bloom is masterful. When one sifts through the polemics, Bloom does indeed show us much about this Jewish God."

—Walter Brueggemann, *Theology Today*

"An illuminating attempt to liberate the origins of the Bible . . . a classic of translation." —Greil Marcus, *California Magazine*

The Book of J

THE BOOK
OF J

TRANSLATED FROM

THE HEBREW BY

David Rosenberg

INTERPRETED BY

Harold Bloom

GROVE PRESS
New York

Printed in the United States of America
Published simultaneously in Canada

FIRST GROVE PRESS PAPERBACK EDITION

Library of Congress Cataloging-in-Publication Data

Bible. O.T. Pentateuch. English. Rosenberg. Selections. 1990.
The book of J/David Rosenberg & Harold Bloom.
Translation by D. Rosenberg of the portions of the Pentateuch
which derive from the so-called J document, with introd. and
commentary by H. Bloom.
ISBN 0-8021-4191-9
1. J document (Biblical criticism) 2. Bible. O.T. Pentateuch—
Criticism, interpretation, etc. I. Rosenberg, David. II. Bloom,
Harold. III. Title.
BS1223 1990 222'.105209—dc20 90-37391

Grove Press
an imprint of Grove/Atlantic, Inc.
841 Broadway
New York, NY 10003

05 06 07 08 09 10 9 8 7 6 5 4 3 2 1

For Moshe Idel

Contents

Acknowledgments

My share in this book is indebted to John Hollander, Michael Dietz, Joy Beth Lawrence, Barry Qualls, and to Aaron Asher and Joy Johannessen, my editors.
      —H.B.

I wish to acknowledge the support I received at crucial junctures from Grace Schulman, Susan Pensak, Alba Arikha, Walter Brown, and Sanford Rosenberg. I am grateful for the refuge of The Writer's Room, and to Lewis Warsh, for the first push. Aaron Asher, Joy Johannessen, Lew Grimes, and Lynn Nesbit nurtured with great skill. Finally, credit is due the Jewish Publication Society, for stimulating the critical questions about translation: my work on the Book of J began during my tenure as editor in chief.
      —D.R.

The Author J

HAROLD BLOOM

Preface on Names and Terms

THE HEBREW BIBLE, of which the Book of J is the origin, ought not to be confused with the Christian Bible, which is founded upon it, but which amounts to a very severe revision of the Bible of the Jews. The Jews call their Holy Scriptures Tanakh, an acronym for the three parts of the Bible: Torah (the Teaching, or Law, also known as the Five Books of Moses, or Pentateuch); Nevi'im (the Prophets); and Kethuvim (the Writings). Christians call the Hebrew Bible the Old Testament, or Covenant, in order to supersede it with their New Testament, a work that remains altogether unacceptable to Jews, who do not regard their Covenant as Old and therefore superseded. Since Christians are obliged to go on calling Tanakh the Old Testament, I myself suggest that Jewish critics and readers might speak of their Scriptures as the Original Testament, and the Christian work as the Belated Testament, for that, after all, is what it is, a revisionary work that attempts to replace a book, Torah, with a man, Jesus of Nazareth, proclaimed as the Messiah of the House of David by Christian believers.

Biblical scholars use "Israelite" (as distinguished from "Israeli," meaning a citizen of the post-1947 state of Israel) to refer to the people of ancient Israel down to the Return from Babylonian Exile. "The Jews" are thus the Israelites from the Return until the present moment. "Jew" comes from the Hebrew *yehudi*, meaning a Judahite, or Judean, a descendant of Judah, who was Jacob's (Israel's) fourth son and heir, the historical carrier of the Blessing of Yahweh, first given to Abram (Abraham). "Hebrews" tends not to be used anymore for the ancient Israelites; "Hebrew" refers to what is now the language of contemporary Israel, and to what was, in its ancient form, the Old Canaanite language of the Bible.

The Christian Old Testament is arranged differently from the Hebrew Bible, and that makes a considerable difference. The first five books of this very mixed work, Scripture, follow the same order in the two faiths but take different names. It is always worth remembering that the word "bible" suggests diversity, since it comes from *ta biblia,* Greek for "the books." "Pentateuch" as a name derives from a Greek term, *hê pentateuchos biblos,* meaning "the book of the five scrolls." The Christian Genesis is the Hebrew Bereshith, "In the Beginning," following the Hebrew Bible's frequent practice of naming a book after its opening words or first crucial term. Thus, the Christian Exodus is the Hebrew Shemoth, "Names," while Leviticus is the stirring Wayiqra, "And He Called." Even better is the Hebrew title for Numbers: Bemidbar, "In the Wilderness." The resounding Deuteronomy has the terser and more accurate Debarim, "Words."

After Torah, or Pentateuch, there is little in common between the Jewish and Christian ordering. What is most worth noting is that the Christian Old Testament ends with the latecomer prophet Malachi, proclaiming a new appearance of Elijah, who in Christian typology is seen as the forerunner of John the Baptist. But the Hebrew Bible ends with 2 Chronicles, so that the final word is given to the Return to Jerusalem and the rebuilding of Solomon's Temple: "Any one of you of all His people, the Lord his God be with him and let him go up."

The reader ought to remember also that the division of the Hebrew Bible into chapters and verses is purely arbitrary and does not reflect the intentions of the original authors. Jewish exegetes divided up the verses in a long process that was not concluded until the ninth century C.E. ("of the common era," equivalent to A.D. in

Christian parlance), while the chapter divisions were made by Christian editors of the thirteenth century.

"The Book of J" is used here as the title for what scholars agree is the oldest strand in the Pentateuch, probably composed at Jerusalem in the tenth century B.C.E. ("before the common era," or "before Christ," as Christians traditionally say). J stands for the author, the Yahwist, named for Yahweh (Jahweh, in the German spelling; Jehovah, in a misspelling), God of Jews, Christians, and Muslims. The later strands in Genesis, Exodus, and Numbers are all revisions or censorings of J, and their authors are known as E, or the Elohist, for "Elohim," the plural name used for Yahweh in that version (J always uses "Elohim" as a name for divine beings in general, and never as the name of God); P, for the Priestly Author or School that wrote nearly all of Leviticus; D, for the author or authors of Deuteronomy; and R, for the Redactor, who performed the final revision after the Return from Babylonian Exile.

The name "Abram" in J means "exalted father"; the now more familiar "Abraham," which means "father of a host of nations," was introduced by P.

Chronology

c. 400	The Redactor (JEPD)
c. 250–100	The Septuagint
c. 90	Canonization of the Hebrew Bible completed

C.E.

c. 400	Saint Jerome's Latin Vulgate translation of the Bible
1530	William Tyndale's Pentateuch
1534	Luther's Bible (Old Testament)
1535	Miles Coverdale's Bible
1560	Geneva Bible (Shakespeare's Bible)
1611	King James (Authorized) Version
1952	Revised Standard Version
1966	Jerusalem Bible (Catholic)
1970	New English Bible (Protestant)
1982	New American Jewish Version

INTRODUCTION

IN JERUSALEM, nearly three thousand years ago, an unknown author composed a work that has formed the spiritual consciousness of much of the world ever since. We possess only a fragmentary text of that work, embedded within what we call Genesis, Exodus, and Numbers, three of the divisions of Torah, or the Five Books of Moses. Since we cannot know the circumstances under which the work was composed, or for what purposes, ultimately we must rely upon our experience as readers to justify our surmises as to what it is that we are reading. Scholarship, however deeply grounded, can reach no agreement upon the dating of what I am calling the Book of J, or upon its surviving dimensions, or even upon whether it ever had an independent existence at all.

For reasons that I will expound, I am assuming that J lived at or nearby the court of Solomon's son and successor, King Rehoboam of Judah, under whom his father's kingdom fell apart soon after the death of Solomon in 922 B.C.E. My further assumption is that J was not a professional scribe but rather an immensely sophisticated, highly placed member of the Solomonic elite, enlightened and ironic. But my primary surmise is that J was a woman, and that she wrote for her contemporaries as a woman, in friendly competition with her only strong rival among those contemporaries, the male author of the court history narrative in 2 Samuel. Since I am aware that my vision of J will be condemned as a fancy or a fiction, I will begin by pointing out that all our accounts of the Bible are scholarly fictions or religious fantasies, and generally serve rather tendentious purposes. In proposing that J was a woman, at least I will not be furthering the interests of any religious or ideological group. Rather, I will be attempting to account, through my years of reading experience, for my increasing sense of the astonishing differences between J and every other biblical writer.

Feminist literary critics curiously condemn as what they term "essentialism" any attempt to describe particular literary characteristics as female rather than male. Surely feminist criticism should also exclude as "essentialism" every description of J's writing as possessing male characteristics. We simply do not know whether J was a man or a woman, but our moral imaginations can calculate the passage of possibilities into probabilities when we compare J to the other strands in Genesis, Exodus, Numbers, or when we compare J to all other extant literature of the ancient Middle East. What is new in J? Where do J's crucial originalities cluster? What is it about J's tone, stance, mode of narrative, that was a difference that made a difference? One large area of answer will concern the representation of women as compared with that of men; another will concern irony, which seems to me the element of style in the Bible that is still most often and most weakly misread, even by the latest-model literary critics of the Hebrew Bible.

Misunderstandings of J's irony have continued for two millennia and have produced the curious issue of "anthropomorphism," of J's representation of Yahweh as human-all-too-human. They have produced also the deadly issue of J's supposed misogyny and championing of "patriarchal religion." William Blake, in *The Marriage of Heaven and Hell,* taught us that a crucial aspect of religious history is the process of "choosing forms of worship from poetic tales." That historical irony remains so prevalent, in its consequences, that it continues to affect all our lives. Jimmy Carter, former president of the United States, recently chided

Salman Rushdie for meddling with the poetic tales of the Koran, and also denounced Martin Scorsese for his liberties with the poetic tales of the New Testament. I myself do not believe that the Torah is any more or less the revealed Word of God than are Dante's *Commedia*, Shakespeare's *King Lear*, or Tolstoy's novels, all works of comparable literary sublimity. Yet even I am shadowed by the residual aura of the Book of J, despite my conviction that the distinction between sacred and secular texts results from social and political decisions, and thus is not a literary distinction at all. Because the peculiar status of the Bible, from at least the Return of Israel from Babylonian Exile on to the present day, is the decisive factor in the misreading of J, I must begin by speculating upon whether it is at all possible to recover the Book of J, even on my own rather free premises of imaginative surmise.

How does one begin to read more severely a writer whose work one has been misreading, necessarily and rather weakly, all of one's life? The investment, societal and individual, in the institutionalized misreading of J is extraordinarily comprehensive, since it is divided among Jews, Christians, Muslims, and members of the secular culture. There are profound reasons for not regarding the Bible as a literary text comparable to *Hamlet* and *Lear*, the *Commedia*, the *Iliad*, the poems of Wordsworth, or the novels of Tolstoy. Believers and historians alike clearly are justified in finding the Bible rather more comparable to the Koran or the Book of Mormon. But what if one is neither a believer nor a historian? Or what if one is a believer, of some degree or kind, and yet still a reader, unable or unwilling to keep reminding oneself that the pages one reads are sacred or holy, at least to millions of others? If one is an Orthodox Jew, then one believes the marvelous fiction that the historical Moses wrote Genesis, Exodus, and Numbers, so that J never existed. J, whether female or male, may be a fiction also, but a less irrational fiction than the author Moses.

Religion can be the greatest of blessings or the greatest of curses. Historically it seems to have been both. There are myriads more Christians and Muslims than there are Jews, which means that the Hebrew Bible as such is more important in its revised form as the Old Testament than it can now be as itself. And there are many more normative Jews, few as they are compared with Christians and Muslims, than there are secular readers, Gentile and Jewish, who are prepared to read the Bible in something like the same spirit in which they read Shakespeare. This means that the Five Books of Moses, that grand work of the Redactor, are more important than the Book of J. And yet, whether we speak of the Hebrew Bible or of the Old Testament, we are speaking of a work that takes as its original the writing of J. And that returns me to the profound reason for regarding the Bible as a library of literary texts, which to me and many other readers it must be. Yahweh, in transmogrified forms, remains the God of the Children of Abraham, of believing Jews, Christians, and Muslims. But Yahweh, in the Book of J, *is a literary character,* just as Hamlet is. If the history of religion is the process of choosing forms of worship from poetic tales, in the West that history is even more extravagant: it is the worship, in greatly modified and revised forms, of an extraordinarily wayward and uncanny literary character, J's Yahweh. Churches are founded upon metaphors, such as rocks and crosses, but the Western worship of God is in one sense more astonishing than the foundation of any church. The original Yahweh of the Bible, J's, is a very complex and troublesome extended metaphor or figure of speech and thought. So is Hamlet. But we do not pray to Hamlet, or invoke him when we run for political office, or justify our opposition to abortion by appealing to him.

I am neither a believer nor a historian, but the dilemma I cite seems to me as much theirs as mine. Why does Yahweh attempt to murder Moses? How can God sit under the terebinth trees at Mamre and devour roast calf and curds? What can we do with a Supreme Being who goes nearly berserk at Sinai and warns us he may break forth against the crowds, who clearly fill him with great distaste? As I insist throughout this book, J is anything but a naive writer; she is rather the most sophisticated of authors, as knowing as Shakespeare or Jane Austen. I am frightened by the ironies of belief and of history when I contemplate the enormous differences between J's Yahweh and the God of Judaism, Christianity, and Islam, and indeed the God of the scholars and literary critics, both sectarian and secular. We, whoever we are, have been formed in part by strong misreadings of J. This is as it must be, but is there not value in returning to J, insofar as it can be done? The return may produce only another misreading, strong or weak, but the spirit of that misreading can be brought closer to what may have been J's own strong misreading of an archaic Jewish religion, or if not a religion, then a body of traditions and stories.

The largest assumption of nearly all writers on the Bible is that it is a theological work, as well as historical and literary. J was no theologian, and rather deliberately not a historian. To call J the composer of a national epic also seems to me misleading. Genre is an inoperative category when the strongest of authors are involved. Is Shakespeare's *Troilus and Cressida* a comedy or a tragedy, or is it an ancient history play, or a satirical romance of chivalry? All and none. The Book of J fits no genre, though it established whatever genre the authors of the E, P, and D texts sought to follow. J tells stories, portrays theomorphic men and women, links myth to history, and implicitly utters the greatest of moral prophecies to post-Solomonic Judah and Israel. Yet J is something other than a storyteller, a creator of personalities (human and divine), a national historian and prophet, or even an ancestor of the moral fictions of Wordsworth, George Eliot, and Tolstoy. There is always the other side of J: uncanny, tricky, sublime, ironic, a visionary of incommensurates, and so the direct ancestor of Kafka, and of any writer, Jewish or Gentile, condemned to work in Kafka's mode. This other side of J will receive the largest share of my exegesis, because it is this antithetical element that all normative traditions—Judaic, Christian, Islamic, secular—have been unable to assimilate, and so have ignored, or repressed, or evaded.

Many contemporary literary critics of the highest distinction have turned their labors of cognition and description upon the

Bible, but almost without exception they chose to deal not with J but with R, the triumphant Redactor, who seems to have been of the Academy of Ezra, insofar as it existed. To that diverse company of eminent readers—Northrop Frye, Frank Kermode, Robert Alter, and Geoffrey Hartman among them—the Bible is the received Bible of the normative traditions. Perhaps there can be no other Bible, in which case my attempt at a literary analysis of the Book of J is bound to be a failed experiment. But Frye's Bible is the Protestant Bible, in which the Hebrew Scriptures dwindle down to that captive prize of the Gentiles, the Old Testament. Kermode, shrewdest of empiricists, reads what is available to an objective scrutiny. Alter reads a work of "composite artistry," in which the artist is the Redactor, masterfully blending his somewhat incompatible sources. Hartman, questing after some shred of the normative garment, holds on fiercely to what he can, as though revisionism at last must touch its limit. Somewhere is such a kingdom, but not in the Hebrew Bible, not here, not now. Nothing is more arbitrary than the endless misprisions of J, who has served nearly every purpose except those I believe to have been her own. The God of the Jews and the Christians, of the Muslims, of the secular scholars and critics, is not the Yahweh of J. What J portrays, with loving irony, is an archaic Judaism now largely lost to us, though to call it a Judaism at all is bound to be an error. I know of only two paths back to some acquaintance with that lost strangeness. One is the way of the Israeli scholar of Kabbalah, Moshe Idel, who finds in Kabbalah not a Gnosticism but the surviving elements of an archaic vision that the Gnostics parodied. The other, equally speculative, is to search the giant fragments of J's text for just those areas of fable and surmise that the normative tradition could accommodate only with unease, if at all. But by what authority can such a search be undertaken, and for what purpose? What use can it be to recover a hypothetical Book of J?

The allegorization of Homer by Alexandrian Neoplatonists and their heirs led eventually to the *Commedia* of Dante, though Dante never read Homer, who was hardly available to him. To recover J is to recover a great ironist, a revealer who works through the juxtaposing of incommensurates. Though I attempt throughout *not* to allegorize J but to seek her plain sense, I am aware that such a sense is unavailable to me. Presumably it was available to her contemporaries, so that we can find some clues to it in 2 Samuel, but it was lost forever by the time of the Deuteronomists, the Priestly Author, and the Redactor. Those who came after the Redactor read the Redactor, and explained away whatever of J could not be passed over in rabbinical silence. If J can be recovered, it must be by a reading that is partly outside every normative tradition whatsoever, or if inevitably inside, however unwillingly, then inside with a considerable difference. What matters most about J is what is sublime or uncanny, which can be recovered only by a criticism alert to the vagaries of the Sublime. But that returns us to the center of reading J: what are we to do about J's Yahweh, the uncanniest of all Western metaphors?

Jews, Christians, Muslims, and secularists fortunately are now less touchy about God than Jews are about Moses, Christians about Jesus, Muslims about Muhammad, and secularists about the idol they call Objectivity. Yahweh is less a personal possession, even for fundamentalist American Protestants, than Jesus is, and no one, in any case, is going to be tempted to make a film called *The Last Temptation of Yahweh,* or to write novels in which Yahweh appears as a travestied character. Safely transcendentalized, the Yahweh of normative tradition has become a kind of gaseous vapor, fit only for representation through the resources of science fiction. J's Yahweh is quite another story, an imp who behaves sometimes as though he is rebelling against his Jewish mother, J. Like J herself, we ought always to be prepared to be surprised by him, which is the only way we can avoid being surprised.

No one in the West can now hope to read the Bible without having been conditioned by it, or by the various misreadings it has engendered. Throughout my commentary on the Book of J, I have tried to keep in mind certain observations by Ralph Waldo Emerson, founder of the American Religion, which is post-Christian yet somehow also Protestant, or shall we say Protestant-Gnostic. Emerson, properly wary of those who convert the Bible into an idol, warned against mistaking the figure for the figuration of Jesus Christ, in a great sentence of "The Divinity School Address": "The idioms of his language and the figures of his rhetoric have usurped the place of his truth; and churches are not built on his principles, but on his tropes." Much the same can be said of Moses, or of Freud, or of many another founder. In two journal entries Emerson beautifully caught the double edge of what is now even more problematic about the Bible. In 1839 he wrote, "People imagine that the place which the Bible holds in the world, it owes to miracles. It owes it simply to the fact that it came out of a profounder depth of thought than any other book." And yet in 1865 the American sage remarked that "the Bible wears black cloth. It comes with a certain official claim against which the mind revolts." The two statements retain their force, and help define my own project for me. J's cognitive power is unmatched among Western writers until Shakespeare, yet J, converted to the official uses of the rabbis, priests, ministers, and their scholarly servants, is made to wear black cloth, hardly appropriate garb for that ironic and sophisticated lady (or enigmatic gentleman, if you would have it so).

I am aware that it may be vain labor, up Sinai all the way, as it were, to seek a reversal of twenty-five hundred years of institutionalized misreading, a misreading central to Western culture and society. Yet the Book of J, though fragmentary, is hardly Mr. David Rosenberg's creation or my own. All I have done is to remove the Book of J from its context in the Redactor's Torah and then to read what remains, which is the best and most profound writing in the Hebrew Bible. What emerges is an author not so much lost as barricaded from us by normative moralists and theologians, who had and have designs upon us that are altogether incompatible with J's vision.

ENFOLDING AN AUTHOR

A UNIVERSAL AUTHOR provokes highly contradictory responses, depending upon the student or reader. Political scientists read Shakespeare rather differently than I do, and these days Shakespeare is perpetually reduced by Foucault-inspired historicists who fold him back into his age, as though he were Thomas Kyd or John Marston and not the author of *Hamlet, King Lear, Othello,* and *Macbeth.* Similarly, J is read as a historian, a theologian, an antiquarian, or what you will, depending upon your own profession or inclination. Yet the Book of J is clearly not history, theology, or folktale collecting. A responsible recent study by a literary scholar, David Damrosch's *The Narrative Covenant* (1987), insists upon dividing J into several Yahwists, thus contravening Gerhard von Rad and Frank Moore Cross, who have assumed one Yahwist writing in the great age of what von Rad memorably dubbed the Solomonic Enlightenment, and probably writing at or under the sponsorship of the indubitably literary Solomonic royal court. For Damrosch, the extraordinary diversity and mixed genres of J's work make a single author seem unlikely.

> To take Genesis alone, the text actually contains not three epics but three very distinct literary forms: a creation-flood epic, a collection of oral sagas and saga cycles, a wisdom-oriented novella. To unite these materials would have seemed

even stranger to a tenth-century audience than the amalgamation of Hesiod and Homer would have seemed to eighth-century Greece. It is possible to imagine a later Alexandrian editor who might have tried to unify and harmonize the old Greek epics in such a manner. The result, however, would certainly have looked shapeless and unwieldy to the poets who crafted the original texts, and this is how "the Yahwistic epic" would have looked to any practitioner of Near Eastern epic. Here I am speaking only of the material in Genesis; the whole body of Yahwistic material in the Pentateuch would have presented an even stranger violation of known narrative forms.

It is little wonder that Damrosch goes on to envision the several scrolls of several Yahwists being combined by an editor centuries later. Yet the reply to Damrosch, himself a gifted representative of many biblical scholars, is that great originals among the world's strongest authors are precisely those who violate known forms. Doubtless J's work startled those to whom it was read in the tenth century B.C.E., but such startlement is an attribute of the strongest literature. Shakespeare wrote five-act dramas for stage presentation, yet Shakespeare wrote no genre. What, again, is *Troilus and Cressida*? It is comedy, history, tragedy, satire, yet none of those singly, and more than all of them together. What is Dante's *Commedia*? Is it an epic, a comedy, a spiritual autobiography, or a prophecy in the mode of the wild Joachim de Flora? J mixes everything available to her and produces a work so comprehensive and so universal that the entire Hebrew Bible, Greek New Testament, and Arabic Koran could be founded upon it. Scholars have a way of dividing up strong ancient works and assigning them to several authors, or to that curious scholarly fiction, an oral tradition. Recent critics of the French variety have joined in, cheerfully destroying what they regard as the capitalistic social myth of individual creativity. In sophisticated ways, they want to persuade us that a demiurgical "language" dictates and authors merely serve as a medium. We are left with poems without poets, narratives without narrators, with "the Yahwists" and "the *Iliad* poets." Still worse, sometimes we are left with the odd vision of committees, virtual congresses of scholars of orality who scamper about posting up mosaics such as the *Iliad* and the Book of J.

Somebody wrote the Book of J, using the Phoenician–Old Hebrew script, either marking a leather scroll with a dull knife or more likely writing in ink with a reed pen on a papyrus, with the sheets then glued together to make a scroll. We can think of J keeping her scrolls in one place but probably never making them into a composite unit. But these physically separate entities reflected a remarkably unified consciousness, not a bevy of Yahwists or a desultory network of legendary gossipers, but a single, magnificent mind, holding reality together in the grand, single image of Yahweh, whom we may call J's awakened imagination. This J is my fiction, most biblical scholars will insist, but then each of us carries about a Shakespeare or a Tolstoy or a Freud who is our fiction also. As we read any literary work, we necessarily create a fiction or metaphor of its author. That author is perhaps our myth, but the experience of literature partly depends upon that myth. For J, we have a choice of myths, and I boisterously prefer mine to that of the biblical scholars. I will put all my cards on the reader's desk here, face up. My J is a *Gevurah* ("great lady") of post-Solomonic court circles, herself of Davidic blood, who began writing her great work in the later years of Solomon, in close rapport and exchanging influences with her good friend the Court Historian, who wrote most of what we now call 2 Samuel.

If that is a sketch of my J, I must at this point locate J in the history of scholarly speculation upon the Hebrew Bible, a history already centuries old and likely never to culminate. In particular, I must deal with what scholars call the Documentary Hypothesis, which asserts the multiple authorship of the Five Books of Moses (I would call it the Authorial Hypothesis) and is largely associated with the nineteenth-century German master scholar Julius Wellhausen. In a way, questions of Pentateuchal authorship can be reduced to the formula "From Moses to Wellhausen"—an ironic descent almost worthy of J. Deuteronomy, composed centuries later than J, tells us that Moses wrote down a Torah, or Teaching, and perhaps on that basis Jewish and Christian opinion ascribed the authorship of the Five Books to a historical Moses. The formidable Umberto Cassuto, who rejected the Documentary Hypothesis, can be said to represent normative Jewish judgment in opening his *Commentary on the Book of Genesis* (1961) thus: "The purpose of the Torah . . . is to teach us that the whole world and all that it contains were created by the word of the One God, according to His will, which operates without restraint." That is the impressive language of normative trust in the Covenant, and it reminds us why Moses is still the author of the Five Scrolls for so many Christians and Jews. If the Five Scrolls indeed are divine instruction for you, whatever your belief, then I think it still poetically apt to regard Moses as their composer.

Though there were some earlier doubts through the ages, the superb materialist philosopher Thomas Hobbes seems to have been the first person to deny in print that we are reading Moses when we read the Five Books. Spinoza followed the path of Hobbes, as did some other speculators, but it was a trio of nineteenth-century German scholars who actually broke through to the realization of the different "sources" intermeshed in the Pentateuch, or Torah. Behind these three investigators was a direct precursor, W. M. L. De Wette, who established that Deuteronomy, the Fifth Book of Moses, was by a separate author (most would now say authors), distinct from the writers who mingled in the other books. Those writers had been established in the eighteenth century as the Elohist, or E, and the Yahwist, or J. Subsequently a third source was found and named P, for Priestly Author (or Authors), as priestly concerns dominated the texts in question. Readers may feel they are being tormented by a serving of alphabet soup, when after J, P, E, and D they are also called upon to remember R, for the Redactor or Redactors who put the Torah together, presumably in the time of Ezra.

The crucial nineteenth-century German biblical scholars were the triad Karl Heinrich Graf, Wilhelm Vatke, and Wellhausen, who died in 1918, and whose name has become synonymous with the Documentary (or Source) Hypothesis. Graf concentrated on establishing the temporal order of the sources, while Vatke worked to decide whether the sources represented earlier or later phases of the cult (as what we now call Judaism was in the time of J). Wellhausen combined both enterprises so as to render a supposedly clear portrait of the historical development of the religion of Israel. Unfortunately, these grand savants were all Hegelians, and like Hegel, they saw Israelite faith as a primitive preparation for the sublimities of the true religion, high-minded Christianity, a properly Germanic belief purged of gross Jewish vulgarities and superstitions. The idealist anti-Semitism of this biblical Hegelianism is almost enough to explain the strong resistance of normative Jewish scholars to the Documentary Hypothesis. But one can throw away all the anti-Semitic nonsense and hold on to what remains valuable in the Wellhausen theory. Most Jewish and secular scholars now join Christian exegetes in working with severely modified accounts of source study, though there remains very little agreement on the exact distribution or dating of sources.

I myself am wary of falling into the abyss of what Damrosch describes as the critic's "arbitrary plucking out of a convenient theory to support a preexisting literary judgment." "Preexisting" is the problematic word there; I have read the Hebrew Bible since I was a child, with the growing sense that there is a great authorial voice in Genesis, Exodus, and Numbers that is very much at variance with the composite voice all too frequently heard therein. My experience over half a century as a reader teaches me the authorial reality of J as against a frequently numbing context of communal or normative voices. I would grant Damrosch, or any scholar, that to recognize the tone or stance, the rhetorical art, of J does not tell one anything whatsoever about J's date of composition, which might be later than I guess it to be. But literary experience teaches one when an authorial voice is belated, and I hear in J an ever early freshness, long preceding all the other voices in the Pentateuch. That hardly dates J either, except to suggest on intuitive aesthetic grounds (of no interest to scholars) that J stands at the start of what the late E. A. Speiser liked to call "the Biblical Process." I can prove nothing; I can only invite other readers to the hypothesis that there is one J, and that she precedes any other substantial biblical writer, with the single exception of the Court Historian, who seems to me her contemporary.

The long, sad enterprise of revising, censoring, and mutilating J began with someone you can call the Elohist, if you want to, though I do not think that as an author he existed at all; more often than not, E strikes me as revised or censored J, doubtless with other material mixed in. If J finished writing at about 915 B.C.E., as I would guess, then the Elohistic revisionist could well have been at work about two generations later, in 850 B.C.E. or so. He combined J's text with a variety of material, doubtless from written sources that are now lost, reworked the Binding of Isaac and perhaps Jacob's wrestling with the angel, and so began the tradition of reducing the extraordinary J to something more normative. The Deuteronomists (two or three, at least) wrote about two hundred years later, focusing on the violent moment of King Josiah's puritan reform, 621 B.C.E. A generation later, after the fall of Jerusalem to Babylon in 587 B.C.E., the Priestly Authors began to compose an alternative text, comprising all of what is now Leviticus and the larger share of what is now Genesis, Exodus, Numbers. That labor of composition, by several hands, continued deep into the Exile. A redactor of undoubted genius, thought by some to be Ezra the Scribe, or at least a member of the putative Academy of Ezra, working soon after 458 B.C.E., produced the Torah probably pretty much as we have it now. This Redactor, a formidable fellow, has received very distinguished praise in our time, but I am afraid he is the villain of this book, since I am convinced that but for him we would have a much fuller Book of J. However, R can sustain my disesteem, for whatever it is worth. Franz Rosenzweig, the most eminent modern Jewish theologian, who with Martin Buber produced the grand German Jewish translation of the Hebrew Bible, observed that for him R was not merely the Redactor but *Rabbenu,* "our teacher." R is Robert Alter's "composite author" of the Torah, credited by Alter with a high aesthetic, novelistic intermin- gling of the J, E, D, and P texts. The most singular praise for R has come from the indubitably great critic Northrop Frye, who commended the pulverization of the various sources as being so thorough that we are totally unable to reconstitute any of them, J included. The Redactor certainly splintered imaginative literature for the sake of heaven, but J is not mocked with impunity. This book attempts a restoration of the greatest Jewish writer, for the writing's sake and for ours. What it will show is that the whole company of normativizing scribes and priests—E, D, P, R—performed a work of *avodah,* of service, to Yahweh, but not to that writer of genius, the Yahwist.

T H E   L O N G   H I S T O R Y   of what is called "the problem of anthropomorphism" brought about by J's depictions of Yahweh constitutes one of the curious cultural comedies of Western religious tradition. Embarrassment caused by the impishness of J's Yahweh presumably began with the early revisionists, attaining a first culmination with the work of the Redactor. But such puzzlement or resentment at the Yahwistic text became far more overt among the Jews of Hellenistic Alexandria during the last two centuries before the common era. Greek philosophy demanded a dehumanized divinity, and Jewish Hellenists rather desperately sought to oblige, by allegorizing away a Yahweh who walked and who argued, who ate and who rested, who possessed arms and hands, face and legs.

Philo of Alexandria, the founder of what I suppose must be called Jewish theology (which is the antithesis of J's lively vision), was particularly upset by J's Yahweh, since Philo's God had neither human desires nor a human form, and was incapable of passion, whether anger or love. But even the less Platonized great rabbis of second-century-C.E. Palestine tended to argue these same difficulties, as in the celebrated disputes between Akiba and his colleague Ishmael, who also followed allegorical procedures in order to expunge the anthropomorphic. Christian attacks upon Judaism, starting with Justin Martyr in the time of Akiba, insisted on the anthropomorphism of the Jews, and this suggestion that Judaism is theologically cruder and more primitive than Christianity survives even now in some Christian scholarship.

J's uncanny sophistication as a writer is so subtle and nuanced as to suggest Shakespearean dimensions to her irony. There is considerable social irony in portions of 2 Samuel, but nothing like the high, even exalted irony that is the continuous condition of the Book of J. It is at first disconcerting to realize that J is essentially a comic writer, not wholly as Chaucer is, but more in the difficult mode of Kafka, who seems to me the author closest to J's irony, undoubtedly because Kafka is the authentic inheritor of J's legacy among the Jewish writers of our own century. But what kind of irony is it that J and Kafka share, and why do we have so much difficulty in seeing that it is indeed irony, and not some other literary mode?

"Irony" goes back to the Greek word *eiron*, "dissembler," and our dictionaries still follow Greek tradition by defining irony first as Socratic: a feigned ignorance and humility designed to expose the inadequate assumptions of others, by way of skilled dialectical questioning. With this Platonic irony, J has no affinities, and we may put it aside here. Two broader senses of literary irony are also irrelevant to our reading of J: the use of language to express something other than supposedly literal meaning, particularly the opposite of such meaning, and also the contrast or gap between expectation and fulfillment. A touch closer to J is what we call dramatic irony or even tragic irony, which is the incongruity between what develops in a drama or narrative and the effect of what develops on adjacent words and actions that are more fully apprehended by the audience or readers than by the characters. J is a master of such irony, yet it tends to be one of her minor modes. Her major ironic stance is very different and must be regarded as her own invention.

What happens to representation when altogether incommensurate realities juxtapose and clash? How can Abram haggle with Yahweh? How is Jacob able to wrestle a nameless one among the

Elohim to a standstill, whether the angel be Michael, Sammael, or the messenger of death? Or far more starkly, how can we find it persuasive that the rough hunter Esau should barter his birthright for that celebrated mess of pottage? The catalogue could go on very extensively but would center finally upon the representation of Yahweh as at once human-all-too-human, even childlike, even childish, and yet Yahweh and none other, which is to say, wholly incommensurate even with himself.

J's attitude toward Yahweh resembles nothing so much as a mother's somewhat wary but still proudly amused stance toward a favorite son who has grown up to be benignly powerful but also eccentrically irascible. Such a stance feels ironic, but again, how are we to categorize such an irony? E. A. Speiser, in his very useful edition of Genesis in the Anchor Bible (1964), emphasized that J is marked by "his incisive style, his economy and boldness of presentation, his insight into human nature." Certainly economy is the particular strength of J; the most elliptical of all great writers, she shows continually that leaving something out is the best way of compelling the auditor or reader to be severely alert. An elliptical style derives from a shrewd sense that a reader's preconceived responses need to be evaded, or provoked into freshness by dissociative means. In J, the characteristic ellipsis is related to endless wordplay, to an incessant harmony of puns, false or popular etymologies, homonyms, virtually Shakespearean in their witty profusion. Pointing out where these occur in the Hebrew is rarely an aid to a reader of J in translation; what matters far more is the central difficulty and yet the central literary glory of J, which is the ironic complexity of her tone. J is at once the greatest and the most ironic writer in the Hebrew Bible; she *is* essentially a comic author, however surprising that judgment at first must seem. If one could imagine a Jewish Chaucer writing with the uncanny ironies of Kafka and Isaak Babel and Nathanael West, but also with the high naturalistic wisdom of Tolstoy and Wordsworth, then one would approach the high humor of J, ultimate ancestor of *The Canterbury Tales* as well as of Tolstoy's fictions and Kafka's parables.

J, in the text as we now have it, begins with Adam, Eve, and Eden, which I do not think was her own start but rather represents a triumph of redaction over J's originality. Not that what remains is not stark, incommensurate, and ironic to the highest degree. Yahweh shapes man out of dust or clay; perhaps we might speak of a "dust of clay" that has been moistened by the rising up of underground springs. The Hebrew word *va-yitser*, "shaping" or "forming," belongs to the work of the potter, or *yotser*, but Yahweh has no potter's wheel, unlike Egyptian and Mesopotamian maker-gods who stand in front of a potter's wheel in the ancient texts and fashion man upon it. And when Yahweh blows the *nishmat hayyim* ("breath of life") into the nostrils of the clay figurine, he creates a monistic "living being" rather than an animated carcass. Monism is one of J's inventions; as Cläus Westermann observes in his *Genesis 1–11: A Commentary* (1984), "A 'living soul' is not put into one's body. . . . any idea that one is made up of body and soul is ruled out." We can sum up J's originality here in her depriving Yahweh of the potter's wheel, and depriving him also of a dualism common to the ancient Near East, one that rose again with Christianity, which captured J when it took the Hebrew Bible captive.

A reader of the Authorized Version (or King James Holy Bible) experiences an extraordinarily harmonious and unified style, one of the handful of truly sublime styles in the English language. The deepest residuum of that style is constituted by the rhetorical stances of William Tyndale, martyred pioneer of English Bible translation, and of his follower Miles Coverdale. Their work, brought to culmination by the skilled inheritors who made the Authorized Version, gave us so powerful a composite text that we have real difficulty in assimilating an awareness that Genesis, Exodus, and Numbers are a palimpsest, a tangled skein or coat of many colors, a work of "composite artistry," in Robert Alter's deft phrase. That composite artist was R, the Redactor, who would presumably rejoice at our inability to disentangle J from P in the strong style of the King James Bible. But even the composite artistry of the Authorized Version cannot mask the profound differences that abound throughout the three books of Genesis, Exodus, and Numbers, differences between J and P in particular when they present accounts of the same event. One path into the understanding of the problematical J is to contrast her story of the Creation with the altogether different vision of P.

The Redactor unsurprisingly chose to begin what we now call Genesis with P's version of the Creation, since it was doubtless much easier for him to assimilate than J's lively chronicle of the ultimate origins. Even what the Redactor retained has not lost its fundamental sense of incommensurateness. Yahweh molds the clay, not as the potter does, but in the manner of a child making mud pies, freestyle with his own hands. J does not tell us whether Yahweh blows his breath through his own nostrils, or by his own mouth, into the newly formed mouth of the moistened red clay creature, but either way the image is powerfully grotesque. Perhaps even more original, and more ironic, is the uniqueness of the creation of woman, since there is absolutely no other story of the forming of a human female in all of the surviving literature of the ancient Near East. That J gives six times the space to the woman's creation as to the man's may well reflect J's gender, but that I will discuss in other contexts.

Can we recover J's true opening, assuming that my surmise as to its exclusion by the Redactor is accurate? Shrewd arguments on the composite artistry of the Creation accounts in Genesis as it has come down to us have been made by Alter and others, and yet the contrasts between P's cosmological fantasy and J's earthbound irony are quite overwhelming. I would suggest that what is now Genesis 1–2:4a was deliberately composed to replace a rather outrageous Yahwistic vision of a very combative cosmological Creation, so that the Redactor merely followed a pious tradition in preluding J's story of Eden with P's hymn to divine order. It is crucial to realize that P did not care to give us a rival narrative of the creation of Adam, perhaps because an archaic Judaism, now largely lost to us, began with an even more grotesque version of

Adam's making. One can speculate that J's lost account of cosmic beginnings was also an ironic revision of an archaic combat myth, Yahweh's battle with the Dragon and the Deep.

The Psalms and the Book of Job reverberate with passages in which Yahweh triumphs in a grand fight with a dragon or sea serpent, sometimes named Rahab, sometimes Leviathan. Some of these passages make God's adversary the sea itself, which struggles vainly to oppose the act of Creation. Behind the combat between Yahweh and the sea, or its representatives, is a Canaanite myth that tells how the storm god Baal and his sister (and wife) Anat fought Yamm, or the sea, emblem of chaos. Certainly J knew this story, and probably she knew also the Babylonian epic *Enuma Elis,* in which the storm god Marduk battles Tiamat, goddess of the sea. Every trace of this world-making conflict has been obliterated by P in his account of Creation, for reasons readily understandable. The God of the Priestly Author is too transcendent, and too powerful, for anyone to imagine his stooping to a struggle with a sea serpent. When the Redactor chose to begin with P's Creation, what did he choose against? Visions of a warlike Yahweh elsewhere in the Hebrew Bible may help to answer that difficult question. Here is a cento of such visions, from the King James Version; did they come from recollections of a J cosmogony that we have been defrauded of knowing?

For God is my King of old, working salvation in the midst of the earth.

Thou didst divide the sea by thy strength: thou brakest the heads of the dragons in the waters.

Thou brakest the heads of leviathan in pieces, and gavest him to be meat to the people inhabiting the wilderness.

Thou didst cleave the fountain and the flood: thou driedst up mighty rivers.

The day is thine, the night also is thine: thou hast prepared the light and the sun.

Thou hast set all the borders of the earth: thou hast made summer and winter. (Ps. 74:12–17)

Thou rulest the raging of the sea: when the waves thereof arise, thou stillest them.

Thou hast broken Rahab in pieces, as one that is slain; thou hast scattered thine enemies with thy strong arm.

(Ps. 89:9–10)

Awake, awake, put on strength, O arm of the Lord; awake, as in the ancient days, in the generations of old. Art thou not it that hath cut Rahab, and wounded the dragon?

Art thou not it which hath dried the sea, the waters of the great deep; that hath made the depths of the sea a way for the ransomed to pass over? (Isa. 51:9–10)

The extraordinary metaphor of Psalm 74 actually identifies the flesh of the slain Leviathan with the manna fed to the wandering Israelites in the Wilderness, an identification that flowered in Kabbalistic stories that the companions of mystical contemplation would feast again upon Leviathan in the days of the Messiah. Isaiah, like the Psalms, seems to recall a more archaic account of Creation even as he equates that making with the miracle of deliverance at the Red Sea. Job, if combined with the Psalms and Isaiah, and with passages scattered through Kings, Nahum, Proverbs, Jeremiah, and Habakkuk, would give one a composite vision of the archaic cosmogony something like this.

Yahweh with one word created the Sun, the Moon, and the Stars. He stretched out the skies like a tent cloth to shroud the Deep, and placed his secret court above the skies, founding it upon the Higher Waters. In creating, Yahweh rode above the Deep, which rose against him. Tehom, queen of the Deep, sought to drown out Yahweh's Creation, but he rode against her in his chariot of fire, and bombarded her with hail and with lightning. Yahweh destroyed her vassal Leviathan with one great blow to the monster's skull, while he ended Rahab by thrusting a sword into her heart. The waters fled backward, awed by the voice of Yahweh, and Tehom fearfully surrendered. Yahweh shouted his triumph, and dried up the floods. He set the Moon to divide the seasons, the Sun to divide day and night. Observing Yahweh's victory, the Morning Stars sang together, and all the sons of God shouted for joy. Thus the work of Creation was completed.

If J began in some such way, it seems clear enough why the Redactor chose to do without her at the very origin, and began instead with P's stately vision of Creation.

As I have said, few fixed ideas are as difficult to dislodge as the notion that the Bible is a "holy book" in an altogether unique way. The Koran, the Book of Mormon, the sacred writings of the Asian religions, not to mention other rival works, somehow do not have the curious prestige that the Bible retains even for secularists and unbelievers. It is of absolute importance for the reader of the Book of J to begin with a realization that J did not think in terms of sacred texts as she composed the scrolls that constitute her achievement. The stories of the Creation, of the Patriarchs, of Joseph, of Moses, were not for her holy tales, not at all. Of all the extraordinary ironies concerning J, the most remarkable is that this fountainhead of Judaism, Christianity, and Islam simply was not a religious writer. This is not because, as some scholars insist, Yahweh was All-in-All to her. The Yahwist, unlike every subsequent biblical writer, shows no awe or fear of Yahweh. Her Yahweh is a lively fellow, dynamic in the extreme, who has very little in common with the God of the Priestly Author or of Jeremiah, though something in common with the Davidic God of the Court Historian. J's marvelous contemporary is not primarily a comic and ironic writer, as she was, but his sophistication matches her acute consciousness of paradox, and I will argue later that both can be said to have left their hearts behind them in the heroic age of David and the urbane civilization of Solomon. We can fantasize them as two mature survivors of a greater time, pondering the splendors of their people while enduring the equivocal reign of Solomon's inadequate son, Rehoboam, under whom the United Monarchy and its empire came apart. The age into which J survived was hardly an era of heroes.

I think it accurate to observe that J had no heroes, only heroines. Sarai and Rachel are wholly admirable, and Tamar, in proportion to the narrative space she occupies, is very much the most vivid portrait in J. But Abram, Jacob, and Moses receive a remarkably mixed treatment from J. If she had a male hero, then it was David the King, who is not an overt part of her story, though Joseph, his surrogate, is.

Abram, like Adam before him, reflects J's vision of human reality as familial rather than royal or priestly. Community and society for J are extensions of the relations between husbands and wives, parents and children, brothers and sisters. The Court Historian has a very different sense of society, one that apprehends power as administrative and military. Again I risk being charged by feminist critics with that hideous sin, "essentialism," when I suggest that J sees power as marital and familial for the same reason that she has no male heroes: because she is a wise woman. Consider the basic structure of her book: her great originality is to retell the story of her people from the Creation to the death of Moses so that the Patriarchs become the connecting link between the origins of humankind and the return of their descendants, the Jewish people, into their own land. For J, the Patriarchs are her narrative center; Creation and Exodus frame the lives of Abram and Jacob, and take most of their significance from the stories she tells about Abram and Jacob. I do not believe that J had any precedent for linking the primordial vision of Adam in Eden to the national celebration of the redemption from Egypt by way of the fathers: Abram, who made the Covenant with Yahweh, and Jacob, who became Israel, and so brought forth and named the tribes. Literary originality achieved one of its crucial breakthroughs in what was to become Western tradition when it occurred to J to so fuse what we call myth and history. The result was a new kind of narrative, closer to Tolstoy than to Homer, and departing radically from the archaic narratives available to J as models.

That departure has been much studied, but interests me less than departures we only can hypothesize because we have only fragmentary Hebrew texts, of any kind, that predate the Yahwist. Supposedly the Yahwist revised oral traditions, but I am highly skeptical that writing as sophisticated and complex as the Yahwist's comes out of any full relation to largely oral traditions. Great originals—even Dante, Shakespeare, and Freud—cunningly revise the written texts of precursors. "I created psychoanalysis because it had no literature," Freud joked, and he denied ever having read Schopenhauer and Nietzsche, who nevertheless inform him pervasively. The Yahwist, as I read her, is the greatest of all ironists, and every mode of literary irony depends upon prior writings, works more naive, literal, straightforward, than the ironist's interventions. But that brings me to one of the truly vexed aspects of biblical literature. How are we to proceed when nearly all writing that has survived reflects the canonical choices and redactions of normative Judaism? How are we to receive an irony whose antecedents are lost? The normative tradition in Judaism did not censor; it simply ignored what it disapproved in its own backgrounds. Archaic Judaism is all but totally unknown to us. We know the rabbinical Judaism that has been dominant since the second century C.E., and we know, more or less, what that Judaism judged to be the chain of tradition that extended from Ezra the great Redactor to the Pharisees and then on to Akiba, central among all the second-century rabbis. What we do not know is the Judaism that was available to the Yahwist, and the history, or the mythology, of that Judaism. All that I can see is that the Yahweh of the Yahwist has very little to do with the God of Ezra or the God of Akiba. I cannot see whether her Yahweh came to her from her people's past or their beliefs in her own day, or from her own humorous and subtle imagination. Most likely, an amalgam of the three formed in her work, and remains with us still, despite all the revisionary labors of normative Judaism.

3 4 The proper use of a fiction of authorship is not to aid in an interpretation but to clarify an interpretation once it has developed out of a sympathetic and imaginative reading of a difficult text. My own obsession with the J writer goes back a decade, but it was only in the last year that I began to wonder whether the voice I encounter in the text is that of a woman. My starting point of wonder came when I heard yet once more the familiar contention of feminist criticism that my own theories of influence are patriarchal. Why, I reflected, are the portraits of the Patriarchs and of Moses so mixed, and even at moments so unfavorable, in what the older scholarship found to be the Yahwistic, or earliest, portion of the Pentateuch? This reflection rapidly assimilated itself to my long-standing sense of J's quite prevalent tone of irony. J begins in irony, with Yahweh's childlike molding of clay, and concludes in irony, with Yahweh's uncanny burial of Moses. Why does a child bury a beloved creature in isolation and then refuse to divulge the location of the grave? Perhaps to preserve the memory for himself or herself alone, but why? A kind of wounding and wounded intimacy seems to be the answer. J's Yahweh has a tormented relationship with his own chosen prophet, Moses, whom he even attempts to murder, for no reason, and whom he excludes from Canaan, for no good reason. Possessiveness, rather than affection or even regard, is the stance of J's Yahweh toward Moses. A poor thing, but mine own, Yahweh seems to think, and we are left again wondering at the extravagant strangeness of J's Yahweh.

It is perfectly clear to me that J neither loved nor feared her Yahweh, which is why normative Jews and Christians and their scholarly expositors make such weak readers of Yahweh. Since Yahweh is clearly male, and considerably less mature and sophisticated than the aristocratic ironist J, it is appropriate that his author handles him with a certain reserve. If we had J's written sources, such as they may have been, we could experience the fascination of seeing precisely what J invented for herself. I have implied throughout that only part of the Book of J can be a twice-told tale, but I can only surmise precisely what she chose to create for herself.

As soon as we rid ourselves of the arbitrary presupposition that J's prime motive for writing was piety in any normative sense, we become free also of the exuberant varnish that has discolored J since the time of the early revisionists—the so-called E and the Priestly Authors and Deuteronomists and scribal Redactor—on through the enormous tradition of what became at last the normative Judaism of the rabbis in the second century C.E. If J existed at all for the great Rabbi Akiba and his colleagues, it was only as a rather annoying if colorful remnant of weird anecdotes that had somehow gotten into the majestic text composed by Moses himself, if not written down by Moses at Yahweh's dictation. Talking animals, lustful Elohim, deceitful Patriarchs, ambitious women anxious to break into the Blessing, murderous founders of the tribes of Israel, a drunken Noah, a raging Yahweh out of control even by himself, inheritances suborned by imposture: somehow these were shrugged off by the rabbis (though not by the Pharisees, to judge by the famous and badly written Book of Jubilees, sometimes called the Little Genesis).

Few cultural paradoxes are so profound, or so unnerving, as the process of religious canonization by which an essentially literary work becomes a sacred text. When script becomes Scripture, reading is numbed by taboo and inhibition. Even if imagining an author and calling her J is an arbitrary and personal fiction, something like that imagining is necessary if we are to be stirred out of our numbness.

DAVID: J AND

THE COURT HISTORIAN

I HAVE ADMITTED that to identify J as a woman is a fiction, but so, of course, is the usual easy assumption that J was a man. I now elaborate upon the sublime fiction that J was either a princess of the Davidic royal house or else the daughter or wife of a court personage, perhaps directly related by blood or marriage to her great contemporary the Court Historian, the author of 2 Samuel, with whom she exchanged influences. The anagrammatic references to Rehoboam (J, as we shall see, has a way of punning ironically on Rehoboam's name) and the many unfavorable allusions to Jeroboam indicate Rehoboam's reign in the curtailed kingdom of Judah as a likely time and place for the writing careers of J and the Court Historian, both of whom look back through the Solomonic splendor to the heroic origins of the royal line in David.

The effect of 2 Samuel seems to me strongest at the beginning of J's work but wanes in what is now Exodus and Numbers. My speculation is that as J wrote on and revised herself, a darker age came, in which Rehoboam succeeded his dead father, Solomon, and the Davidic kingdom fell apart, with the larger share falling to Jeroboam as the Northern Kingdom of Israel. I place J and the Court Historian under Rehoboam because a nostalgia for David, a dubiety about the Solomonic splendor, and an ironic disdain for Rehoboam and the people all characterize the inner workings of J's text, for me, and because the Court Historian is so rueful about the whole matter of royal transitions. To be the grandson of David, and the son of Solomon, would have been a heavy burden upon the best of kings, but all that is memorable about Rehoboam is his promise to Israel to go Solomon one better in the art of chastise- ment: "My father beat you with whips, but I will beat you with scorpions!"

J's cultural situation, and the Court Historian's, as we can derive it from their works, seems to suit both the Solomonic glory and the time of troubles that came after. We need not look to the Exile for such a time, as some scholars have done in suggesting that there were two Yahwists. David Damrosch gives a useful summary of the argument.

> The Yahwist who arises in the triumphant moment of the establishment of the kingdom of Israel is a different figure from the Yahwist who writes at the time of the virtual destruction of Israel's national life; a Davidic-Solomonic Yahwist is to be seen as celebrating and consolidating a new religious and social order, whereas an exilic Yahwist would instead be trying to recreate a distant past as a way to understand what went wrong.

But one need not assume that the Exile was "what went wrong"; the transition from Solomon to Rehoboam is more than enough. If you were a younger contemporary of Solomon, then you began your mature life in Solomonic security but lived to see the collapse of the United Monarchy soon after Solomon's death.

Because of J's elitist and aristocratic preferences, I incline to the fiction that she was of the royal house rather than in the family of one of Rehoboam's scribes, as I take the Court Historian to have been. A further intimation for my surmise comes from J's approach to David only by innuendo through the surrogate of Joseph, and from the tradition that made David, her possible grandfather, into the poet of the Psalms, and ascribed authorship of Proverbs and the Song of Songs to Solomon, her possible father. One doubts that

Solomon himself wrote the Song of Songs, which is probably the work of a single great court poet, but it is quite possible that Solomon, like Queen Elizabeth I of England, was a poet, and even likelier that he originated some of the Proverbs, as befits his reputation for wisdom. It is even more possible that David indeed was a poet, and that the lament for Jonathan and some of the Psalms began as his work. If J was a princess of the same house, then she had a considerable family literary tradition to inspire her, while royal decorum would have excluded David (or Solomon) as her overt subject. And if she wrote under Rehoboam, then both tact and personal safety would have suggested a certain wariness in praising figures whose heritage Rehoboam had marred and even destroyed forever.

If we are to piece together J's social vision, we can begin by observing that she does not share in what has been termed the "nomadic ideal" of her descendants, the Prophets. Cain is punished by nomadism, and Ishmael's geographical destiny is hardly presented as a blessing. The wanderings in the Wilderness are dramatized by J almost as a nightmare or phantasmagoria. Perhaps there is something male about the nomadic ideal, or perhaps J herself feared exile, since her work is haunted by images of exile. What seems certain to me, on the basis of the Book of J, is that it was the normative misreaders who fostered a patriarchal ideal that is certainly alien to J, who mocks such an ideal throughout. Nor are her visions of polygamy very cheerful: Sarai persecutes Hagar, Rachel is violently jealous of her sister, Leah, and the strong-minded Rebecca cannot be conceived as ever allowing a rival, even if Isaac could be conceived as risking such audacity. Evidently only the king was allowed (or perhaps could afford) more than one wife after the monarchy was instituted. Jacob, for all his flaws, seems to earn J's regard because of his love for Rachel, the supreme love of J's story, transcending any other relationship between man and woman in the Hebrew Bible.

One wonders whether the instances of Rachel and Rebecca were not J's implicit critiques of royal self-indulgence in these matters. David, as fervent in love as in war, had an abundance both of wives and concubines, though nothing like his son Solomon, who is supposed to have enjoyed seven hundred wives and three hundred concubines, on how regular a basis we are not advised. Rehoboam, whom I like to think of as J's unworthy nephew, managed to finance eighteen wives and sixty concubines, who presumably consoled him for having lost much the largest portions of David's and Solomon's empire. Richard Friedman, in his *Who Wrote the Bible?* (1987), points to six passages in J that play on the root of Rehoboam's name, a root that suggests spaciousness or openness, like the name itself. I think that all these passages are hidden, ironic critiques of Rehoboam, and that they would suit the outlook of a consciousness that matured under Solomon and then survived to suffer the disintegration of the kingdom under Rehoboam.

Taken together, the passages constitute an ironic epilogue to the glory of David and Solomon. In Genesis 13:17, after Abram and Lot part, Yahweh tells Abram to look in all directions around Canaan, for all of it will belong to him and his descendants: "Rise, walk around on this land—open and broad—it is to you I will give it" (34).* That "open and broad" of the promise reverberates against the root of Rehoboam's name—the man who has reduced the open and broad vista to the pent-up little hill kingdom of Judah. In Genesis 19:2, Lot tells Yahweh's angels to "stay the night, wash your feet, rise refreshed, then go on—the road will wait," but they reply, "No, we will lie by the broad road" (44), the last phrase savagely intimating Rehoboam, who feared to war against Jeroboam to preserve his realm. Isaac, departing from the Philistines in Genesis 26, provides J with another irony: "Moving on from there, he dug another well; they didn't struggle over this one, so he named it Rehovot, or Open: 'Now that Yahweh has

---

*Parenthetical references following quotations from the Book of J indicate the chapter of David Rosenberg's translation from which the quotation comes. The corresponding passage in the Hebrew Bible (where not given in the text) can be found in Appendix B: Biblical Sources.

opened a broad road for us, we can take root in the land' " (59). King Rehoboam is hardly open or broad but is rather the lord of a closed and narrow land.

Shechem, site of Jeroboam's coronation as king of Israel, is the setting of a doubtful passage, revised from J, in Genesis 34:21, where Hamor and Shechem speak to their townspeople, saying of the sons of Jacob, "Look: the land is broad enough to embrace them" (75). J's irony is double: poor Hamor, Shechem, and those they address will soon lie slaughtered on the broad land, and those who live under Rehoboam have seen the revenge of Shechem under the leadership of Jeroboam, who has taken away Israel, or the north of Canaan. In Exodus, this ironic refrain continues, first in 3:8, when Yahweh says to Moses, "I beheld the burden my people held—in Egypt. I come down to lift them out of Egypt's hand, to carry them to a broad, open land" (115). Here the allusion to Rehoboam contrasts the return to the Promised Land with the hapless king's truncation of the work of Yahweh.

The sequence of J's hidden dirge for Rehoboam's disgrace culminates precisely as one might expect, in the sonorous declaration of the Commandments in Exodus 34, where Yahweh chants, "So be it: I will disperse a nation in your path, broaden your road and borders; so no one dreams he can embrace your land on your way to Yahweh; as you go up to face your God three times a year" (165). Nothing could be darker for Rehoboam than the echo of his name's root in Yahweh's commandment. Yahweh broadens the borders, and poor Rehoboam shrinks them. J's art of wordplay leaves nothing of Rehoboam, who has been shredded by ironic allusion. Those ironies overtly refer to the stories of the Patriarchs and of Moses, but it is the imperial theme of David and Solomon that provides the sense of glory from which Rehoboam falls away.

In coming at last to David and Solomon, paradoxically we arrive at the center of J, who never mentions either of them. Like anyone else exploring this paradox, I am deeply indebted to the great scholar Gerhard von Rad, who pioneered in seeing that the undersong of the Yahwist is always the achievements of the monarchy under the charismatic hero David and the prudent Solomon. Another precursor for me is E. A. Speiser, who shrewdly surmised the contemporary relation between J and the author of 2 Samuel. Following von Rad's lead, Hans Walter Wolff and Walter Brueg- gemann, in *The Vitality of Old Testament Traditions* (1975), have developed some of the implications of what David in particular meant to J, while Joel Rosenberg, in *King and Kin* (1986), has gone further than Speiser in reading Genesis and 2 Samuel as companion works. Since I am not a biblical scholar, I am uninhibited enough to go further still, and to suggest that the J strand in Genesis, Exodus, and Numbers was written in close association with the composition of 2 Samuel. The two works echo one another, use one another, and are available to one another, so that it is quite possible that the two authors traded concepts and images as they went along. Certainly there is nothing unusual, in the context of later literary history, in my suggestion that J and the Court Historian were friendly rivals, at work side by side, reading aloud to one another and thus exchanging influences. As I remarked earlier, imagining an author may not be a mode of positivist scholarship, but it cannot be evaded in the reading process.

Though the Court Historian is quite as sophisticated as J, he is a less consistent ironist, and his vision is neither as exuberant nor as ultimately foreboding as J's. Great artist though he is, the author of 2 Samuel does not have or need J's range, but after J he is the strongest writer of narrative in the Hebrew Bible. Like the author or authors of 1 Samuel, the Court Historian begins with a grand asset, the figure of David, who far more than Moses is the hero of the Hebrew Bible, if so startling a role or position can be granted. As with Moses, David's crucial relation is with Yahweh, but Yahweh is in love with David and not with Moses. That the greatest of the kings should be preferred to the greatest of the Prophets tells us much that is crucial about J's Yahweh, and about J.

It is difficult to locate in Western literature and history a more charismatic figure than David. The Achilles of the *Iliad* scarcely yields his aesthetic supremacy to the David of 2 Samuel, but Achilles remains a child compared to David, compared even to the child David. One could juxtapose David to the charismatic complexity of Hamlet, except that David, unlike Hamlet, is the beloved of God, and again David was a very considerable historical figure. But just as we know what came before the Conquest, the Judges, and the monarchy primarily through J, even so we do not know the historical David. What we know is the David of 1 and 2 Samuel, 1 Kings, 1 Chronicles, and in quite another way, the Psalms. David therefore is a literary character, as is J's Yahweh, and like Yahweh, David has become a religious force, if only because of Yahweh's peculiar favor.

That there is a highly recognizable personality in all the versions of David does not mean that a historical reality necessarily underlies them. A literary character can retain his or her spirit and singularity as he or she undergoes several treatments. The figure of David appears to transcend its representations, even in the masterly 2 Samuel, but we are in a kind of whirlpool here, since David is as much the imagination of the people Israel as Yahweh is J's imagination. I seem to be veering upon the notion that David is divine, one of the Elohim, as it were, but that suggestion does not belong to the Hebrew Bible. Unlike his supposed descendant Jesus, David is not the son of God, even though Yahweh proclaims that he will be a father to David's children. David most simply is the object of Yahweh's election-love, and yet we are not tempted to apply Freud's definition of love as the overvaluation of the object. Yahweh does not overvalue David, in our judgment or in his own. Like everyone else, from Samuel, Saul, and Jonathan down to the present, Yahweh is charmed by David.

I use "charmed" in its deep sense, as there is something magical in the charismatic personality of David. In literary terms, the magic is originality, since that was and remains David's dominant characteristic. He is an original, yet of that rarest sort whose advent establishes a new center, whose freshness has nothing of the eccentric in it. His story is an astonishment; before him comes the primitive kingdom of Saul, and after him the advanced empire of Solomon. In between is only David himself, who in his own person carries his people from an obscure hill clan to a high culture dominant in its part of the world. Before David, there is almost no Hebrew literature. After David, and because of him, J and the writer of 2 Samuel appear, establishing the sublime limits of Hebrew literature almost at its beginnings. It is as though Achilles, Pericles, and Pindar were combined in one individual, a blend that dazzles our powers of imagining and interpreting. David clearly was a difference that made a difference, one that took its origins in the elusive matter of personality. For a people to move so rapidly, in a single generation, from an inward-turning community to an international power, must have been bewildering. The shift in perspective from Saul to David finds its permanent emblem in the City of David, Jerusalem, so that we are confronted by present realities as soon as we think of David.

Scholars are united in seeing that for the Israelites David was a new kind of man, or perhaps a new image of human existence, with all human potentialities fulfilled in him. Supposedly, David's is a secularized image, but the distinction between sacred and secular vanishes in David's career. The Yahweh of 2 Samuel is considerably less interventionist than J's Yahweh, and so David is even freer than Jacob is to struggle for his own fulfillment, while enjoying also the favored status of Joseph, knowing that Yahweh is with him. Since David is as complex and dialectical a consciousness as Hamlet, describing his personality is a Shakespearean task. There is David the fugitive chief of outcasts who insists that he and his men are worthy to devour consecrated bread. There is another David who dances before the Ark, enraptured by an exuberant piety that breaks all limits. And there is the man of power and no scruple who acts instantly to liquidate Uriah the Hittite when that loyal soldier stands in the way of his monarch's illicit lust. Perhaps most revealing is David's conduct when his first child by Bathsheba, Uriah's not very bereft widow, is born ill, being under the curse of Yahweh. In the week when the infant ebbs toward death,

David mourns fanatically, risking his own life in fasting and abnegation. Directly the child dies, David snaps out of his mourning and returns to the full vitality of his intense existence. We behold a pragmatist of the spirit, in whom the fruits of the Blessing are overwhelming. David himself is more life, and the promise of yet more life, into a time without boundaries.

I am arguing that the image of David is precisely what informs J's particular sense of the Blessing; David is what, in J's judgment, Abram, Jacob, Tamar, and the others strive toward becoming. As the elite image, David is to be distinguished from Moses, at least from J's Moses, who has more affinities with the host he leads. The difference is in Yahweh's attitude, as well as in our own. To no one in J does Yahweh speak as he speaks to David, through the prophet Nathan, in 2 Samuel 7:12–16. I quote from the Jewish Publication Society Translation (1985).

> When your days are done and you lie with your fathers, I will raise up your offspring after you, one of your own issue, and I will establish his kingship. He shall build a house for My name, and I will establish his royal throne forever. I will be a father to him, and he shall be a son to Me. When he does wrong, I will chastise him with the rod of men and the affliction of mortals; but I will never withdraw My favor from him as I withdrew it from Saul, whom I removed to make room for you. Your house and your kingship shall ever be secure before you; your throne shall be established forever.

This astonishing promise of Solomon's reign, and of the perpetuity of the House of David after Solomon, is Yahweh's unique risk in the Hebrew Bible, a risk he ventures nowhere in the Book of J. Yahweh is not making a covenant here, but a gift of his love to his adopted son David, for whose sake Solomon will be adopted after him. The Blessing will not be withdrawn, even if it is not merited—an astonishing notion that is illuminated by an extraordinary later passage, 2 Samuel 12:1–13, when Yahweh speaks through Nathan again to express his wrath at David's crime against Uriah. In J, Yahweh would speak to his elite directly, not through a prophet, but nowhere do we hear in J's Yahweh the accents of a hurt lover whose trust has been betrayed. I like the eloquence here of the King James Version, where the outraged Yahweh cries out:

> And I gave thee thy master's house, and thy master's wives into thy bosom, and gave thee the house of Israel and of Judah; and if that had been too little, I would moreover have given unto thee such and such things.

Having awarded David Saul's kingship, his queens, and the United Monarchy of Israel and Judah, Yahweh is in the desperate position of the giver who has run out of gifts, and is reduced to the incoherence of "such and such things," or twice as much, or what you will. Yahweh has discovered that David is insatiable, and that the Blessing of more life nevertheless must have its moral limits even for the most favored of all men. I like to think that J had read this passage, or heard it read aloud by the author of 2 Samuel, because her uncanny and incommensurate Yahweh, who touched his limits at Sinai while confronting a whole people to whom the Blessing was to be passed, confronts here a very different and more intimate limit. David, whose only limitations are those of our common mortality, is also Yahweh's limit, the unique object of Yahweh's altogether incommensurate love.

If my fiction of J has any force, then it must have cost her a great deal not to take David as the subject of her work. When Nietzsche reminds me that the motive for metaphor, for fiction, is the desire to be different, the desire to be elsewhere, I think always of J, for whom the difference, the elsewhere, was David. No one in J, not even Joseph, behaves with the grace and chivalry of David, who pours out the water of Bethlehem that he longs to drink, precisely because his best men have risked their lives to bring it back, merely to satisfy his passing whim. That superb acknowledgment of their response to his charisma is itself the enhancement of everything that is most charismatic about David. All by himself, David inaugurates an order of being not available in J's world, whether in its actuality of the transition from Solomon to Rehoboam or in its representation in that long agon from Yahweh's molding of Adam to his digging of the grave for Moses. The meaning of what goes from Adam to Moses, for J, is what came with David and departed with Rehoboam, the splendor both fulfilled and parodied by Solomon and his world. Adam receives Eden, and Moses his unwilling mission, because David is to be. I affirm this odd proposition not in the spirit of the theologian Walter Brueggemann, for whom Eden is a question of trust, or of the scholar Joel Rosenberg, who reads the Eden story as political allegory. I see the parallels between J and 2 Samuel as they (and von Rad and Speiser) have seen them, but I do not believe that J's interests were either theological or political. They were what we would now call imaginative or literary, and concerned the elite image of the individual life, rather than the relation between Yahweh and the Israelites, or the fortunes of the Davidic monarchy as such.

The Book of J exalts open and broad vision, or the personality of David. Tamar, David's ancestor, quests to join herself to the promise of a name that will not be scattered. Do we not have here, and in David, a paradigm that for the secular individual transcends either strictly religious or political interests? Poets from Pindar to Petrarch, and beyond to the Shakespeare of the Sonnets, have sought to build powerful rhymes that would outlast marble or the gilded monuments of saints and monarchs. David is eternally memorable not because he was a crucial political and religious leader, but because he so moved the imagination of his own people and of other peoples after them. It is an eternal irony that J is so memorable that all of the West's principal religions have been able to found themselves upon her stories, even as they have argued for spiritual codes that fit those stories most imperfectly, and fit the stories of David just as badly. Shakespeare is a truer inheritor of J than Rabbi Akiba or Saint Paul, because Shakespeare, like J and David, is the dramatist of personality and its possibilities.

Perhaps the largest obstacle to our reading J as J is that we cannot cease thinking of the Book of J as the heart of that composite work the Torah, or Five Books of Moses, and so as the central element in those even more composite works the Hebrew Bible and the Christian Bible, with its Old Testament / New Testament structure. But such thinking perspectivizes J in a most misleading way. The Torah is the product of the middle of the fourth century before the common era; J wrote at the end of the tenth century, almost six hundred years before the time of Ezra the Scribe, the time of the Redactor. The reign of Solomon has nothing in common with the era of the Return from Babylonian Exile. J lived in the age of the First Temple and seldom mentioned or alluded to it, so little did it mean to her. In the time from Ezra to the destruction of the Second Temple in 70 C.E., we gradually move from a cultic Yahwism to the worship of Torah, and so to the birth of Judaism as a book religion. More than nineteen hundred years later, the Jews still worship a book, as Ezra perhaps intended them to do, but nothing could be further from J than the assumption that she was writing a text for worship. Her idea of heroism was the heroic David. Her idea of order was Solomon. Cult and priests meant nothing to her, and Torah worship would have meant even less. To read the Book of J, we need to begin by scrubbing away the varnish that keeps us from seeing that the Redactor and previous revisionists could not obliterate the original work of the J writer. That varnish is called by many names: belief, scholarship, history, literary criticism, what have you. If these names move or describe you, why read the Book of J at all? Why read the *Iliad,* or the *Commedia,* or *Macbeth,* or *Paradise Lost*? The difference is that those works have not been revised into creeds and churches, with a palimpsestic overlay of orthodox texts obscuring what was there to be revised. Recovering J will not throw new light on Torah or on the Hebrew Bible or on the Bible of Christianity. I do not think that appreciating J will help us love God or arrive at the spiritual or historical truth of whatever Bible. I want the varnish off because it conceals a writer of the eminence of Shakespeare or Dante, and such a writer is worth more than many creeds, many churches, many scholarly certainties.

ONE OF OUR MANY DIFFICULTIES in reading J as J is the lasting literary power of the King James Bible, or Authorized Version (1611). That Bible, never to be surpassed in English, revises many previous translators, but two great writers in particular, the martyred William Tyndale and Miles Coverdale. The style first developed by Tyndale, and amplified by Coverdale, has become biblical style in English, and has had an effect upon writing in English second only to that of Shakespeare. Tyndale, the pioneer in translating directly from the Hebrew Bible into English, translated the Pentateuch with a homely power (1530), and Coverdale, who knew little Hebrew, maintained the base of Tyndale's rough eloquence while adding his own extraordinary flair for English prose rhythm (1535). The Geneva Bible (1560), put together by English Calvinist exiles, stands out among many subsequent revisions of Tyndale and Coverdale because it was the text used by Shakespeare, with frequent effect throughout his work. The King James Version can be considered essentially a correction, as the Geneva Bible was, of Tyndale-Coverdale, and most of its literary strength can be traced back to those pioneers.

I am not much impressed by any of the subsequent Christian or secular translations of the Hebrew Bible into English, because they lack the plain power of Tyndale and the lyrical force of Coverdale. Jewish Bible translation pragmatically began with the

Septuagint, the Greek version of the Hebrew Bible prepared in the third century B.C.E. for the great Alexandrian Jewish community. The Septuagint (from the Latin for "the Seventy" translators who were supposed to have finished the work in seventy-two days on the island of Pharos) was considered sacred by the Jews until the Christians adopted it as their official text for what they called the Old Testament. Jewish vernacular versions since the Septuagint include the ancient Aramaic Targum Onkelos and Aramaic Pseudo-Jonathan, the Arabic version of Saadia Gaon in the tenth century C.E., and the modern American versions of the Jewish Publication Society (1917, 1985). Unfortunately, the American Jewish versions, despite their scholarly accuracy, compare poorly with the King James Bible in literary value. In particular, all flavor of J has vanished in those versions, whereas much of J's strength (though little enough of her individuality) can still be felt in the text founded upon the Tyndale-Coverdale base.

The primary virtue I find in David Rosenberg's translation of what we have ventured to call the Book of J is that he has preserved the Yahwist's ironic tone and stance, while remembering throughout how individual her irony is. I want to illustrate this by contrasting four versions of the Tower of Babel, Genesis 11:1–9. In order I give Tyndale, King James, E. A. Speiser's Anchor Genesis, which I prefer to the American Jewish Version, and finally Rosenberg.

And all the world was of one tonge and one language. And as they came from the east, they founde a playne in the lande of Synear, and there they dwelled. And they sayd one to a nother: come on, let us make brycke and burne it wyth fyre. So brycke was there stone and slyme was there morter. And they sayd: Come on, let us buylde us a cyte and a toure, that the toppe may reach unto heaven. And let us make us a name, for peraventure we shall be scatered abrode over all the erth.

And the Lorde came downe to see the cyte and the toure

which the childern of Adam had buylded. And the Loᴙde sayd: See, the people is one and have one tonge amonge them all. And thys have they begon to do, and wyll not leave of from all that they have purposed to do. Come on, let us descende and myngell theire tonge even there, that one understonde not what a nother sayeth. Thus the Loᴙde skatered them from thence uppon all the erth. And they left of to buylde the cyte. Wherfore the name of it is called Babell, because that the Loᴙde there confounded the tonge of all the world. And because that the Loᴙde from thence, skatered them abrode uppon all the erth.

And the whole earth was of one language, and of one speech.

And it came to pass, as they journeyed from the east, that they found a plain in the land of Shinar; and they dwelt there.

And they said one to another, Go to, let us make brick, and burn them thoroughly. And they had brick for stone, and slime had they for morter.

And they said, Go to, let us build us a city and a tower, whose top may reach unto heaven; and let us make us a name, lest we be scattered abroad upon the face of the whole earth.

And the Loᴙd came down to see the city and the tower, which the children of men builded.

And the Loᴙd said, Behold, the people is one, and they have all one language; and this they begin to do: and now nothing will be restrained from them, which they have imagined to do.

Go to, let us go down, and there confound their language, that they may not understand one another's speech.

So the Loᴙd scattered them abroad from thence upon the face of all the earth: and they left off to build the city.

Therefore is the name of it called Babel; because the

LORD did there confound the language of all the earth: and from thence did the LORD scatter them abroad upon the face of all the earth.

The whole world had the same language and the same words. As men migrated from the east, they came upon a valley in the land of Shinar and settled there. They said to one another, "Come, let us mold bricks and burn them hard." Brick served them for stone, and bitumen for mortar. Then they said, "Come, let us build ourselves a city, and a tower with its top in the sky, to make a name for ourselves; else we shall be scattered all over the world."

Yahweh came down to look at the city and the tower that the earthlings had built. And Yahweh said, "If this is how they have started to act, while they are one people with a single language for all, then nothing that they may presume to do will be out of their reach. Let me, then, go down and confound their speech there, so that they shall not understand one another's talk." Yahweh dispersed them from there over the whole earth, and they stopped building the city. That is why it was named Babel, since Yahweh confounded the speech of the whole world, as he dispersed them from there over the whole world.

Now listen: all the earth uses one tongue, one and the same words. Watch: they journey from the east, arrive at a valley in the land of Sumer, settle there.

"We can bring ourselves together," they said, "like stone on stone, use brick for stone: bake it until hard." For mortar they heated bitumen.

"If we bring ourselves together," they said, "we can build a city and tower, its top touching the sky—to arrive at fame. Without a name we're unbound, scattered over the face of the earth."

Yahweh came down to watch the city and tower the sons of man were bound to build. "They are one people, with the same tongue," said Yahweh. "They conceive this between them, and it leads up until no boundary exists to what they will touch. Between us, let's descend, baffle their tongue until each is scatterbrain to his friend."

From there Yahweh scattered them over the whole face of earth; the city there came unbound.

That is why they named the place Bavel: their tongues were baffled there by Yahweh. Scattered by Yahweh from there, they arrived at the ends of the earth. (29)

Tyndale ruggedly catches J's fundamental wordplay between *balal,* "confused" and Babel or Babylon, and his fine word "confounded" is retained in King James and by Speiser. Rosenberg's "baffle their tongue" plays on *balal* and Babel, so that Babylon becomes a universe of bafflement. This reinforces Rosenberg's care in repeating the subtle J's play upon "bound," "boundary," "unbound." J's Yahweh curses the snake with a crucial setting of boundaries.

"Since you did this, you are bound apart from flocks, from any creature of the field, bound to the ground, crawling by your smooth belly: dirt you shall taste from first day to last. I make you enemy to woman, enmity bound between your seed and hers." (7)

This belongs to the same complex as Yahweh's warning to Moses.

"The people will be a boundary, warn them to watch themselves, approach but not climb up, not touch the mountain. For those who overstep boundaries, death touches them, steps over their graves." (160)

J plays incessantly, in these passages and elsewhere, upon the Hebrew stem *'rr,* which means "to restrain or bind, as by a magical spell." In J, *'rr* is not quite a curse but does constitute an antithesis to the Blessing of Yahweh, in which time loses its boundaries. My penultimate section in this book, "The Blessing: Exiles, Boundaries, Jealousies," deals in part with this complex. Rosenberg's version of Babel seems to me admirable at bringing into American English the Yahwist's ironic playfulness with binding and unbinding, boundaries and the unbounded. The men of what will be called Babel, after it is scattered or unbound, converge on the site in order to make a common purpose and name, implicitly against Yahweh. To become men with a name, so that one's renown is not scattered, is to be like the Nephilim, those "giants in the earth" who were the children of the mismatches of the Elohim and earthly women (Gen. 6:4). Bringing or binding themselves together in alliance, the men of Babel compare themselves to building stones, hard-baked bricks of resentment against oblivion. To be nameless is to be unbound and scattered, and Yahweh descends to bring about just that when he comes down "to watch the city and tower the sons of man were bound to build." They are "bound to build," covenanted to one another yet also overdetermined by their ambitions. Hence Yahweh's grimly deliberate irony.

> "They are one people, with the same tongue. They conceive this between them, and it leads up until no boundary exists to what they will touch. Between us, let's descend, baffle their tongue until each is scatterbrain to his friend."

But we hear also a dramatic irony, intended not by Yahweh but by J. Yahweh's "between us" must be addressed to the Elohim, or angels, his own creatures, not his friends or fellow building stones. Impish to a high degree, Yahweh overthrows by mischief, the baffling or confusion of languages. The scatterbrains indeed will be scattered, will become men without a name, because they would reach beyond Yahweh's boundaries, as though they were commensurate with the incommensurate. Scattered, their city unbound, stone falling away from stone, "they arrived at the ends of the earth." All the world has become Babylon, permanently baffled. The play of J's language emerges in Rosenberg's version as it does not in Tyndale, King James, or Speiser. That verbal play tends to give our dramatic sympathies to the builders of Babel even as we apprehend the fierce irony of J's Yahweh. As always, what we are likeliest to miss in J when we read her previous translators is given back to us by Rosenberg.

The Book of J

TRANSLATED BY

DAVID ROSENBERG

For Michal Govrin

1

Before a plant of the field was in earth, before a grain of the field sprouted—Yahweh had not spilled rain on the earth, nor was there man to work the land—yet from the day Yahweh made earth and sky, a mist from within would rise to moisten the surface. Yahweh shaped an earthling from clay of this earth, blew into its nostrils the wind of life. Now look: man becomes a creature of flesh.

2

Now Yahweh planted a garden in Eden, eastward, settled there the man he formed. From the land Yahweh grew all trees lovely to look upon, good to eat from; the tree of life was there in the garden, and the tree of knowing good and bad.

3

Out of Eden flows a river; it waters the garden, then outside, branches into four: one, Pishon, winds through the whole of Havila, land with gold—excellent gold, where the bdellium is, the lapis lazuli. The second, named Gihon, moves through the length of Cush; Tigris, the third, travels east of Asshur; and Euphrates is the fourth. Yahweh lifts the man, brings him to rest in the garden of Eden, to tend it and watch. "From all trees in the garden you are free to eat"—so Yahweh desires the man know—"but the tree of knowing good and bad you will not touch. Eat from it," said Yahweh, "and on that day death touches you."

4

"It is no good the man be alone," said Yahweh. "I will make a partner to stand beside him." So Yahweh shaped out of the soil all the creatures of the field and birds of the air, bringing them to the man to see how he would call them. Whatever the man called became the living creature's name. Soon all wild animals had names the man gave them, all birds of the air and creatures of the field, but the man did not find his partner among them. Now Yahweh put the man into a deep sleep; when he fell asleep, he took a rib, closed the flesh of his side again. Starting with the part taken out of the man, Yahweh shaped the rib into woman, returned her to the side of the man.

"This one is bone of my bone, flesh of my flesh," said the man. "Woman I call her, out of man she was parted." So a man parts from his mother and father, clings to his wife: they were one flesh.

And look: they are naked, man and woman, untouched by shame, not knowing it.

Now the snake was smoother-tongued than any wild
creature that Yahweh made. "Did the God really
mean," he said to the woman, "you can't eat from
any tree of the garden?"

"But the fruit of the trees we may," said the woman
to the snake. "Just the tree in the middle of the
garden, the God said. You can't eat from it, you can't
touch—without death touching you." "Death will
not touch you," said the snake to the woman. "The
God knows on the day you eat from it your eyes will
fall open like gods, knowing good and bad."

Now the woman sees how good the tree looks, to eat
from, how lovely to the eyes, lively to the mind. To
its fruit she reached; ate, gave to her man, there with
her, and he ate.

And the eyes of both fall open, grasp knowledge of
their naked skin. They wound together fig leaves,
made coverings for themselves.

6
Now they hear Yahweh's voice among the evening
breezes, walking in the garden; they hide from the
face of Yahweh, the man and his woman, among
trees of the garden. "Where are you?" Yahweh called
to the man.

"I heard your voice in the garden," he answered. "I
trembled, I knew I was smooth-skinned, I hid."

"Who told you naked is what you are?" he asked. "Did you touch the tree I desired you not eat?"

"The woman you gave to stand beside me—she gave me fruit of the tree, I ate."

7
"What is this you have done?" said Yahweh to the woman.

"The smooth-tongued snake gave me, I ate."

"Since you did this," said Yahweh to the snake, "you are bound apart from flocks, from any creature of the field, bound to the ground, crawling by your smooth belly: dirt you shall taste from first day to last. I make you enemy to woman, enmity bound between your seed and hers. As you strike his heel, he shall strike your head."

8
To the woman he said: "Pain increasing, groans that spread into groans: having children will be labor. To your man's body your belly will rise, for he will be eager above you."

To the man he said: "You bent to your woman's voice, eager to eat—from the tree of which you knew my desire: 'You will not eat from it.' Now: bitter be the soil to your taste; in labor you will bend to eat from it, each day you live.

"Thorns and thistles will bloom before you; you will grasp the bitter herbs the field gives you.

"As you sow the sweat of your face so you will reap your bread, till you return to earth—from it you were taken. Dust you are, to dust you return."

9

The man named his wife Hava: she would have all who live, smooth the way, mother.

Now Yahweh made clothes from skins of the wild animals for the man and woman, dressed them.

10

"Look," said Yahweh, "the earthling sees like one of us, knowing good and bad. And now he may blindly reach out his hand, grasp the tree of life as well, eat, and live forever."

Now Yahweh took him out of the Garden of Eden, to toil—in the soil from which he was taken.

The earthling was driven forward; now, settled there—east of Eden—the winged sphinxes and the waving sword, both sides flashing, to watch the way to the Tree of Life.

11

Now the man knew Hava, his wife, in the flesh; she conceived Cain: "I have created a man as Yahweh has," she said when he was born. She conceived again: Abel his brother was born. Abel, it turned out, was a watcher of sheep, Cain a tiller of soil.

12

The days turned into the past; one day, Cain brought an offering to Yahweh, from fruit of the earth. Abel also brought an offering, from the choicest of his flock, from its fat parts, and Yahweh was moved by Abel and his holocaust. Yet by Cain and his holocaust he was unmoved. This disturbed Cain deeply, his face fell.

"What so disturbs you?" said Yahweh to Cain. "Why wear a face so fallen? Look up: if you conceive good it is moving; if not good, sin is an open door, a demon crouching there. It will rise to you, though you be above it."

13

Cain was speaking to his brother Abel, and then it happened: out in the field, Cain turned to his brother, killing him.

Now Yahweh said to Cain: "Where is your brother, Abel?" "I didn't know it is I," he answered, "that am my brother's watchman."

14

"What have you done?" he said. "A voice—your brother's blood—cries to me from the earth. And so it be a curse: the soil is embittered to you. Your brother's blood sticks in its throat.

"You may work the ground but it won't yield to you, its strength held within. Homeless you will be on the land, blown in the wind."

"My sentence is stronger than my life," Cain said to
Yahweh. "Look: today you drove me from the face
of the earth—you turned your face from me. I return
nowhere, homeless as the blowing wind. All who
find me may kill me."

"By my word it will be known," said Yahweh, "any
killer of Cain will be cut to the root—seven times
deeper." Now Yahweh touched Cain with a mark: a
warning not to kill him, to all who may find him.

Cain turned away from Yahweh's presence, settled
in a windblown land, east of Eden.

15

Now Cain knew his wife in the flesh; she conceived,
Hanoch was born. The days turned into the past: he
has founded an ir—city—calling it by the name of
his son, Hanoch.

Now Irad—a city lad—was born, to Hanoch; Irad
fathered Mehuyael; Mehuyael fathered Methusael;
and Methusael, Lamech.

16

Lamech rose up and married two wives for himself;
one was named Adah, the second, Tzilah.

Adah bore Yaval, who became father to tent dwell-
ers, watchers of flocks.

Yuval was his brother's name, father to musicians,
masters of flute and lyre.

Tzilah also gave birth: Tuval-Cain, master of bronze and iron, to whom Naamah was sister.

"Hear my voice," sang Lamech to his wives, to Adah and Tzilah, "hear what's sung to Lamech's wives: A man I've killed if he wounded me; a boy too, for a blow—merely. If Cain's justice cuts seven deep—for Lamech, it reaches down seven and seventy."

17

Now Adam still knew his wife in the flesh; she bore a son, called him Seth—"God has settled another seed in me, reaching beyond Abel, whom Cain cut down"—which became his name. Now Seth grew to father a son, Enosh by name—"sweet mortal," he called him. And in that time began the fond calling by name of Yahweh.

18

Now look: from the earthling's first step man has spread over the face of the earth. He has fathered many daughters. The sons of heaven came down to look at the daughters of men, alive to their loveliness, knowing any they pleased for wives.

19

"My spirit will not watch man so long," Yahweh said. "He is mortal flesh." Now his days were numbered: to one hundred and twenty years.

20

Now the race of giants: they were in the land then,
from the time the sons of heaven entered the rooms
of the daughters of men. Hero figures were born to
them, men and women of mythic fame.

21

Yahweh looked upon the human, saw him growing
monstrous in the land—desire created only bad
thoughts, spreading into all his acts. Now Yahweh's
pain was hard, having watched the man spread in the
land; it saddened his heart. "I will erase the earthlings
I created across the face of earth," said Yahweh,
"from human creature to wild beast, crawling creature to bird in the air—it chills me to have made
them." But innocent Noah warmed Yahweh's heart.

22

"Come—you, your household," said Yahweh to
Noah. "Enter the ark. It was you my eyes found
upright in this generation, righteous before me.

"Gather in seven by seven—seven male and female
mates—from each of the clean creatures; from the
unclean creatures a male and female mate; also from
the birds of the air, seven by seven, male and female:
to spread life's seed over the whole face of earth.

"In another seven days rain spills on the land unceas-
ing: forty days, forty nights. I will erase all that rose

into living substance, spreading over the face of earth—all which I made."

Now Noah did it, all as Yahweh desired. Noah and his sons, his wife, the sons' wives—all came with him to the ark, facing the flood water.

23

Now look: the seven days and the flood water is on the land. Look: the rain would be on the land, forty days, forty nights.

Yahweh shut him in at the door.

24

So it was: forty days on the land, the flood; the water rose, the ark lifted up above the land.

The water overcame everything, overran the land; the ark made its way over a face of water.

Now the water was swelling fast, the earth was subdued: all the high mountains under the sky were covered.

Fifteen cubits higher grew the water, above the submerged mountains.

All living spirit on dry land—the wind of life in its nostrils—died. Erased: all that arose from the earth, earthlings from man to beast, creatures that crawl and creatures that fly. They ceased to exist, all but Noah, left alone in the ark with all his company.

25

Now it was held back, the rain from the sky. The
water rolled back from over the land: so it had come
and so it was going.

Now look: the window of the ark which Noah made
opens, after forty days. He reaches out, lets go a
dove—to see if the water slipped away from the land.

But the dove found nowhere to settle its feet, returning to him, to the ark, since water covered the face
of the land. He reached out his hand, caught it,
pulled it back to him, into the ark.

Another seven days passes: again the dove is sent
away from the ark. Toward evening it comes back
to him, the dove, but look: an olive twig dangles from
its beak. So Noah knew that the water was slipping
away from over the land.

Another seven days passes, again; once more he
sends the dove. And now it didn't return to him, he
didn't hold it again.

26

Noah rolled back the cover of the ark and looked: so,
firm earth it was, facing him.

Now Noah built an altar to Yahweh, took from all
the clean creatures, all the clean birds, offering them
up: holocausts on the altar.

Now Yahweh smelled a soothing scent; in his heart,
Yahweh was moved: "Never again will I judge the

earth because of the earthling. Imagination bends his human heart to bad designs from the very start. Never again will I cut off all that lives, as I have done.

"Never again, for all the days on earth—sowing turning to reaping, cold turning hot, summer turning to winter, day turning into night—never ending."

27
And here they were: the sons of Noah leaving the ark, Shem, Ham, Yafat. It is Ham who is father to Canaan. From these three sons of Noah, man spread over the earth.

28
So it was: Noah, who tills the soil, is the first to plant a vineyard. Now he drank from the wine, now he was drunk, now he lay uncovered in the middle of his tent.

The one who fathered Canaan, Ham, enjoyed his father's nakedness: now he tells it to the two brothers outside.

But Shem and Yafat took a cloak, draped it over their shoulders, walked in backward, covered their naked father, faces averted: they never saw their father naked.

Roused from his wine, Noah learned what happened, what his youngest son made of him. "A bitter curse on Canaan," he said. "A servant to his brothers' servants.

"A blessing on Yahweh, Shem's God," he said. "But Canaan—his servant.

"God will fatten Yafat, make him welcome in Shem's tents. But Canaan—his servant."

29
Now listen: all the earth uses one tongue, one and the same words. Watch: they journey from the east, arrive at a valley in the land of Sumer, settle there.

"We can bring ourselves together," they said, "like stone on stone, use brick for stone: bake it until hard." For mortar they heated bitumen.

"If we bring ourselves together," they said, "we can build a city and tower, its top touching the sky—to arrive at fame. Without a name we're unbound, scattered over the face of the earth."

Yahweh came down to watch the city and tower the sons of man were bound to build. "They are one people, with the same tongue," said Yahweh. "They conceive this between them, and it leads up until no boundary exists to what they will touch. Between us, let's descend, baffle their tongue until each is scatterbrain to his friend."

From there Yahweh scattered them over the whole face of earth; the city there came unbound.

That is why they named the place Bavel: their tongues were baffled there by Yahweh. Scattered by Yahweh from there, they arrived at the ends of the earth.

30

"Bring yourself out of your birthplace," Yahweh said to Abram, "out of your father's house, your homeland—to a land I will bring you to see. I will make of you greatness, a nation and a blessing; of your name, fame—bliss brought out of you.

"One who blesses you I will bless; curse those who curse you; bring all families of earth to see themselves blessed in you."

Now Abram comes out, follows Yahweh's words to him. Lot went out with him.

31

Abram crossed into the land, as far as the sanctuary of Shechem, the oak of Moreh; he found the Canaanites in the land, back then. Now Yahweh revealed himself to Abram: "I will give this land to your seed." He built an altar there: to Yahweh who appeared to him.

He rose, came to the hills east of Beth El, pitched his tent there—Beth El to the west, Ai to the east. It was there, building an altar to Yahweh, he called on him by name, Yahweh. Yet Abram kept on, journeyed down toward the Negev.

Now look: a famine grips the land. Abram went down further, toward Egypt, to live—starvation ruled the land.

At the point of entering Egypt, listen: "To look upon," he said to his wife, Sarai, "you are as lovely a woman as I have known. Imagine the Egyptians when they see you—'That one is his wife.' Now I am killed; you, kept alive.

"Say you are sister to—and for—me, for my good and on your behalf. As my flesh lives, it is because of you and with you."

So it was: Abram crosses into Egypt; the Egyptians see the woman, how lovely. Pharaoh's officers see her, praise her to Pharaoh. Now the woman is taken away, into Pharaoh's palace.

On her behalf, it was good for Abram. Look: he had sheep and cattle, donkeys and asses, servants and maids, and camels. But Yahweh struck Pharaoh with disease as if with lightning—his whole house stricken—on behalf of Sarai, Abram's wife.

32

Now Pharaoh called for Abram: "On whose behalf have you done this to me? Why not tell me this is your wife? Why say, 'This is my sister'—I would of course take her in, for my wife. Yet now, look: a wife that's yours—take her out of here, for life."

Pharaoh hurried his men to take him out of the country—with his wife and his whole household.

Now Abram rose up from Egypt—wife, household, and Lot with him—up toward the Negev. He was surrounded with livestock, slowed with silver and gold.

33

His journey took him from the Negev to Beth El, to arrive at the very place he pitched his tent in the beginning, between Beth El and Ai. Here was the calling: the first altar made, he called the name Yahweh.

Lot who traveled with Abram—he too was surrounded by many sheep, cattle, tents. Now look: argument breaks out between Abram's shepherds and Lot's—this was when the Canaanites were settled on the land, along with the Perizzites, back then. "Please, hold off this quarreling between us, between our shepherds," Abram said to Lot. "We are men who hold each other as brothers. You may let go of me and face the whole country, open before us. Please yourself, make your own way: left, and I'll go right; south, I'll go northward."

Now Lot lifted his gaze, drank in the whole Jordan valley—how moist the land was everywhere (this was before Yahweh destroyed Sodom and Gomorrah)—like Yahweh's own garden, like Egypt—gazing as far as Zoar.

Lot chose all the Jordan valley for himself; he set out toward the east—and so a man let go of his brother. Abram settled in Canaan's land; Lot in the cities of the valley, his tents set beside Sodom.

34

Now the people of Sodom had gone bad, parading contempt in Yahweh's eyes.

"Open your eyes, and may it please you look around you," said Yahweh to Abram after Lot had parted, "from the place you are standing to the north, then down to the Negev, to the sea and back, westward. The whole land you see I will give you: to your seed for all time.

"I have planted that seed, made it true as the dust— like each grain of dust no man could ever count. Rise, walk around on this land—open and broad—it is to you I will give it."

Abram folded his tents, moved on; he settled by the oaks of Mamre, beside Hebron, built there an altar to Yahweh.

35

These things had passed when Yahweh's word came to Abram in a vision passing before him: "Have no fear Abram, I am your shield and reward, a shield that prospers."

"Lord Yahweh," said Abram, "what good is prospering when I walk toward my death without children, my inheritance passed to a son of Damascus, Eliezer, accountant of my house. Look at me," Abram continued, "you have given me no seed; and look, a son not mine—though under my roof—inherits my household."

Now hear Yahweh's word that passed before him: "Not this one for your heir—only what passes between your legs may inherit from you." He drew him outside: "Look well, please, at heaven; count the stars—if you can count them. So will be your seed"—and so it was said to him. He trusted Yahweh, and it was accounted to him as strength.

36

"I am Yahweh, who drew you out from Ur, of the Chaldeans," he said to him, "to give you this land as heir."

"Lord Yahweh," he said, "how may I show it is mine to possess?"

"Bring me a heifer of three," he said to him, "a she-goat and ram, three-year-olds also, a turtledove and a fledgling dove." All these he brought, cut down the middle, placed each one's half opposite the other; the birds he left unparted.

And the vultures descended on the carcasses, but Abram scared them off. Now look: as the sun goes down, a deep sleep falls over Abram—a covering darkness thrown over him: underneath he is plunged in fear.

"Know this within," he said to Abram, "your seed will be strangers in a land not theirs; slavery will be their state—plunged in it for four hundred years. Yet the nation which enslaves them will also know judgment.

"After, they will come out prosperous, surrounded with it.

"You will come to your forefathers peacefully, when good and old be settled in your grave. They will be a fourth generation before they return: that long will Amorite contempt build, until the glass is full."

So it was: the sun gone, darkness reigns. Now look: a smoking kiln and its blazing torch pass between the parted bodies.

It was that day Yahweh cut a covenant with Abram: "I gave this land to your seed, from the river of Egypt to the great river, Euphrates—of the Kenite, the Kenizzite, the Kadmonite; of the Hittite, the Perizzite, the Rephaim; of the Amorite, the Canaanite, the Girgashite, the Jebusite."

37

Now Sarai, his wife, had no children with Abram; she had an Egyptian maid, Hagar her name. "See how it is," Sarai is saying to Abram, "Yahweh has held me back from having children. Please go into my maid now; maybe a child will come out of it." Abram grasped Sarai's words; his wife Sarai had taken in Hagar the Egyptian, her maid (it was ten years since Abram had settled in the land of Canaan), and hands her to Abram to go into as a wife.

Now he came into Hagar so that she conceived; she saw that she was pregnant and looked down at her mistress with contempt in her eyes. "I have been hurt on behalf of you," said Sarai to Abram. "I gave my maid into your grasp and now, seeing that she's pregnant, she looks down at me—may we know Yahweh's judgment between you and me."

"See how it is: your maid is in your hands," said Abram to Sarai. "Do as you see best." Now Sarai punished her; she fled beneath her eyes.

38

Yahweh's angel found her by a watering hole: a spring in the desert on the track to Shur. "Hagar, maid of Sarai," he called, "from where have you come, where are you going?"

"I am escaping," she said, "the cold eyes of my lady, Sarai." "Go back to your lady," Yahweh's angel said to her, "hand yourself back to her desire."

Now Yahweh's angel said to her: "Your seed I will sow beyond a man's eyes to count." "Look," said Yahweh's angel again, "you have been made pregnant. You will give birth to a boy: Ishmael, you will name him. Yahweh heard your pun*ish*ment: you will hear a *male*.

"Impudent, he will be stubborn as wild donkeys, his guard up against everyone and theirs raised against him. The tents of his rebellion will rise before the eyes of his brothers."

Yahweh had spoken to her and the name she called him was "You are the all-seeing God," having exclaimed, "You are the God I lived to see—and lived after seeing." That is why the hole was called "Well of Living Sight"—you can see it right here, between Kadesh and Bered.

39

Now Yahweh was seen by Abram among the oaks of Mamre; he was napping by his tent opening in the midday heat.

He opened his eyes: three men were standing out there, plain as day. From the opening in the tent he rushed toward them, bent prostrate to the ground.

"My Lord," he said, "if your heart be warmed, please don't pass your servant, in front of his eyes. Take some water, please, for washing your feet; rest a moment under the tree. I will bring a piece of bread to give your hearts strength. Let your journey wait; let your passing warm your servant—to serve you."

"You may," they said, "make what you've said true."

40

Abram rushed toward the tent, to Sarai. "Hurry, three measures of our richest flour, to roll into our finest rolls."

From there to the cattle he runs, chooses a tender calf—the best—gives it to the servant boy, who hurries to make it ready.

Now Abram gathers curds, milk, and the tender meat he had prepared, sets it down for them under the tree, stands near, overseeing: they ate.

41

"Your wife—where is Sarai?" they asked of him. "Look, she is here," he said, "in the tent."

"I will appear again to you—in the time a life ripens and appears. Count on it and see: a son for Sarai, your wife." Sarai was listening by the tent opening—it was right behind them.

But Sarai and Abram were old, many days were behind them; for Sarai the periods of women ceased to exist. So within her Sarai's sides split: "Now that I'm used to groaning, I'm to groan with pleasure? My lord is also shriveled."

"Why is Sarai laughing," asked Yahweh of Abram, "when she says, 'Now I can count on giving birth, when I'm elderly?' Is a thing too surprising for Yahweh? In the time a life ripens and appears I will appear to you—and to Sarai, a son."

Sarai hid her feeling: "No, I wasn't laughing"—she had been scared. "No," he said now, "your sides split, count on it."

42

The figures rose, starting down toward Sodom; from there they could see its upturned face. Abram walks with them, showing the way.

"Do I hide from Abram," said Yahweh within, "what I will do? Abram will emerge a great nation, populous, until all nations of the earth see themselves blessed in him. I have known him within; he will fill his children, his household, with desire to follow Yahweh's way. Tolerance and justice will emerge— to allow what Yahweh says to be fulfilled."

Now Yahweh says: "The noise from Sodom and Gomorrah grows; as their contempt grows heavy, it rises. It weighs on me to go down, to see what contempt this disturbance signifies. If brought down to find offense, I will pull them down. If not, I will be pleased to know."

So the figures, leaving there, descend toward Sodom. Now Abram stands aside, facing Yahweh.

43

Abram drew close. "Will you wipe away the innocent beside those with contempt? What if there are fifty sincere men inside the city, will you also wipe the place away? Can you not hold back for the fifty innocent within it?

"Heaven forbid you bring this thing to light, to erase the innocent with the contemptuous—as if sincerity and contempt were the same thing. Can it be— heaven forbid—you, judge of all the earth, will not bring justice?"

"If I find fifty innocent inside the city," said Yahweh, "I will hold back from the whole place on their behalf."

"Listen please," said Abram, pressing further, "I have imagined I may speak to Yahweh—I, mere dust and ashes. What if we have less than fifty sincere, five less—for these five will you wipe away an entire city?"

"I will not pull down," said Yahweh, "if I find forty-five there."

Yet he found more to say. "Consider," he pressed on, "you find forty there." And he said, "On behalf of these forty I will not act."

"Please, do not lose patience my lord," he continued, "if I speak further. Consider thirty are found there." And he said, "I will not act if I find thirty there."

"Listen please," said Abram, pressing further. "I have imagined I may speak to Yahweh—I, made of mere dust and ashes. Consider twenty are found there." "I will not pull down," he said, "on behalf of these twenty."

"Please, do not lose patience my lord," he continued, "if I speak further—for the last time. Consider ten are found there." And he said, "I will not pull down on behalf of these ten."

Now Yahweh, having finished speaking to Abram, went on. Abram turned back, toward his place.

44

In the evening two angels arrived in Sodom. Lot was
sitting in the courtyard of Sodom's gate. As he saw—
then recognized—them, Lot rose, then bent prostrate, face to the ground. "Please hear me, my lords,"
he said, "and stop at the house of this humble servant.
Stay the night, wash your feet, rise refreshed, then
go on—the road will wait."

"No," they said, "we will lie by the broad road."

Then he begs them, until they stop, to go with him
to his house. Now he makes them a feast, complete
with fresh-baked matzah and drink: they ate.

Yet before they had fallen asleep, the townsfolk—
Sodomites—press round the house, from boys to
graybeards, the whole population from as far as the
outskirts. "Where are the people who visited you
tonight?" they call to Lot. "Bring them out for us,"
they ask. "We want to know their intimate ways."

Now Lot came to the door, closing it behind him.
"Brothers, please don't act by showing contempt.
Listen, I have two daughters who have not known
a man intimately. Let me bring these out for you:
handle them as you please. Only leave the visitors
untouched, bring no hand to them: I have brought
them under my roof's wing."

"Get out of the way," one said. "He comes here to
share our shelter and already he hands down the law.
Now you will know more than them, a touch of our

contempt." They pressed against the man, against Lot, were ready to break down the door.

But from within a hand stretched out, brought Lot toward those visitors in the house. Now they shut him in. They blinded them with light: the people at the door, boys as well as graybeards. They would grope for the door handle vainly.

The visitors with Lot said: "Are there others of yours—a son-in-law, sons, daughters—anywhere in the city, to be gathered from this place? The offense has risen to Yahweh's ear. Yahweh sends us—to bring down this loud violence."

Lot hurries to speak to his sons-in-law—those his daughters prepared to marry. "Pack up now, leave this place," Lot said. "Yahweh is prepared to over-turn the city." Now watch: the sons-in-law see only—in him—a joke on them.

Now the sun began to rise; the angels pressed Lot on. "Get up," they said, "gather your wife, your two daughters that are left—or be gathered into the crush of citizens—in this city's sin." He wavered; the fig-ures grasped his arm, his wife's, the hands of his two daughters—it was Yahweh reaching out to him. They brought him out, stopping only outside the city.

45
So it was: while being brought out, one said to them, "Pity your lot—run, don't look back, don't stop until

the end of the valley. Escape to the mountain—or be crushed."

"My lord," Lot said to them, "please not so. Listen to me: if this servant has warmed your heart, evoked your tender pity—you have kept me alive—then see: I cannot survive in the mountains, where the hand of contempt brands me. Look instead at this town within my chosen lot, small enough to overlook. Let me fly there, please, it is small, insignificant—and so will I be there."

"Hear," he answered, "I pity your lot again, will not overturn this city you speak for. Hurry, run—I will do nothing until you're there." And this is how one came to call this city Smallah.

The sun rose above the earth as Lot came to Smallah.

46

Now Yahweh spilled on Sodom and Gomorrah a volcanic rain: fire from Yahweh, from the sky. These cities he overturned, with the whole valley, all the citizens in the cities and plants in the earth.

Behind him, Lot's wife stopped to look back—and crystallized into a statue of salt.

Abram arose that morning, hurried to the place he had last faced Yahweh, had stood there with him. Looking out over the upturned faces of Sodom and Gomorrah, over the whole face of the valley, he saw—so it was—a black incense over the earth climbing like smoke from a kiln.

47

But Lot went out from Smallah, toward the mountains, his two daughters with him—he grew afraid to stay in Smallah, settled in a cave alone with his daughters.

"Father is getting old," the firstborn said to the youngest. "There are no men left on earth to enter us—to follow the way of the earth.

"We'll pour drink for our father; with wine we will lie with him—life will follow from our father's seed."

On that night their wine poured out for their father. The eldest now comes, lies with her father; he recalls no sense of her lying there, nor when she rises.

Now listen: "I lay last night with my father," said the eldest to the youngest. "Follow me. We will have him drunk with wine tonight again, so you may have from him. At his side, we will give life to our father's seed."

The wine flows on this night also, for their father. The youngest rises, to lie with him; he senses nothing of having her, nor her rising.

So Lot's two daughters became pregnant by their father. The eldest gave birth to a son named Moab—"from father"—the father of the Moabites we see today. A son was born as well to the youngest, whom she called Ben Ami—"son of my kin"—the father down through today's sons of Ammon.

48

Now Yahweh conceived for Sarai what he had said.

Sarai became pregnant and, the time ripe, gave birth: a son appearing from Sarai, for Abram in his ripe old age.

"Now who would conceive of Abram having children at Sarai's breast? But I gave birth to a son—not to wisdom—for his old age."

49

These things had passed when Abram would hear: "Listen carefully, Milcah too gave birth to children, for your brother, Nachor. Uz, the eldest; then Buz his brother, and Kemuel, father of Aram; then Chesed, Hazo, Pildash, Jidlaph, Bethuel. Bethuel fathered Rebecca—but these eight were mothered by Milcah for Nachor, Abram's brother. His second wife also gave birth: Reumah mothered Tebah, Gaham, Tahash, and Maacah."

50

Now Abram was very old, his better days—thoroughly blessed by Yahweh—behind him.

"Please put your hand under my thigh," said Abram to the senior servant, head of all under his roof. "Swear for me, by Yahweh, God of sky and earth, that you will choose no wife for my son from Canaanite daughters, though I'm settled among them. Instead, visit my homeland, my birthplace, bring out a wife for Isaac, my son."

"What if the woman won't come, following me back to this land?" the servant asked him. "Do I then bring out your son—from here, back to the land you left behind?"

"Watch yourself," Abram said to him. "Don't turn to returning, especially my son. Yahweh, God in the skies, who took me out of my father's house, my homeland, who spoke to me, giving his word—'I will give this land to your seed'—will place his angel by your side, until you choose a wife from there, for my son. If she won't follow, won't be beside you, be cleansed of this vow—so long as my son doesn't settle there."

Now the servant places his hand under Abram's thigh—the lord to whom he vows in this matter. Ten camels he chooses, from among his master's camels.

He departs with precious goods in hand, his lord's; he comes out as far as the city of Haran, in Mesopotamia. He has the camels kneel outside the city by the well, toward evening, the time the women come to carry water.

"Yahweh," he said, "my lord Abram's God, let it happen please, today in my presence. Show tenderness for my lord, Abram. Look, I've placed myself by the watering place, the city's daughters are coming to draw from it. Allow that the young woman I am drawn to—to whom I will say, 'Please, lower your jug so I can drink'—will say, 'Drink, and let me water your camels also.' Let her prove the one unveiled for Isaac's servant, and for your servant Isaac. Through her may I see the tenderness you show to my lord."

51

Now before he had finished speaking, look: Rebecca appeared out of the city, child of Bethuel—a son to Milcah, the wife of Nachor, Abram's brother—and on her shoulder the jug. The young woman was lovely as an apparition, as fresh, one no man had known, and she went down to the well.

Now she fills her jug; as she ascends the servant runs toward her. "A sip, please," he says, "a little water from your jug." "Drink, my lord," she says, lowering her jug down quickly to her hands, letting him drink.

Allowing him all he could drink, she said, "For your camels I will pour too, until they've drunk enough." Quickly she turned over her jug, into the trough, then hurried back to the well to draw up more, watering all his camels.

52

The man stood staring but silent, not to disturb the outcome: has Yahweh proved his journey fertile?

Look: as the camels finish drinking, the man takes a nose ring of gold—a half shekel its weight—and two bracelets for her arms, ten gold coins their weight.

"Whose daughter are you?"—he has spoken. "Please say—and of your father's house, tell: is there room for us to stop?"

"I am Bethuel's daughter," she said to him. "He is the son of Milcah, whom she had with Nachor." She continued, "There is straw and yes, there is feed, more than enough, and there's room to stay over."

Now the man was awed, fell prostrate to Yahweh. "Bless Yahweh, my lord Abram's God, who has not held back tenderness nor hidden his trust from my lord. And I—Yahweh ushered my feet to my lord's family."

The young woman hurries, tells those in her mother's house.

53

Rebecca had a brother, Laban his name. Laban rushes outside to the man, toward the well. He had seen the nose ring, the bracelets on his sister's wrists. And "So the man spoke to me," he heard his sister say—after hearing all her words. He approached the man and so it was: he was still standing by the camels, beside the well.

"Come, Yahweh's blessed," he said. "You are standing outside, yet I've already made room in the house and a place for the camels." Now the man draws near the house; the camels are unloaded, straw and feed provided for them, and water for washing feet—his, and the feet of the men who accompanied him. Yet when meat was placed in front of him, he said, "I won't open my mouth to eat until the words I bring are out." "Speak out," came the response.

"A servant of Abram am I," he began. "Yahweh has blessed my master, enriched him, given him sheep and cattle, silver and gold, servants and maids, camels and donkeys. My lord's wife, Sarai, gave birth to a son for him—in her old age—and he made him heir to all he has.

"He made me swear by these words: 'Do not choose a wife for my son from Canaanite daughters,' he said. 'I am settled in their land; instead, to my father's house journey, to my family, to choose a wife for my son.'

" 'Yet what if the woman won't follow me?' I questioned. 'Yahweh,' he answered me, 'who has walked beside me, will send his angel with you. Your way will be smoothed, you will find my son a wife, among family, among my father's relations.

" 'You will be cleansed from your vow only then— when you approach my family; if they won't give you, you are cleansed of it.'

"Today I came to the well, said, 'Yahweh, my lord Abram's God, if you are smoothing the way I walk, look: I've placed myself beside the well of water—let it happen the young woman comes out for water, so I may utter, "Let me drink, please, a little water from your jug." "Not only you," she will say, "but your camels will drink also"—let her be the woman Yahweh unveils for my lord's son.'

"I hadn't finished voicing these words to myself before—look—Rebecca comes out, jug on her shoulder, goes down toward the well, draws—and I say, 'Please, a sip.' Quickly she lowers the jug down from herself—'Drink,' she says, 'I will water your camels too.' I drank, along with the camels.

" 'Whose daughter are you?' I asked—the words leaping out on their own. 'The daughter of Bethuel, son of Nachor—whom Milcah gave birth to,' she would say. I set the ring in her nostril, the bracelets on her wrists.

"I knelt, prostrated myself to Yahweh. 'I bless Yahweh, God of my lord Abram, who guided me in the true path, to the daughter of my lord's brother, to choose her for his son.' So, if you will generously act, genuinely on my lord's side, tell me; if not, speak also: I will turn to the right hand or to the left."

Then Laban and Bethuel answered: "This thing has unfolded from Yahweh," they said. "We could not say anything against it, bad or good. See: Rebecca is there beside you, provided; bring her out for a wife to your lord's son, just as Yahweh spoke."

54
So it was: as he heard their words, Abram's servant knelt face down, prostrate to Yahweh.

Now the servant draws out gold and silver jewelry, garments, gifts for Rebecca; and for her brother and her mother, precious objects.

They ate, drank—he and the men with him—and stayed over. Rising in the morning, he asked, "Send me back to my master."

"Let a virgin prepare. Even a few days, no more than ten," the brother and the mother answered. "Then she will come."

"Don't hold me back," he said to them. "Now that Yahweh has smoothed my path, let me follow it to my lord."

"We'll bring the young woman," they said, "and have it from her own lips." Calling Rebecca, they asked her, "Will you leave beside this man?" "I'll go," she said.

Now they go out with their sister, Rebecca and her maids, see her off with Abram's servant and his men.

So it was they blessed Rebecca: "Our sister," they said, "may you mother thousands and thousands, until your descendants inherit the gate their enemy goes out."

55
Now Rebecca was ready, along with her maids; she mounted the camels, followed the man—the servant who chose her, who is departing.

Now Isaac was coming home by way of the well known as "Well of Living Sight," since he had settled in that area of the desert. Out in a field in contemplation as evening approached, Isaac opened his eyes, looked up—and there were the camels, approaching.

Rebecca gazed out and Isaac was there. She leaned over on the camel, asking the servant, "Who is the man, that one walking in the field toward us?" "That is my lord," said the servant. She reached for the veil, covered herself.

The servant told Isaac the story of what he had done, the things that happened.

Isaac brings her inside his mother Sarai's tent; he chooses Rebecca, she becomes his wife; he loves her, is consoled when his mother passes away.

So Abram passed down all he had to Isaac. To his sons by concubines, Abram gave gifts, sent them away eastward—while he was still alive—away from his son Isaac, to the country in the East.

Now look: after Abram's passing, his son Isaac is blessed by God. So Isaac settled near Beer Lahai Roi (Well of Living Sight).

56
Now Isaac appeals to Yahweh on behalf of his wife: she is childless. Yahweh responds, Rebecca becomes pregnant.

The children are struggling inside her; "Is this what I prayed for?" she said, questioning Yahweh.

"Two nations," Yahweh said to her, "are inside you—two peoples already at odds in your belly. One country grows stronger on the strength of the other; youth grows senior over age."

Her time for giving birth grown ripe, look: twins are in her belly. The first comes out ruddy, hairy all over as a coat, so they named him Esau, ruffian.

Then his brother comes out, his hand latching onto Esau's heel, like a figure J. He named him Jacob, heel-clutcher; Isaac was sixty when she gave birth to them.

When the youths are grown, look: Esau is a man with knowledge of the hunt, the outdoors; Jacob is quiet, keeping to the tents. Isaac loved Esau, whose game tasted sumptuous in his mouth. But Rebecca loved Jacob.

One day Jacob was cooking a stew of beans; Esau came back from the fields exhausted. "Please, pour me some mouthfuls from that reddish stuff," Esau asked Jacob. "I can barely speak." That's why he was called "Red," Edom.

"Sell me your birthright," said Jacob, "right now."

"Look, I'm fit to die," Esau said. "So what use is this blessing to me now?" "Vow it this very day," said Jacob. He swore to Jacob, selling his birthright to him.

So Jacob gave Esau bread, a stew of beans; he ate, he drank, got up and left—a blessing slighted by Esau.

57
Now look: starvation grips the land—not the earlier famine in Abram's day, but again. Isaac journeys to Abimelech, Philistine king, to Gerar.

Yahweh appears to him: "Do not go down toward Egypt, stay on the land I envision for you.

"Reside in this land: I will be with you, bless you; it is to you, your seed, I will give all these lands. I will bring you to see the blessing I vowed to your father, Abram. I will make your seed numerous as stars, I will give your descendants all these lands; all the nations of earth will see themselves blessed in your future.

"For so it was: Abram heard my voice, kept watch by my word, my desire, by my laws, my way."

58
So Isaac remained in Gerar. The men around asked about his wife. "She is my sister," he said, afraid to say "my wife"—"What if the men here kill me over Rebecca?"—for what a vision she was.

Now see: he had been there for some time when Abimelech, the Philistine king, was looking out the window: there is Isaac fondling Rebecca, his wife. Abimelech called to Isaac, "It's plain as day she's

your wife—how did you dare say, 'She is my sister.' "

"Because I thought, 'What if I'm killed for her?' "
Isaac answered him.

"What drama have you brought us?" said Abimelech. "What if one man had acted in a moment, slept
with your wife. You would have brought us guilt."

Now Abimelech proclaimed for all: "One who
touches this man and his wife has felt his own death."

59
Isaac sowed seed in that land. Now look: he reaps a
hundredfold, that same year; Yahweh was his blessing.

The man grows prosperous, success sprouts from
success, blossoms into wealth.

Look: flocks of sheep, herds of cattle, throngs of
servants. Philistine envy also bloomed. The wells
dug by his father's servants, in Abram's day, were
blocked by the Philistines, filled in with dirt.

"Go out from our people," said Abimelech to Isaac.
"You have sprung up too strong for us."

Isaac went away from there, set up camp in the
Gerar valley, took root there.

Isaac dug again for water, by the wells unearthed in
his father's day, those covered by the Philistines after

Abram's death. He called them names like those his father used.

While digging in the valley, Isaac's servants discovered a well with virgin water.

But the Gerar shepherds argued with those of Isaac: "The water is ours." So he named the well Opos, "they opposed." Yet another well, another argument over it—he named it Striving.

Moving on from there, he dug another well; they didn't struggle over this one, so he named it Rehovot, or Open. "Now that Yahweh has opened a broad road for us, we can take root in the land."

From there he went up to Beersheba. Yahweh appeared to him on that night: "I am Abram's God, your father's. Have no fear, I am in back of you. I will bless you, further your seed, on behalf of Abram, my servant."

He built an altar and there called Yahweh by name. He pitched his tent, began to dig—Isaac's servants dug it—a well there.

Now Abimelech goes out to him from Gerar, along with Ahuzzath, his adviser, and Phichol, his army chief. "Why have you come to me?" Isaac asked them. "You let anger come between us, pushed me out from among you."

"We see how Yahweh is with you, viewed it and reviewed the vow between us—please, let's remake it personally between us, a covenant cut with you. If you turned against us . . . Yet we haven't touched you, and just as we acted—only for the best, turning you away in peace—now turn us to saying, 'Yahweh be blessed wherever you be.'"

He made them a feast; they ate, they drank.

When they awoke in the morning they swore as a man to his brother. Isaac walks with them as they turned to go, sent off in peace.

Now listen: on that same day, Isaac's servants approach with news about the well they are digging: "We have found water," they said. He called it Sworn-oath—"Sheb-oath"—which is why the city is named the Well of Sheba—Beersheba—to this day.

60
Now see: Isaac is old, his sight a dim blur, as he calls his older son, Esau. "Son of mine," he began. "Here I am. As you can see," he said, "I am old enough that any new day may be my deathday.

"Listen, please gather your weapons—your quiver, your bow. Go out in the field to gather game for me, then prepare the dish I love. Serve it to me: I will eat so that my flesh may bless you before death comes."

Rebecca listened as Isaac spoke to Esau, his son. Now Esau leaves for the fields to hunt, gathering game to serve.

"Listen," said Rebecca to Jacob, her son, "I heard your father speak to your brother Esau. 'Serve me game, serve me a sumptuous dish, so I may eat and bless you in the presence of Yahweh, in the face of my death.'

"You must go—see that my words guide you, dear son of mine—go out to the herd. Choose two perfect kids for me, and I will cook the delicacy he loves from them. Serve it to your father; he will eat so that he may bless you, before dying."

"But wait," said Jacob to his mother, Rebecca. "My brother Esau is hairy and I—my skin is bare. I would be in his eyes an impostor, should he touch me. I would be serving myself a curse, not a blessing."

"My son, any curse would be mine," his mother said to him. "My voice guides you—only follow, choose them for me."

He goes out, chooses, hands them to his mother. Now his mother cooks the dish, sumptuous as his father loves it. Rebecca chooses some of her older son Esau's clothes, those in the house ready for washing, gathers them for Jacob her younger son. With the skins from the goats she gloves his hands, covers the bare nape of his neck. She put the dish, along with the bread she baked, into her son Jacob's hands.

He comes to his father, saying, "Father," and then, "Here I am." "Which one are you, my son?" "I am Esau, your firstborn," Jacob said to his father. "I followed your words to me. Get up, please, sit now and eat from my hunt, so your flesh may bless me."

"Can it be you've found it this fast, my son?" asked Isaac. "Because Yahweh your God put it into my hands," he said.

Now Isaac asked Jacob, "Please, come near, so I may touch you, my son, and know for sure that you are my son Esau."

So Jacob approached his father Isaac, who embraced him: "The voice is Jacob's voice, yet the hands are the hands of Esau."

So it was: he did not know him—his hands were the hands of Esau, his brother, hairy. He is prepared to bless him yet he asks, "Is it you, my son Esau?" "It is I," he says.

"Put it near me," he said. "I will eat my son's game so my flesh may bless you." He serves it; he eats. He serves him wine; he drinks. "Come near, my son," his father Isaac said to him. "Please kiss me."

He approaches, kisses him. Now he smells the scent of his clothes and he blesses him. "So it is: the smell of my son is the smell of a summer field blessed by Yahweh. May God grant you sky's water, earth's milk—an overflow of grain, flowing wine. May countries cater to you; and people, be anxious to please. May you seem a lord to your brothers: your mother's sons look up to you. May your haters become hated; those who bless you, blessed."

61

So it was: Isaac finishes the blessing of Jacob, and in the moment Jacob is gone from facing his father Isaac—in comes Esau, his brother, back from his hunt.

Now he too prepares the delicacy, bringing the dish to his father. "May my father get up, to eat of his son's game, and so his flesh bless me."

"Who are you?" his father Isaac asked him. "It is I, your son," he said, "your firstborn, Esau."

Isaac shuddered; heavy trembling overcame him as he spoke: "Who then was he, who hunted game, who served me? I ate it all before you came, I blessed him—and blessed he must remain."

62

As Esau heard his father's words he moaned; bitter sobbing shook him as he spoke: "Bless me—me too, my father." He could only answer, "Your brother came as an impostor to clutch your blessing."

"Was he named Jacob, heel-clutcher," he groaned, "that he might jaywalk behind me, twice? My birthright and now look: he clutches my blessing. Can it be," he mouthed, "that you have no blessing for me?"

Isaac looked down. "Look hard, a master I've given you," he uttered to Esau. "His brothers I've given for his servants; I've backed him with grain and wine. Is there anything I would have held back?—for you, my son, what's left me to do?"

Of his father, Esau asked, "The one blessing is all you have, father? Bless me too," his voice tearfully burst, "my father."

63

Now Isaac looked up. "Look all around you, the creations of earth must serve you as walls, heaven's dew as a roof. You will live by your sword, use it to serve your brother. But if held back, you will use it to cut his yoke from your neck."

Yet Esau held a grudge against Jacob for the blessing his father bestowed. His feelings found words: "It's not so many days to my father's mourning time. Then my brother's day will come, when I can kill Jacob."

Rebecca was informed of these words of her eldest son Esau. She sent for Jacob her younger son, calling out for him. "Pay attention: your brother Esau is reconciled only to the aim of killing you. It is again time your mother's voice be your guide. Hurry, escape as you are, to my brother Laban in Haran. Stay over with him, as long as it takes your brother's feelings to lose their aim. When they go away, turn from what you've done to him—then I'll send for you to return from there. Could I ever be reconciled to losing you both in one day?"

64

Now Jacob comes out from Beersheba, journeys toward Haran. Encountering the spot, he stays over there: it is already sunset. So it was: Yahweh stood beside him.

"I am Yahweh, your grandfather Abram's God, Isaac's God," he said. "The ground you camp upon belongs to you: I bestow it on your seed. Like grains of dust on the ground your seed will be; you will burst out toward the sea and toward the east, northward and toward the Negev. All families of earth will see themselves blessed in you, in your descendants.

"Now look: I am beside you, to watch you wherever you go, to see you return to this soil. I will not abandon you before I have made these words deed— on your behalf."

In the morning Jacob said: "It must be Yahweh stands by this spot, only I didn't know it."

Beth El, a place of God, is what Jacob called the spot—although the city there was named Luz in the past.

65

Now Jacob broke camp, walking toward the eastern people's land.

He gazes out and there it is: a well in the field. Look: three herds of sheep lie there, around the well that waters them. The stone is huge over the mouth of the well.

When all the herds are gathered there, together the shepherds roll the stone from over the well's mouth, water the sheep, then lay the stone back in place, over the mouth of the well.

Now Jacob speaks to them: "From where do you come, my friends?" "We are from Haran," they answer.

"Do you know Laban, Nachor's son?" he asked. "We know him," they said. "Is he well?" he continued. "Well," they answered. "Turn and see: his daughter Rachel is coming with the flock."

"Yet observe," he responded, "it is still midday, long before time to gather in livestock. Why do you not water the flock, then go back to graze?"

"That can't be done," they said. "Only when all the shepherds are gathered can the stone be rolled away from the mouth of the well, to water the sheep."

As he continues speaking with them, Rachel approaches with her father's flock: she is a shepherd.

So it was: when Jacob saw Rachel, daughter to Laban—his mother's brother—he went to the stone and rolled it off the well's mouth. Then he watered his uncle Laban's flock.

Now Jacob kisses Rachel, bestows a deep sigh, weeps. He is her father's brother, Jacob tells Rachel, and Rebecca's son. Rachel runs to her father, telling him.

So it was: Laban knew the news of Jacob, his sister's son, and ran out to him, hugging him. Now Laban kissed Jacob, bringing him to his house, and he was told all Jacob knew.

"Of my bone and flesh you are," Laban said to him, "undoubtedly."

66

He stayed on with him until the end of the month. "Just because you are my nephew you are at my service for nothing?" Laban said to Jacob. "Tell me, what can I pay you?"

Two daughters had Laban, the older named Leah, the younger's name, Rachel. The eyes of Leah were exquisite but Rachel was finely formed, a vision to grasp.

Jacob fell in love with Rachel, and he answered: "I will stay in a seven-year service—for Rachel, your youngest daughter."

"Better I give her to you," said Laban, "than give her away to another man. Stay on with me."

So Jacob would work for Rachel the seven years; they seemed in his eyes a few days, in the grasp of his love for her.

To Laban, Jacob now said: "Now let me enter my wife's arms; my service has been filled, so that we may fulfill each other."

Then Laban gathered all the people of the place for a feast with wine. But that night it was the daughter Leah who was brought in fulfillment; he grasped her body. For a maid to his daughter Laban had given Zilpah.

Now look: it is morning, it is revealed; she is Leah. "With what practice have you filled my arms?" Jacob asked Laban. "You undoubtedly know I stayed with you to work for Rachel. Why did you disarm me with empty words?"

67

"In our region it's not the custom to give away the younger one before the firstborn," said Laban. "Finish the bridal week for this one; then we can give you the other also, in return for her seven-year service."

This Jacob did, finishing the week for this one. Then Laban gave his daughter Rachel to him as a wife. For a maid to his daughter he had given Bilhah.

So he entered as well Rachel; he was in love with Rachel, instead of Leah. He worked with him seven more years, starting again.

68

Now Yahweh paid attention to the neglected Leah; he opened her womb, while Rachel remained unfruitful. Leah conceived, would have a son she named Reuben: "Yahweh has rued my emptiness," she said. "Now my husband will bend over me."

Again she conceived; having a son, she said: "As Yahweh heard my sigh—manless—he has given me this one also"—whom she named Simon.

And again she was pregnant, giving birth to a son. "Never," she said this time, "will my husband leave, for I've given him three sons." So she called him Levi.

Fruitful once more, a son was born and she said: "For this jewel I laud Yahweh." Judah was his name, the finish to her having of children.

69

Now the time of the wheat harvest found Reuben out in the field; there he unearthed a mandrake, carrying him home for his mother, Leah. "May I, please," Rachel said to Leah, "employ your son's mandrake?"

"Is it just a small thing that you have already employed my husband?" Leah answered. "You would also carry off my boy's manikin?"

"To be fair," said Rachel, "you may employ him tonight, in trade for your son's mandrake."

Now Jacob was coming in from the field in the evening as Leah went out toward him: "You must come into me," she was saying, "because I have em-

ployed you in outlay of my son's mandrake." On
that night, he came to lie with her.

And she profited, bearing another son.

70
"May this son en*joy safe*ty from Yahweh," said Rachel. So it was: Rachel had Joseph. Then Jacob
turned to Laban: "Let me go to my birthplace, return
to my family.

"Bestow my wives and children, for whom I worked
with you, so I may leave. You know my service has
brought good fortune to you."

"Please, if there is warmth in your heart, stay with
me," said Laban. "I've seen the work of Yahweh in
your service, as he blessed me with you. Fix your
own wage for me," he continued, "and I'll pay it."

"You know the service my work performs for you,
the fortunes of your livestock under me. That little
you had before has built up, to encircle you with
Yahweh's blessing—so it appears from where I
stand. When comes the time to build a family—to
serve myself?"

71
Jacob was ready to leave; settling sons and wives on
his camels, he drove off with his livestock, surrounded by all his goods (the good he had carried out
in Padan-aram)—on his way to Isaac, his father in
the land of Canaan.

Laban was off to his sheepshearing when Rachel carried off the hearth idols her father kept. She and Jacob made off while Laban's attention was elsewhere; Jacob drove away beneath Laban's eyes, not to disturb his thoughts.

As Laban headlong caught up with Jacob: "What are you doing, making off with my daughters like prizes of war? Why did you just walk away—to walk all over my trust? Why not call my attention? I could have sent you off with music, harps and drums. You did not even call me to kiss my daughters and grandchildren—it's as if you walked all over appearance in your going. But even if you walked out—out of your own desire to go home again—why steal my gods?"

"I was worried," Jacob said to Laban. "I thought, 'Who knows what next: he may steal his daughters back from me.' But if someone is found with your gods—take his life. See for yourself, here among relatives: if I have taken something, take it for yourself." Jacob did not know that Rachel had stolen them.

Now Laban enters Jacob's tent, then Leah's, then into the two maids' tents—but he finds nothing. Leaving Leah, he enters Rachel's tent.

But Rachel had gathered up the idols, stowed them under the saddle cushions—now she sits upon them while Laban searches through the tent, finding nothing.

"Let it not inflame my lord if I do not appear beside you," she said to her father, "but I am in the way of women: my period is with me." Though he searches he does not find the idols.

Now Jacob has become inflamed by Laban's head-long pursuit, moves on.

72

On the way, Jacob was informed: "Your brother Esau is coming to meet you—along with four hundred men." A shudder went through Jacob, a deep unease. He began to divide his people into two camps, along with the cattle, sheep, camels. "If Esau arrives at one camp and attacks it, the other camp flees.

"Watch over me, please"—he asked Yahweh—"if the hand of Esau, my brother, overreaches its boundary—to destroy me, mother along with child."

He waited there that night, gathered whatever was at hand as a gift for Esau, his brother. Then he sent the gift ahead, as he waited there in the camp.

He rose in the night and led his wives, their maids, and his children to the river Jaboc. He sent them over with all he possessed.

73

That night Jacob waited alone. There some man struggled with him, even until daybreak. It was clear he could not overcome Jacob, so he broke his thigh at the hip. Jacob's thigh was limp as he struggled with him.

"Let me go, day is breaking," he said. "I won't let go of you," said the other, "until I have your blessing."

Now he asked him: "What is your name?" "Jacob," he said. "Not anymore Jacob, heel-clutcher, will be said in your name; instead, Israel, God-clutcher, because you have held on among gods unnamed as well as men, and you have overcome."

Now Jacob asked the question: "Please, what is your name?" "Why is it just this—my name—you must ask?" he answered. Instead, he blessed him there.

The name of that place Jacob called Deiface: I've seen God face to face, yet my flesh holds on.

Now the sun rose over him as he passed through the place called Deifus; he was limping on his hip.

74

Now Jacob looked out afar and there he was: Esau was coming, four hundred men with him. He divided the children among their mothers: Leah, Rachel, the maids. The maids and their children were placed first, Leah and her children behind them; Rachel and Joseph were in back. Then Jacob went out ahead, fell prostrate sevenfold—before Esau came running toward him.

And Esau fell on his neck—with kisses, embraces, weeping. Then he looked around, seeing the women and children. "Whose are these?" he asked. "The children," Jacob answered, "with whom God has blessed your servant."

The maids with their children bowed; Leah and her children approached afterwards, bowing also. Finally Joseph and Rachel came and bowed. "But why have these come forward—and the whole camp you sent ahead?" Jacob answered: "To melt your heart, my master."

"I am rich enough, my brother. What is yours—should be."

"—Please don't," Jacob appealed. "If I may warm your heart, accept my gift. What came from my hand allows me to see your face—as if God's face had turned toward me, in peace.

"Accept my gift please, as it came to you. Embraced by God—now I have everything." Since he urged it, Esau took it.

"Let's travel on together, beside each other," said Esau.

Jacob responded: "My lord knows the children are delicate. The calves and kids as well: I must take account of them. If they're driven all day, the flock might end up destroyed.

"Let my lord go on ahead, please, while your servant makes his way at the pace of his charges—and in stride with the legs of his children. Eventually I will reach my master in Seir."

"Let me appoint to you some of the men with me," said Esau.

"But why? The warmth of my lord's heart is enough."

So Esau returned that day toward Seir. But Jacob traveled to Succot, building himself shelter. For his flocks he made succahs; after those sheds they called the place Succot.

75

Now Dinah went out—she was Leah's daughter by Jacob—to see some girlfriends in the country. It was then Shechem saw her—he was son to Hamor, the local governor—and seized her. Lying with her, her guard was broken.

But she had touched his heart: he had fallen in love, his reserve broken by tenderness for the young woman.

Jacob heard how he had fallen upon his daughter Dinah. Because his sons were out herding the cattle, Jacob restrained himself until they came in.

Yet Jacob's sons heard it out in the field; they came home hurt and angry the man had stained Israel's honor. To just lie with a daughter of Jacob—a desire never to be acted upon.

But Shechem said to her father and brothers, "Open your hearts, whatever you ask of me is yours. Set the dowry as high as you wish and I will give whatever you say; you need just give the girl in marriage."

The young man had no reservation about anything they might ask, because he had fallen in love with Jacob's daughter—and in his own family, he was held in the highest honor. "I will say to them," he said, " 'Look: the land is broad enough to embrace them.' "

76
Now two of Jacob's sons, Simon and Levi, Dinah's brothers, buckled their swords and entered the city unsuspected.

So Hamor and his son, Shechem, died by the edge of the sword—as they seized Dinah from Shechem's house, slipped back out.

77
"You have stained me for the population," Jacob said to Simon and Levi, "and stirred up a scent to reach the Canaanites and Perizzites. There are few of us; they'll gather to destroy me, extinguish my whole household."

But they answered: "Should he just seize our sister as a whore?"

78

Now Joseph was a shepherd's helper to his brothers;
he was still a boy among the sons of Bilhah and
Zilpah, his father's wives. And Joseph was a little
tattletale, straight to their father. For Israel loved him
above all his children: the child of his old age.

A many-colored coat was made for Joseph. His
brothers grasped that it was him their father loved
most; they hated him, could not speak warmly to
him.

79

Joseph dreamed and told this dream to his brothers,
so that their anger toward him only grew. He had
begged them to listen. "So it was," he had begun,
"we were binding bundles in the field when, to my
surprise, my bundle lifted itself up, was standing
upright. And then it happened your bundles got up,
encircled mine, and fell prostrate before it."

Yet another dream followed which Joseph could
not contain. "So it was," he concluded, "that the sun,
the moon, eleven stars—all were prostrate before
me."

"What kind of dream is that?" his father teased him,
when Joseph told him as well. "Are we going to
crawl before you, fall prostrate at your feet—myself,
your mother, all your brothers?" On account of his
telling of dreams, his brothers hated him more.

80

Now his brothers were pasturing their father's flock near Shechem when Israel said to Joseph: "I'm worried about your brothers when they pasture near Shechem. If you're prepared, I'll send you to them." "I'm ready," he replied.

"Then go, and please inform me about your brothers: are they safe, are the flocks secure? Bring me your news." He sent him from near Hebron.

When he came near Shechem, a man found him wandering in the fields. "Whom are you looking for?" asked the man. "I'm searching for my brothers," he said. "Could you tell me where they're pasturing?"

"Not here. 'Dothan,' I heard them say."

81

As Joseph approached Dothan: "Look, here comes our master of dreams," the brothers said among themselves. "Now is a time to kill him, then throw him down an abandoned well. 'A mad animal has eaten him,' we will say. We will see what becomes of his dreams."

Now look: as Joseph greets his brothers they grasp his coat from off his back—the many-colored coat he is wearing. They seize him and put him down the well. It is an abandoned well, with no water in it.

Some Midianites are camping nearby. They are merchants who discover Joseph and draw him up from the well. For twenty pieces of silver, they sell him to Ishmaelites from Gilead when their caravan comes by—camels loaded with gum, balm, ladanum—on the way down to Egypt.

82

Now with Joseph's coat in hand they killed a small goat, then dipped it in the blood.

The many-colored coat was conveyed to their father. Then they followed: "We found this coat. Can you tell if it's your son's?"

He grasped it. "My son's coat. Eaten by a wild animal. Torn limb from limb—Joseph!"

Jacob tore his shirt, covered his male parts with sackcloth, mourned his son a very long time.

All his sons and daughters gathered to console him, but he fought against consolation: "I will follow my son in grief, straight down to Sheol." So his father spoke, fighting his tears.

83

Now look: soon afterwards Judah moves south from his brothers, down to the neighborhood of an Adullamite named Hirah. There a Canaanite named Shuah has a daughter and she catches Judah's eye. He asks her to be his wife, enters into her arms. Pregnant, she gives birth to a son he names Er.

Pregnant again, she bears a son whom she names Onan. She continues to conceive, this time a son she names Shelah; they are at Chezib when he is born.

Now Judah asks for a wife for Er, his firstborn; her name, Tamar. It happens Er turns corrupt before Yahweh's eyes; Yahweh hastens his death.

"Enter the arms of your brother's wife," Judah says to Onan. "Be a good brother-in-law: bear the seed for your brother." But Onan conceives the seed will not count as his. So it is: whenever he enters the arms of his brother's wife, he spills it to the ground—to keep his seed from counting for his brother.

But in Yahweh's eyes this conception was corrupt; he too was brought to his death.

"Settle as a widow in your father's house," says Judah to Tamar, his daughter-in-law. "Stay there while Shelah, my son, grows up." He thinks: "Heaven forbid death touch him too, like his brothers." So Tamar goes to live in her father's house.

84

A long time later Judah's wife died, Shuah's daughter. Consoled after mourning, Judah rose to join his sheepshearers in Timnath, along with Hirah, his Adullamite friend.

Now Tamar was informed: "Your father-in-law has arisen, goes to Timnath for sheepshearing."

She lays aside her widow's clothes, veils herself; cloaked in disguise, she lingers openly by the crossroads on the way to Timnath. She recognized that while Shelah had now grown up, she was engaged—yet not offered marriage to him.

Now Judah sees her, imagines she is a whore: her face is concealed.

He stepped off the road toward her. "Entertain me," he said, "in your arms. I wish to enter there." He did not recognize his daughter-in-law. "What will you pay me," she replied, "if I take you in?"

"I will pick out a kid from the flock by myself," he said.

"Only if you leave me security," she replied, "until you send it."

"What can I give you for security?" he asked.

"Your seal and ring, and the stick in your hand," she answered. So he gives them to her, then enters her arms, and by him she becomes pregnant.

She gets up, goes away, unwraps the veil and cloak around her; once again, she dresses in her widow's clothes.

85
When Judah sent the choice kid—by the hand of his friend, the Adullamite—to recover the security (those things in the woman's hand), she was not to be found.

"Where can I find your ritual prostitute?" he inquired of the local people. "The one standing openly by the crossroads on the highway."

"No holy lady ever stood there."

Returning to Judah, he said: "I could not find her. And more than that, the local people reported, 'No holy lady ever stood there.' "

"Let her take those things," replied Judah. "Heaven forbid we are taken for fools here. They have seen the kid; though you couldn't find her, I sent it."

86
So it was: about three months pass when Judah was abruptly informed. "Your daughter-in-law Tamar has played the whore and now look: she is pregnant by prostitution."

"Take her away," judged Judah, "to be set afire."

When they came for her she would send a message to her father-in-law: "By the man whose things these are, am I pregnant. Please look at them; recognize whose seal, whose ring, whose stick they are."

Judah recognized his own. "She is a truer judge than I: I failed to marry her to Shelah, my son." Yet he would linger from entering her arms again.

87
So it was: the time for giving birth arrived. Now look: twins are within her.

And it happened, as she labored, one put out a hand—the midwife grabbed it, wrapped scarlet thread around it: "This one came out first." Yet look: he draws in his hand, and then, instead, out comes his brother. "With what power he crosses boundaries," was said, and so Peretz was he called.

Scarlet around his hand, the brother came out after, to be named after the red: Zerah, bright one.

88

Joseph had been taken down to Egypt, where an Egyptian bought him from Ishmaelites—out of the hands of those who brought him down. So it was: Yahweh attended Joseph. And so it happened that Joseph grew prosperous.

Now look: he is in the house of his Egyptian lord. His lord could see that Yahweh attended Joseph, in whose hands everything that he tended, matured. Joseph warmed his heart; he appointed him personal attendant, head of his household. All that he had was put into his hand.

So it was: Yahweh blessed the Egyptian's house on behalf of Joseph, from the time he became head over the household and all the holdings. So it happens: Yahweh's blessing covers all that he holds, in the house, in the field.

With everything committed to Joseph's hands, the Egyptian restrains his concern about almost anything—except the bread he ate.

Now look: Joseph is a finely formed man, a handsome vision. It happened that his master's wife, a
good time later, beckoning Joseph with her eyes,
whispered, "Recline by me."

He abruptly declines. "Look, my lord counts on
me," he says to the lord's wife, "to handle the house.
He has left everything in my hands, stands no watch
over me. I am not restrained from anything but
yourself, since you are his wife. How could I commit
this height of offense—and show contempt for the
gods?"

So it was: she would appeal to Joseph day after day,
yet he declined her desire that he lie with her, attend
her.

On one of these days, as he enters the house to work,
he passes no servants, finds none in the room. Now
she grasps hold of his coat: "Recline by me." But he
abandons the coat in her hand, flees, runs outside.

As she stood there, empty coat in her hand, seeing
he had run away, she screamed for the servants: "See
how he has brought us a Hebrew man to handle us.
He entered the room to lie with me. But I started to
scream, and look: he realized I would not restrain
myself and ran outside, left his coat in my hands."

Now the coat lay beside her until Joseph's master
came home. These were her words to him: "That
Hebrew servant—the one you brought us to fondle

me—tried to enter me. Listen well: I raised my voice, I screamed—and he left his coat beside me when he ran outside."

Now look: as his lord hears his wife's words—"This is the way I was handled by your servant"—his anger bursts its bounds.

Joseph's lord took hold of him, threw him into prison—the place where high prisoners of the king were held.

90
See: he lies there in prison. Yet Yahweh attended Joseph, tendered care, putting warmth for him in the prison keeper's heart.

Now the prison keeper put his faith in Joseph's hands: of all the prison inmates and all that went on there, he was the head. Not a fault could the prison keeper find in all that was in his hands—because Yahweh attended him; all that he touched, Yahweh matured.

91
One morning Pharaoh awoke disturbed. He sent for all of Egypt's magicians, called together all its wise men to tell them his dream. Yet none could interpret it for him.

Now the head waiter to Pharaoh speaks up: "This day has brought back to me a past offense. Pharaoh once was angry with his servants; I was put under

guard in the officers' prison—me, as well as the head
baker.

"We had a dream on the same night, he and I—each
with our own personal details. With us was a Hebrew boy, servant to the head guard; we told him and
he interpreted our dreams for us. He interpreted
each dream in a personal way.

"All happened just as he interpreted. So it was: I was
sent back to my position and he—he was sent hanging."

92

Now Pharaoh ordered Joseph sent out; he was
brought abruptly up from the prison depths. He
shaves, changes his clothes, comes to Pharaoh.

"I have dreamed a dream," said Pharaoh to Joseph,
"that there is no one to interpret. Yet I heard it said
of you, that on hearing a dream your interpretation
solves it."

Pharaoh continued: "In my dream I found myself
standing on the bank of the river. Now look:
abruptly up from the river come seven cows in beautiful health—delicious to gaze at. They were grazing
in the reeds.

"Now I find seven other cows come up after them,
emaciated and misshapen, their flesh stretched thin-
ner than anything I've seen—in all Egypt never such
repulsive ones.

"These emaciated and repulsive cows ate up the first seven cows, the hearty ones. Yet when they were fully digested inside them, you could not believe they had entered their bodies: they still looked emaciated as at first. I recoiled and was awake.

"I told this to the magicians, but none could say anything of any good to me."

Now Joseph answers Pharaoh: "The seven good cows are as seven years; the seven emaciated, repulsive cows that came up after them are as seven years. What the gods intend is made known to Pharaoh.

"Now see: seven fertile years approach, overflowing all of Egypt's land. But seven years of famine will come up after them, until the overflowing in Egypt is forgotten, the land swallowed by famine. Even the word for overflowing will be swallowed up by the famine that follows—heavy will it lie on the land.

"So that now Pharaoh must pick a man shrewd and wise—to put in charge, over Egyptian land. Let all kinds of food be gathered from these seven good years when they come; let grain be piled up, to be held in Pharaoh's hands: food to be protected for the cities."

"As a god has made you know all this," said Pharaoh to Joseph, "there is no man like you for intellect or wisdom. You shall be in charge of my house. By your word all my people shall be fed. Only on my throne will I rule over you. I am Pharaoh, yet without your protection no man shall raise his fist or boot in all of Egypt."

Pharaoh gave Joseph the name Zaphenath-paneah. For a wife he gave him Asenath, daughter of Poti-phera, the Priest of On.

Now Joseph rose in charge; he went out over the land of Egypt.

93
The seven years of famine, of which Joseph had spoken, started. Now look: all lands are gripped by famine, yet in Egypt there is bread.

When all the land of Egypt grows hungry too, the people cry to Pharaoh for bread. "Go to Joseph," said Pharaoh to all Egypt. "As he directs you, follow."

The face of the earth was covered with the famine. Now Joseph opens all that has been held, rations it to the Egyptians—as the famine continued growing stronger in the land of Egypt.

Now they come to Egypt from all over the earth, to buy rations from Joseph. The whole world is in the grip of the famine.

94
Jacob understood there was sustenance in Egypt. "Why do you stand around and stare?" he said to his sons.

So the brothers of Joseph—ten of them—went down into Egypt to buy rations. But Benjamin, Joseph's other brother—Jacob would not send him. "Heaven forbid disaster touch him," he thought.

95

Now Joseph was the governor in the land, in charge of selling rations to all peoples. When the brothers arrived, they fell prostrate at his feet, faces to the ground.

Joseph recognized his brothers, but they did not know him. He veiled his heart from them like a stranger. The dream returned to Joseph—the one he had dreamed about them.

At a night lodging on the way, as they return, one opens his bag to feed his ass. There, in the mouth of his sack, look: his money sits there.

"My money returns," he said to his brothers. "Look: it's in my bag." Their hearts sank.

96

The famine in the land had grown bitter.

So it was: the food brought out from Egypt had all been eaten. "Return on our behalf," their father said. "Buy us what rations we may."

"The man in charge warned us to watch ourselves," said Judah. " 'Do not look upon my face,' he warned, 'unless your brother is with you.'

"If you are prepared to send our brother with us, we will go down to secure food for you. But if you won't send him we will not go—the man warned us not to see his face without our brother."

"Why did you make it bitter for me," Israel asked, "by telling the man you had another brother?"

"The man had many questions," they said, "about us, about our family; such as 'Is your father still alive?' and 'Do you have another brother?' We told him what he wanted to know. How could we have known ourselves he would warn, 'Bring your brother down here'?"

"This son will not go down with you," said Jacob. "Just he remains—his other brother is dead. If disaster were to touch him on the way, you would bend my head white with grief—straight down to Sheol."

Now Judah says to his father, Israel: "Let the boy leave with me. Let us go now; better to live than die—for all of us, even the youngest.

"Let me stand for security: you may request him out of my hands, and if I don't return him to stand before you, my life stands in contempt instead. And—if we stand around any longer, we could already have returned a second time."

"If it must be," said Israel their father, "at least do this: pack an assortment of our fruit delicacies in your jars, take it down for a present to the man—

with a little balm, some honey, gum and ladanum, a few pistachios and almonds.

"And for every silver piece in your hands take a second; take in hand as well those which returned in the mouths of your bags—perhaps they were there by mistake.

"As for your brother, take him and go; return to that man." Now the men gather up the presents, doubling the silver they carry in hand, with Benjamin as well, and leave, down to Egypt; they would stand before Joseph again.

97

Now as Joseph observes Benjamin coming with them, he speaks to the head of his house: "Usher the men home and prepare a freshly slaughtered animal; these men will dine with me this afternoon."

That man followed Joseph's words; he escorted the men into Joseph's house.

But the men were alarmed. On being brought into Joseph's house, they imagined "it has to do with the money finding its way back into our bags: we are being summoned here so it may recoil against us and they seize us for slaves, along with our asses."

As they approach the head of Joseph's house, they speak to him at the entrance: "Patience, kind sir. We came down the first time simply to buy food.

"But a surprise awaited us when we came to our night's lodging. We open our bags and look: each man's silver is at the top of his bag—all of it, exactly. Now we bring it back in our own hands.

"We came down again with more money too, bringing it all by hand to buy food. We never knew by whom our money was put back in our bags."

"But you are welcome; there's nothing to cause alarm," he replied. Ushering them into the house, the man had the water brought for washing feet; he provided feed as well for the asses.

Now they unpack their gifts for Joseph, being told he would arrive at noon—to dine with them.

98

When Joseph comes home, they take their presents in hand, enter the house, fall prostrate to the ground before him.

Now he asks about conditions at home: "Is your father doing well, the old man you mentioned? Does he remain healthy?"

"Our father, your humble servant, is safe, still strong." They fall prostrate as a sign of humility.

He gazed out and there was Benjamin, his brother— his own mother's son. "So that is your little brother, the one you spoke about?"

Joseph turns abruptly aside, his heart bursting with tenderness for his brother—he rushes to his room, to cry.

Then he washed his face, came back, restrained his feelings. "Serve the bread," he said.

99
They were served separately from him, and from the Egyptians eating with him. They ate by themselves, because Egyptians could not bear to eat a meal with Hebrews (that would be an outrage in Egypt).

First, the brothers were ushered to their seats as he directed, in order of age, from the firstborn down to the youngest—and the men stared at one another in amazement.

Joseph ordered additional courses sent to them from his own table but made Benjamin's ration five times larger than the others. They drank until they were merrily drunk around him.

100
Now Joseph takes aside the head of his house: "Fill up the men's bags with food, all they can hold. And with my interpreting cup—this silver cup—settle it in the mouth of the youngest's bag." All was done to the letter of Joseph's words.

Watch: the sun rises, the men are seen off, followed by their donkeys. They are out of the city, though not by far, when Joseph turns to his man: "Now go, catch up with them; when you do, say: 'Why pay back bad for good? See: isn't this the one?—the interpreting cup from which my lord would drink and then divine? Your acts speak badly of you.'"

Now he approaches them with these very words. "But sir," they answered, "why do you speak such words to us? Heaven forbid your servants would act on such words. Recall the money we found in our bags: we came back from Canaan with it. Why would we now steal silver or gold out of your master's hands? Find it among any of your servants and that one dies—while the rest of us will become your lord's slaves."

"Just as your words say," he answered. "Yet only the one who has it will be my servant. The rest go free." So quickly each man lowered his bag to the ground, and each opened it.

Now he searches, beginning with the oldest, until he reaches the youngest—and there it is, in Benjamin's bag. Now they tear at their clothes. Then each one returned his bag over his donkey, returning to the city.

Judah and his brothers approach Joseph's house; he is still there, and they fall before him—prostrate on the ground.

"What act is this you have dreamt up? Can it be you didn't know that a man like me practices interpretation?"

"What can we say to my lord?" says Judah. "What words can we find to speak our innocence? Lord, your slaves stand before you: all of us, not just he with the interpreting cup in his hands."

"Heaven forbid it," he interjects. "Such acts are beyond me. Just the one holding the interpreting cup—this one alone will be my slave. But you: go with clear conscience, up to your father."

Judah drew nearer: "Dear lord, allow a word from your servant to his master's ear. Hold your anger from burning your servant—you are like Pharaoh for us.

" 'Have you a father, or a brother?' my lord asked his servants. 'We have a father, an old man,' we answered, 'with a boy of his old age, whose brother is dead. He alone survives his mother, and his father loves him.'

"Now," continued Judah, "please allow your servant to be held in place of the boy—a slave to my lord—so the boy can go up with his brothers. How could I go to my father and the boy not with me—heaven forbid I see the horror that will grip my father."

Now Joseph could hold himself back no longer. "Leave me alone with them," he called out. No witness stood by him when he revealed himself to his brothers.

He burst into sobs—even the Egyptians could hear, even Pharaoh's court heard of it.

"I am Joseph," his brothers were hearing. "Is my father still alive?" No word returned from their lips, stunned into silence.

101

"Now listen: your eyes can see—even Benjamin's eyes understand—it is from a brother's mouth I speak to you.

"And you will tell my father," he continued, "of my great honor in Egypt, all that you have seen. Hurry, bring my father down to me." Then he fell on the shoulder of Benjamin, his brother, weeping; and Benjamin wept, upon his neck.

102

Judah was sent ahead to Joseph, to arrange Israel's way to the Goshen district.

Joseph harnesses his chariot, goes up to meet Israel in Goshen. He rushes to his father as soon as he sees him, falls on his neck, weeping—a torrent of tears falling on his shoulder.

"I can die at last," Israel says to Joseph, "because I have seen your face, still so full of life."

"I will approach Pharaoh"—Joseph was speaking in the presence of his father's household and his brothers. "I will say to Pharaoh, 'My brothers and my father's house from the land of Canaan have made their way to me. The men are shepherds; they have made their way with sheep and cattle—in fact, all they have surrounds them.'

"Now listen: Pharaoh may call you over, ask, 'What is your livelihood?' 'We make our way with live-stock,' you will say. 'Your servants have grown up among sheep—as our fathers before us.' That is the proper way to settle in the land of Goshen; in Egypt proper, a shepherd is a horror."

103

So it was: many years went past—Jacob was properly settled in Egypt—when Joseph would hear, "Listen: your father is sick." He took his two boys with him, Manasseh and Ephraim.

Now Jacob heard—"Hear: Joseph your son comes to you." Israel gathered his strength, rose up in his bed. Gazing at Joseph's boys, Israel exclaimed, "But whose are these?" "My sons." "Gather them by me, so I may bless them."

Now Israel's eyes were blurry with age, he could barely see; as he felt them in his arms, he kissed them, hugged them close. "I never dreamt to see your face, and now look: sweet faces of your seed."

Ephraim was by Joseph's right hand and he directed him to Israel's left side; Manasseh, by his left hand, he directed toward his father's right.

Yet Israel stretched out his right hand, settled it on Ephraim's head—but he was the younger—while his left hand reached over to Manasseh's head—his arms crossing direction, since the firstborn's right was Manasseh's.

Joseph gazed thunderstruck, seized his father's right hand, to reclaim it from Ephraim's head. "It can't be so, my father," he was exclaiming. "Your right hand belongs on the firstborn's head." But his father held back: "I know, my son, I know."

104

Now look: it was his father's face to which Joseph fell prostrate, sobbing over him, kissing him. Then Joseph directed his servants—the physicians among them—to embalm his father. Israel is embalmed; the physicians do it.

It took them forty days to complete; that is the way of the embalmed. And for seventy days, Egypt mourned over him.

Now these mourning days pass and Joseph speaks to Pharaoh's court. "If I touch your heart, please deliver this to Pharaoh's ear on my behalf: 'My father asked my vow with these words: "Look, I will die soon. Bury me in the grave I dug for myself, in the land of Canaan." Please let me go, to bury my father up there, and then return.' "

Then Pharaoh answered: "Go up to deliver your father, as he delivered the vow to you."

Now Joseph ascended to bury his father; going up with him were all the ministers of Pharaoh, the senior princes of his palace, and all the heads of Egypt.

And all of Joseph's household as well, his brothers' and father's households too. Their babies, their sheep, their cattle—just these were left behind in the land of Goshen.

Chariots and horsemen accompany them. Now look: a huge party is going up.

They arrive at Goren ha-Atad, beyond the Jordan, where they stop for lamentation—a huge lament goes up, the chants heavy with emotion. The mourning service he makes for his father lasted seven days.

As the inhabitants of the land, Canaanites, hear the lamentation at Goren ha-Atad, they are stunned: "What a heavy lamentation for the Egyptians." That is why they named it then Mourning-Egypt, though it is beyond the Jordan.

So Joseph returned to Egypt—he, his brothers, and all those who went up to bury his father—once he had delivered his father to his grave.

105
Now Joseph had died, and all his brothers, and all that generation.

106
A new king arose over Egypt, not knowing Joseph. "Look, the people of Israel are growing too large for

us," he said to his people. "Listen, let's deal shrewdly with this, before they grow further. Or else, in a war, they may join those who hate us, or rise up from the land." They organized cadres to control them, harness their labor; yet, enslaved, as they were punished they grew, bursting their borders.

107
Proclaiming a law to his people, Pharaoh said, "All boys of Israel born, throw them into the Nile—the girls will live alone."

108
A man from the family of Levi rose up and married a Levite woman. She conceived, bore a son, and seeing that he was beautiful, kept him in hiding three months. But this couldn't continue; the woman rose, searched out a crib of papyrus; then tarred it with bitumen, with pitch; then she put the child in, placed it in the reeds by the Nile.

109
A daughter of Pharaoh descended to bathe in the river, her maidservants walking along the bank; she saw the crib among the reeds, sent her servant to bring it up. Opening it, she saw the child—"Listen, he is crying"—a youth bringing pity.

110
The child grew; he was a son to the princess: she gave him the name Moses.

III

Those times passed and Moses grew up; now, he goes out among his brothers, sees them suffering. An Egyptian had beaten dead a Hebrew, one of his brothers—he saw it. Turning around, he looked each way; seeing no officers, he struck—the Egyptian fell, the body hidden in the sand.

112

Pharaoh heard of it, this deed; he was ready to kill Moses. But Moses escaped from Pharaoh's power, settling in Midian. He camped by a well.

113

Now a priest of Midian had seven daughters, and they came to lift water, fill the basins for their father's sheep. Shepherds arrived, began to drive them away, but Moses stood up for the women; he watered their flock. "What brought you home so soon today?" asked their father, Reuel. "An Egyptian man," they answered, "intervened for us with the shepherds. He also lifted water for us and watered the flock." "Where is he?" asked the father. "Why did you just leave the man? Go call him to eat with us." Moses was pleased to stay on with this man, who gave him Zipporah his daughter. She gave birth to a son, whom he named Gershom, after saying, "A stranger I have been in a foreign land." Now during these many passing years, the king of Egypt died.

114

Now Moses shepherded the flock of his father-in-law, priest of Midian, guiding it beyond the border of the desert—coming upon the mountain of God. There Yahweh's angel appeared to him as fire in a thorn bush. He looked closely: there a bush blazed with fire, yet the bush was not burnt away. "I must stop, come closer to this luminous thing," Moses thought, "to see why the bush is not eaten away." Yahweh saw that he approached, called to him from within the bush: "Moses, Moses." "I am listening," Moses answered. "You must not advance," he said. "Take the shoes from your feet. The place you are standing borders the holy."

115

"I saw," spoke Yahweh, "I beheld the burden my people held—in Egypt. I come down to lift them out of Egypt's hand, to carry them to a broad, open land."

116

"They won't believe me," Moses said, "they won't even listen to my voice—'Yahweh doesn't appear to you' will jump to their lips." Yahweh asked, "What is that in your hand?" "My stick," he answered. "Throw it to the ground." He threw it down: a snake was on the ground. Startled, Moses turned around. "Put out your hand," Yahweh said to Moses, "grasp it by the tail." He reached out, took hold: in his fist, a stick.

117

"Please," Yahweh spoke further, "put your hand within, to your breast." He put his hand within, and when he brought it out: a hand leprous as snow. "Return your hand to your breast," he said. He put his hand within, and when he brought it out again it was his flesh returned.

118

"Please, my lord," Moses said to Yahweh, "I am not a man of words; neither was I yesterday or the day before. And since you first spoke to your servant I remain heavy-tongued—my mouth strains for words." "Who put the mouth in man?" Yahweh answered him. "Who makes him dumb? And who makes the deaf—or the seeing and the blind? Wasn't it I, Yahweh? Now go; I guide your mouth, teach you what you will say."

119

"Go again to Egypt"—Yahweh spoke to Moses in Midian—"they've died, all those who would have your life." Moses took his wife and sons, saddled the donkeys, returned to the land of Egypt.

120

On the way, at a night lodging, Yahweh met him— and was ready to kill him. Zipporah took a flinty stone, cutting her son's foreskin; touched it between Moses' legs: "Because you are my blood bridegroom." He withdrew from him. "A blood bridegroom," she said, "marked by this circumcision."

121

Moses met with Aaron, went to gather all the elders of Israel.

122

Later, coming to Pharaoh, Moses said, "Yahweh, God of Israel, declares: 'Send me my people, to feast me in the desert.'" "Who is Yahweh?" Pharaoh replied. "To whom should I listen and send out Israel? I haven't known Yahweh, nor would I let go Israel."

He said: "The God of the Hebrews appeared to me. We would go, please, three days into the desert, sacrifice to Yahweh our God—or else he wound us by disease, or send the sword."

123

"The slave-workers' presence is pressing everywhere," Pharaoh said, "—and you would have them rest from labor." Pharaoh directed his officers that same day, and their policemen: "No more straw to make brick, as yesterday and the day before. Let them go—to collect their own straw. The quota of bricks stays the same; we won't relax the weight on those lax shoulders—or leave them time to groan, 'We must go sacrifice to our God.' Pile more work on them; let them groan with labor, not with slippery words."

Coming to the people, the officers and their policemen said, "Pharaoh declares: 'I won't give you straw. You may go out—for straw—wherever you find it, but you may not lose one minute of production.' " Through all the land of Egypt the people spread, searching out stubble for straw. The policemen pressed them: "Each day's quota as before, as a day when there was straw." The policemen who were Israelites—appointed by Pharaoh's officers—were beaten: "Why haven't you finished your baking of bricks, as yesterday, and filled your quota as the day before?" The Israelite policemen came to Pharaoh: "How could you do this to your slave-workers?" they groaned. "No straw is given to your slaves, yet the officers say, 'Make bricks.' Then the workers are beaten, yet it's your own people's fault."

"Idlers," he said, "you want to relax, that's why you idly groan, 'Let us go sacrifice to Yahweh.' Go to your work, instead; straw will not be given—but you will give back the full quota of bricks."

They saw their sad situation, the Israelite policemen having to say: "Each day's quota as before, not a minute's less." Leaving Pharaoh, they met Moses, waiting for them on the way. "May Yahweh see you and judge: you have given a stench to us, we are stained in the eyes of Pharaoh and his officers; you have given them a sword to kill us."

Returning to Yahweh, Moses said, "My lord, for what have you brought your people into this sad situation? For what have you sent me? Since I've spoken to Pharaoh in your name there are only sad consequences for the people. What of your uplifting? You haven't begun to lift out your people."

124

"Now you will see what I do for Pharaoh," Yahweh answered Moses. "With his strong hand he will send them out."

125

"Pharaoh's heart is rigid," Yahweh said to Moses, "he resists sending the people; but you will go to him. Wait, and meet him by the way: it is the morning he goes down to the riverbank. 'Yahweh, God of the Hebrews, sent me'—you will say this to him—' "Send me my people, to serve me in the desert. Until now you have not really heard—Yahweh speaks so—but in this it will be revealed to you: I am Yahweh. The fish in the Nile will die, the river will be a stench: it will be impossible for Egypt to drink from the Nile." ' "

Moses did as Yahweh desired. The Nile fish died; the stench from the river prevented Egypt from drinking there.

126

But Pharaoh turned away, going into his palace, unmoved in his heart even to this. But now Egypt had to dig for water elsewhere, prevented from drinking the Nile. Seven full days passed after Yahweh struck the Nile; then Yahweh spoke to Moses. "You will come to Pharaoh and say, 'Yahweh speaks so: "Send me my people, to serve me. If you resist letting go, look: I strike down all your borders with frogs. The Nile will be pregnant with frogs; they will go out, out into your palace, your bedroom, onto your bed and into your servants' house and all the houses of your people, into your ovens and dough pans. The frogs will go upon you, upon your people, upon all your officers." ' "

127

After the frogs came up, covering Egypt, Pharaoh called Moses: "Mediate with Yahweh—remove the frogs from me, my people—and I will send out your people: they will sacrifice to Yahweh." "You will be praised over me—" Moses answered Pharaoh— "When?" "Tomorrow." "—According to your word, then, not mine: so you will know there is nothing like Yahweh our God. The frogs will move back from you, from your officers, from your people—back to the Nile."

Then Moses left Pharaoh's presence; he mediated with Yahweh about the frogs put even in Pharaoh's lap. Yahweh performed according to Moses' word: the frogs died in the houses, the gardens, the fields. They were piled in bushelsful until the land was full of the stench. Pharaoh had breathing-room again; now his heart swelled with indifference, dismissed Moses.

"Wake early, present yourself to Pharaoh," Yahweh
said to Moses, "it is the morning he goes down to the
riverbank. 'Yahweh, God of the Hebrews, sent
me'—you will say this to him—' "Send me my people, to serve me. If you refuse to let my people go,
I will let go—upon you, upon your servants, upon
your people, upon your houses—flies. The houses of
Egypt will be full, their floors will be one with the
land: hidden under flies. That day I will distinguish
the borders of Goshen—the land my people squat
upon—to be untouched by flies, so you may know
I am Yahweh, here on earth. I will put borders between your people and mine—by tomorrow this
marking will be plain." ' "

Now, Yahweh did so: powerful droves of flies entered Pharaoh's palace, his officers' houses; through
all the land of Egypt land was ruined under the flies.
Now, Pharaoh called for Moses: "Go sacrifice to
your god, but in our country—"

"—and intervene on my behalf." "Listen," Moses
said, "I leave your presence to represent you with
Yahweh; the flies will be removed—from Pharaoh,
his officers, his people—tomorrow; but Pharaoh
must not play with us, not letting go: the people wait
to give sacrifice to Yahweh."

Leaving Pharaoh, Moses returned to Yahweh's presence; and he performed according to Moses' word:

the flies were removed—not one remained. But Pharaoh's heart stiffened this time also; the people were not sent out.

130

Now Yahweh said to Moses, "Approach Pharaoh and say, 'Yahweh—God of the Hebrews—speaks so: "Send my people out, to serve me. Resist letting go—tighten your grasp again—and listen: Yahweh's hand will grasp your cattle in the field, your horses, donkeys, camels, oxen, sheep—a hard thing, a stiff plague. Yahweh will mark out boundaries around the flocks of Israel, distinguish them from the flocks of Egypt, and among the Israelites not one thing will die."'"

Now Yahweh set the time: "Tomorrow Yahweh makes his word deed in the land." The next day: Egyptian cattle died, yet not one cow of the Israelites. Pharaoh sent out for word—"Listen, not even one cow of Israel died." Still, his heart was hard: he resisted sending out the people.

131

Now Yahweh said to Moses, "Wake early, present yourself to Pharaoh. 'Yahweh, God of the Hebrews, speaks so'—you will say this to him—' "Send me my people, to serve me."'"

132

"—Again you play with my people, resist sending them. Listen: tomorrow at this time a hard hailstorm falls, as has never been in Egypt, not from the day of its founding. Send out your word: the cattle, all that belongs to you in the field, all man and beast not in houses—if not brought into your house they will die as the hail falls." Among Pharaoh's men, those in awe of Yahweh's word chased their slaves and cattle inside; those who didn't take Yahweh to heart left their slaves and cattle in the field.

Now Yahweh let go thunder and hail, lightning touched the ground, hail fell on the land of Egypt: a hard hail, unknown since Egypt became a nation, striking throughout Egypt, cutting down everything in the field, from man to beast—plants, bushes were knocked over by the hail, trees shattered. Only in Goshen did the hail not fall, where the Israelites were.

Pharaoh sent for Moses: "This time I've offended; Yahweh is just, while I, my people—are guilty. Pray to Yahweh: it is more than enough, this god's thunder and hail; I will send you out—there is no longer need to hold you." Now Moses said to him, "As I leave the city, I'll spread my arms to Yahweh: the thunder will stop, hail will not exist—you will know the earth is Yahweh's. Yet you and your officers will not hold to awe in the face of God, Yahweh—this I can see."

133

Now Moses left Pharaoh's presence, left the city, opened his arms to Yahweh: thunder and hail faded away, rain was no longer spilling to earth. When Pharaoh saw the rain, hail, and thunder had stopped, he offended further, his heart stiffened even more—he and his subjects.

134

"We will enter Pharaoh's presence," Yahweh said to Moses. Moses entered: "Yahweh, God of the Hebrews, speaks so: 'How long will you hold a hard mask to my face? Send out my people, to serve me. If you resist sending my people, listen: tomorrow I will bring locusts across your borders, to blanket the land's surface until you won't be able to see it, to devour the living remnant that survived the hail—even the trees, that blossom for you in the field: eaten away. Your palace will be filled and the houses of your subjects—all the houses of Egypt overrun as no one has ever seen, not your fathers or fathers' fathers, not in a day they existed, or any until now' "—and Moses turned away, left Pharaoh's presence.

"How long will this man be our pitfall?" said Pharaoh's officers to him. "Send the men out to serve Yahweh their god—before we find out that Egypt is lost."

Moses was brought back to Pharaoh: "Go, serve Yahweh your god. But who—who are the ones going?" "We all go," Moses said, "including our young and our old, sons and daughters, sheep and cattle. It is a feast to Yahweh for all of us." "May Yahweh be with you," Pharaoh said, "—and with your little ones—were I to let you go together. No, schemes are written on your faces. You may go now—just you men, please—to serve Yahweh, since that is your request." And he was swept out of Pharaoh's presence.

135
All that day and night Yahweh drove a desert wind through the land: now it was morning, the desert wind had brought the locusts. Now the locust ascended over Egypt, obliterating all borders, a heavy blanket, no one had ever seen locusts that thick before—or ever will. The ground was smothered in darkness; the locust ate all vegetation and fruit that survived the hail. Nothing green was left on tree or bush in all Egypt. Now Pharaoh anxiously called Moses back: "I've offended Yahweh, your god and you. Please, overlook a first offense—intervene with Yahweh, your god, to roll back this death from over me."

Moses left Pharaoh, intervened with Yahweh. And Yahweh rolled back a strong sea wind, which lifted the locusts and swept them into the Reed Sea: not one locust remained within Egypt's borders.

136
Again Pharaoh summoned Moses: "Go now, serve Yahweh—only your cattle and sheep need wait behind for you. Even your children will go with you."

"You will also give us offerings—and a free hand with our sacrificial needs," Moses answered, "so we can prepare them for Yahweh our God. Not a hoof of ours may stay: we don't yet know what is required of us."

137
"Go as you are, with nothing," Pharaoh said to Moses. "Now leave my presence—but watch yourself. Don't let me see your face one more time; if I do, on that day you will die."

"Well said. I will not see your face another time," Moses answered—

138
"—as Yahweh," he said, "speaks so: 'In the middle of the night I will appear in the midst of Egypt. And he will die—each first-one in Egypt, from the son of the Pharaoh who sits on the throne, to the son of the slave maid sitting behind the millstone—to every beast firstling. There will be a great screaming throughout Egypt—as never before, nor ever to be. Yet not one dog shall snarl to all the children of Israel—not at a man and not even at his beast. Here you will know how Yahweh marks boundaries between Egypt and Israel.' All your subjects will lower themselves, bowing: 'Go: you—and the whole of your people in your footsteps.' And then I shall leave." Now he left Pharaoh's presence burning with anger.

Moses called together the elders of Israel: "Choose
sheep for your families, and slaughter them for the
Pesach offering. You will dip a bunch of marjoram
into the blood now in the basin, and brush the lintel
and the two doorposts, so they are marked from the
blood in the basin. You will not go out again—not
even one man—through the opening of your house,
until morning. Yahweh will pass through, striking
Egypt; when the blood on the lintel and doorposts
is seen, Yahweh will not pass over the opening without holding back the Slaughterer—who enters to
deal death in your home."

140
In awe, the people lowered themselves; they were
prostrate.

141
Now it was midnight; Yahweh struck all the first
sons in Egypt, from the son of the Pharaoh who sits
on the throne, to the son of the prisoner who squats
in the hole—to every beast firstling. Pharaoh awoke
in the night—he, his officers, all Egypt—to a great
scream: there is no house in which there is not a dead
man.

In that night Pharaoh summoned Moses: "Awake,
go out from my people—you and the Israelites—go,
serve Yahweh according to your words. Your cattle,
your sheep—take them too, as you've spoken, and

may you say a prayer for me as well." Now the Egyptians hurried the people in their going out from the land—desperate, they were saying, "We are dead men." Before it was even leavened, the people were loading the dough; the clothes carried on their shoulders were wrapped around the kneading bowls.

142

Now the Israelites traveled from Ramses toward Sukkot, about six hundred thousand adults on foot, besides children. And others went out with them, along with large numbers of animals, cattle and sheep. They baked the dough they brought from Egypt into matzah cakes—since it was unleavened and they had rushed out from Egypt without proper time to prepare their provisions.

143

They moved on from Sukkot, marked out their camp at Eitam, at the border of the desert. Yahweh walks ahead of them each day in a pillar of cloud, marking the way: at night, in a pillar of fire. Day or night, the people can walk. Ahead of them, it never disappears: a pillar of fire by night, a pillar of cloud by day.

144

Meanwhile Pharaoh, with his officers, changed heart again. "What have we done, sending our slaves, Israel, away from us?" He demanded his chariot and his men, took all with him.

145

Pharaoh was near, the Israelites saw him, saw Egypt
moving behind them. Scared, shouts burst out of
them.

146

Moses spoke to the people. "Do not show fear. Draw
together. You will see the freedom Yahweh creates
today. This Egypt you look upon you will never see
again. Yahweh will fight for you. Watch yourself,
hold still."

147

The pillar of cloud moved from in front to the rear
of them. It comes between the two camps, Egypt and
Israel; a spell of darkness is cast, the two lose touch
through the night.

148

It is the dawn watch and Yahweh looks down on the
Egyptian camp, in the pillar of cloud and fire. Egypt
panicked, saying, "We must get away from Israel,
Yahweh fights for them."

149

But Yahweh had fleeing Egypt rocked into the sea.

150

On that day Yahweh freed Israel from Egypt's hand
and Israel saw it in the bodies of Egyptians, dead on
the distant shore. Israel saw Yahweh's great hand in

the work he made of Egypt. As the people saw Yahweh, fear changed heart to belief, in Yahweh and in
Moses who served him.

151
Then Moses and the people sang to Yahweh: Sing
to Yahweh overcoming   He overflows our
hearts   Driver and chariot   turned over
in the sea

152
Moses led Israel from the Sea of Reeds, entering the
desert of Shur. They walked three days into the
desert without finding water. They arrived at Mara
yet couldn't drink there. The water was bitter; Mara,
they called the place. The people grumbled about
Moses, saying, "What will we drink?" He cried out
to Yahweh. Yahweh revealed a tree to him; he threw
it into the water, and the water turned sweet. It was
there he turned the law concrete, putting them to the
test.

153
They came to Elim and there: twelve springs of
water, seventy palm trees. There they marked out
their camp, beside the water.

154
Later, at Rephidim, in the desert, they were thirsty
again for water. The people grumbled about Moses.
They would say, "Why did you lift us out of Egypt?

To die—me, and my children, and my livestock—of thirst?"

155
There were further trials. The place was called Massa and Meriba: one name for the quarrels of the people Israel, the other for their testing, saying, "Is Yahweh near—with us—or not?"

156
Then, at Mount Sinai, Yahweh summoned Moses, "Ascend, you and Aaron, Nadav and Avihu, and seventy of Israel's elders; prostrate yourselves from a distance. Moses will come near Yahweh alone, the others remain afar. The people will not ascend with him." Moses returned to the people with the words of Yahweh, the laws. In a single voice, all responded, "All the words and laws Yahweh desires, we will keep."

157
Mount Sinai was wrapped in smoke. Yahweh had come down in fire, the smoke climbing skyward like smoke from a kiln. The mountain, enveloped, greatly trembled.

158
So Yahweh descended to Mount Sinai, to the summit. He called Moses to ascend to the top. Moses climbed up and Yahweh spoke to him, "Descend, hold the people's attention: they must not be drawn

to Yahweh, to destroy boundaries. Bursting through
to see, they will fall, many will die. Even the priests
who approach Yahweh must be purified—so they are
not drawn to destruction."

159
Yahweh spoke further, "Descend, arise with Aaron.
The priests and the people shall not come up, as
boundaries destroyed will be their destruction."

160
"They must be ready for the third day, the day Yahweh goes down, before the eyes of all, on Mount
Sinai. The people will be a boundary, warn them to
watch themselves, approach but not climb up, not
touch the mountain. For those who overstep boundaries, death touches them, steps over their graves."

161
So Moses came down and spoke to the people.

162
Then Moses ascended, and with him Aaron, Nadav
and Avihu his sons, and with them seventy of Israel's
elders. They saw the God of Israel. Under his feet
a pavement of sapphire was created, a likeness pure
as the substance of the sky. He did not lay a hand on
them, the noble pillars of Israel. They beheld God;
they ate and drank.

163

Yahweh spoke to Moses, "Carve two stone tablets and at dawn prepare to ascend Mount Sinai. In the light of morning you will present yourself to me, there on the top of the mountain. No one goes with you, no one is seen anywhere on the mountain, no cattle or sheep are seen near it." In the morning Moses ascended to the summit as Yahweh desired, two stone tablets in his hands. Yahweh descended in a cloud and stood with him there, calling to him, "Yahweh, Yahweh." Moses fell to the ground, prostrate.

164

"I mark this a covenant," Yahweh said. "Watch yourself, do not march into covenants with those already in the land. Walking among you, they will destroy your boundaries. You will sweep their altars away; their sacred pillars leveled, their poles cut down. You will not fall prostrate to another God, as if Jealous One is my name, Jealous Yahweh. You must not be drawn into a covenant with the inhabitants; they seduce their gods with slaughter; they will beckon you to their sacrifices and you will eat. Their daughters will give you sons yet still embrace seductive gods: your sons will also."

165

Now Yahweh concluded. "So be it: I will disperse a nation in your path, broaden your road and borders; so no one dreams he can embrace your land on your way to Yahweh; as you go up to face your God three times a year.

"You write these words," said Yahweh to Moses. "On the speaking of these words, I have cut with you a covenant—and with Israel."

Now look: he is there beside Yahweh for forty days, forty nights.

He did not eat bread, he did not drink water, as he wrote on the tablets the words of the covenant.

166

Now look: as Moses approaches the camp he sees the calf, and dancing abounds. His bitterness knows no bounds. He heaves the tablets from his hands, smashing them against the mountain.

The calf they cast—he has it melted down, pulverized to a fine ash, then scattered upon the drinking water. He calls the Israelites to drink; they swallow it.

"What could this people have done to you?" Moses asked Aaron. "Why open the door for them to such a great contempt?"

"My lord, do not be consumed in anger's flames," said Aaron. "You know this people, their memory quickly melts away. 'Make gods to go in front on our way,' they said to me. 'This man Moses, who led us up from the land of Egypt—who knows what has happened to him.'

" 'To those with gold,' I said, 'remove it and give it to me.' I cast it into the fire; out of it came the calf."

167

So it was: Moses goes back to Yahweh. "Heaven forbid, this people has shown great contempt, making gods of gold.

"You will forgive their contempt, perhaps; if not, erase me—bless heaven—out from the book you are writing."

"I will erase the one with contempt for me," Yahweh answered Moses, "from my book. Now you will go, lead the people to where I said: follow the words I spoke."

168

After these things passed, listen: "We are beginning a journey, to the country Yahweh spoke of. 'I will give it to you,' he said." Moses was speaking to Hobab, son of Reuel the Midianite—who was his father-in-law. "Join us on the way, join in our good fortune: Yahweh has joined together good words for Israel."

"I will not be going," came the reply, "but will return to my own country, my homeland."

"Please," Moses interjected. "We would not have you leave. You know this desert well and where we may make camp in it. Be our eyes; what good fortune

Yahweh makes us see will make you fortunate as well—if you would only accompany us."

Now they started out from Yahweh's mountain, traveling for three days, Yahweh's covenant-ark in front of them, escorting them toward the place for making camp.

Now look: as the ark sets out, Moses says, "Arise Yahweh, your enemies disappear like stars; your haters fade before you." When it rests, he says, "Come back, Yahweh, you who embody Israel's countless thousands."

169

Now the rabble among them craved flesh; and soon the Israelites also were grumbling. "Who will fill our yearning for flesh? We can see the fish we used to eat in Egypt, so freely available, like cucumbers and melons, like leeks, onions, like garlic.

"But now our spirit dries up from looking at nothing—nothing but manna."

Moses heard the people weeping, all the different families, the men standing there at their tent doors. It was scalding to Yahweh; to Moses, his heart was singed.

"Why do you hurt your servant?" asked Moses of Yahweh. "How have I made your heart so heavy you push the burden of this people on me?

"Could I have conceived this whole people? Did I give birth to them? You say to me, as if I bore them: 'Hold them to your breast, the way a nurse cradles a baby, until you arrive on the earth which I vowed to your fathers.'

"How would I get flesh to feed this whole people? They are crying for it: 'Give us flesh,' they say to me. 'That is what we want to eat.'

"I am unable to bear this whole people alone; they are too heavy for me.

"If this is what you want of me, strike me dead with mercy; if I have warmed you, let me rest from seeing my breaking heart."

170
"You will say to the people," Yahweh said to Moses: " 'Purify yourselves, tomorrow you will eat meat. Your weeping words—"Who will feed us meat as good as we ate in Egypt"—reached Yahweh's ears. Yahweh will deliver your flesh, for you to eat.

" 'And not for just a day or two days, not even for five or ten days, even twenty days—but for a whole month, until it comes out from your nostrils, until you loathe the smell of it.

" 'For you have denied Yahweh, who is in the midst of you, wailing in his ears, "Why did we ever come out from Egypt?" ' "

But Moses responded: "I stand in the midst of six hundred thousand wanderers—and you want me to say you will have meat for them—enough for eating a whole month of days?

"If all the cattle and sheep were slaughtered, could that begin to be enough? Could all the fish in the sea be caught for them?"

Now Yahweh answered Moses: "Is the arm of Yahweh too short? Soon you will see what becomes of my words."

171

Now a boy came running to Moses: "Eldad and Medad are prophesying in the camp."

"Prohibit them, my lord Moses," appealed Joshua son of Nun, a follower of Moses from his youth.

"Do you think I should show myself jealous?" said Moses to him. "If only the people were all Yahweh's prophets; if only Yahweh would make them bear his spirit."

172

"Go up through the Negev," Moses instructed the scouts sent into Canaan, "and into the mountains. Look around, scout the land and the people settled on it—their power, their weaknesses; how thick, or how thinly spread they are.

"And the land that holds them—worthy or bad. And the cities in which they collect—unwalled or strongholds?

"And the shape of earth itself—fat or sparse, dressed in forests or not. Gather your wits, collect some fruits of the land."

Now it was the time the grapes first ripen, and when they reached the Eshkol valley they cut a section of vine packed with grapes; loaded onto a stretcher, it took two of them to carry it back. They carried off as well pomegranates and figs.

They called that valley Eshkol: the section of vine cut by Israel's sons was packed as a *school* of *fish*.

173

After forty days of scouting the land they returned, presented themselves before Moses, Aaron, and the whole congregation of Israel. There in the desert of Paran, at Kadesh, they presented the fruit and word of the land.

Now this is what they said: "We found the land to which you sent us full with earth's milk and honey— an overflow of grain, flowing wine. Look, this is its fruit.

"But it must be said the inhabitants are strong, the huge cities walled; we even saw the breed of giants there. Amalekites live in the Negev desert, Hittites in the mountains—the Jebusites and the Amorites there too—and by the sea, Canaanites, as well as by the Jordan.

"All the people we saw were stunning in their power. The giants are the children of Anak. We felt like grasshoppers, and in their eyes we were."

A loud sigh heaved from the congregation; the whole people wept that night.

They complained and murmured about Moses and Aaron. "We were better off dying in Egypt," the congregation moaned, "or dying in this desert, than finding out Yahweh delivers us to that land. Are we here just to fall under swords, our wives and children delivered up? We would be better off descending to Egypt.

"Let's make a leader," they were whispering among themselves, "to deliver us back to Egypt."

Now Yahweh spoke to Moses: "How long will this people affront me? How long until they attend me, and see the signs I put in front of them? I will put disease in front of them, erase their inheritance. I will make a nation out of you alone, grander than they, enormous."

But Moses said to Yahweh: "Egypt will hear what you have done to the very people your power brought out from them. And then it will reach the inhabitants of the other land."

Speaking to Moses and Aaron, Yahweh said, "To this people you will say, 'So says Yahweh: "Surely as I exist, what you have said for my ears I will be sure you hear spoken of you. The little children you said will be delivered up—those I will deliver to the land, to conquer it, just as you have belittled it. Yet your carcasses will fall in the desert. Your children will wander the desert forty years, conquering your giant words, until your bodies have wasted away in this wasteland." ' "

169

174
After these things passed, now look: Yahweh had become inflamed that Balaam would go with contemptuous men. Yahweh's angel put himself in Balaam's path, like an adversary. Balaam was riding on his ass, two servant-boys in attendance.

As the ass saw Yahweh's angel standing in her path, sword unsheathed in his hand, she stepped off the road into a field. Yet Balaam whipped the ass, to get her back on the road.

Then Yahweh's angel put himself in a narrow path ahead, through vineyards fenced in on either side. As the ass saw Yahweh's angel she swerved into the wall, pinching Balaam's foot against it; he whipped her again.

Once more Yahweh's angel put himself ahead, in a narrow spot with no room for turning either right or left.

The ass saw Yahweh's angel again and sat down under Balaam; he was furious, whipping the ass with his stick.

Now Yahweh opened the ass's mouth. "What did I do to you," she said, "to make you lash out at me on three occasions?" "Because *you* have been riding *me,*" Balaam said to the ass. "If I had a sword in my hand, it would whip you dead this time."

"No! Aren't I your own ass? I'm the ass you've been riding on as long as you've owned me," said the ass to Balaam. "Have I been trying—to this day—to make an ass of you?" And he: "No."

175
Now Yahweh opens Balaam's eyes; he sees Yahweh's angel standing in the road, the sword unsheathed in his hand—and falls prostrate, flat on his face.

"Why did you strike your ass these three times?" says Yahweh's angel. "Look: at the sight of your wayward path, I came as your adversary.

"The ass sees me and shies away three times—if she had not swerved, I would have killed you by now and spared her."

"I was contemptuous," Balaam said to Yahweh's angel. "I couldn't imagine that you would cross my path. Seeing I have crossed you, I will turn back at once."

But Yahweh's angel said to Balaam: "Continue on your way. But not a word to those men—except what I will tell you to say."

176

Now Israel was staying at Shittim when the people entered the arms of Moabite daughters.

They were beckoned to sacrifices for their gods. Soon the people ate, then lay prostrate with them, before their gods.

As Israel is yoked there, embracing Baal-peor, Yahweh is inflamed. "Round up the heads of the people," said Yahweh to Moses. "Hang them before Yahweh, in broad daylight, until Yahweh's fury is burnt away, away from Israel."

To Israel's leaders Moses then said: "Each of you must kill those of your men who yoked themselves nakedly to Baal-peor."

177

"Look: your deathday arrives," Yahweh said to Moses. "Summon Joshua, and direct yourselves to the tent for encounter, so I may appoint him." Moses and Joshua go to the tent for encounter, as directed.

Yahweh came down to the tent through the pillar of cloud. The pillar of cloud covered the tent entrance.

Now he appointed Joshua, son of Nun: "Summon strength and audacity, as you will direct the children of Israel to the land I vowed—for I will attend you."

178

Moses ascends from the Moab valley to Mount Nebo in the direction facing Jericho. There Yahweh reveals all the land, from Gilead to Dan; then all Naphtali, the land of Ephraim and Manasseh, and now all the land of Judah to the Western Sea; then the Negev, past the oasis of palms that is Jericho, and out through the valley to Zoar.

"This is the land I vowed to Abram, Isaac, and Jacob," Yahweh said to him. " 'To your seed I will give it,' were my words. It is revealed to your eyes, though your body cannot follow."

Moses, servant of Yahweh, died there, in Moab's land, following Yahweh's word.

Now he buries him there, in the clay of Moab's land, in a gorge facing Beth-peor: no man has ever seen his grave, to this day.

Commentary

HAROLD BLOOM

A TEMPERAMENT like J's could hardly have resisted the ironic joys of portraying an impish cosmological Creation, probably the total antithesis of the Priestly first chapter of Genesis, as we have it now. But as I have sketched that missing vision of J's already, I repeat here only that what we have as the start of the Book of J is not to be taken as *her* notion of how to begin. And yet it is a superb point of origin.

> Before a plant of the field was in earth, before a grain of the
> field sprouted—Yahweh had not spilled rain on the earth, nor
> was there man to work the land—yet from the day Yahweh
> made earth and sky, a mist from within would rise to moisten
> the surface. Yahweh shaped an earthling from clay of this
> earth, blew into its nostrils the wind of life. Now look: man
> becomes a creature of flesh. (1)

Let us begin with "shaped," which in the Hebrew takes its resonance from the work of a potter. Yahweh, unlike the rival creator-gods of the ancient Near East, does not stand in front of a potter's wheel. Instead, he picks up the moistened clay and molds it in his hands, rather like a solitary child making a mud pie or building clay houses near water. We are in the hard Judean spring, and not in the grand harvest festival of the Priestly first chapter of Genesis. Whether or not J began her scroll with Yahweh vanquishing the Dragon and the Deep Sea, she begins her account of the natural and the human with Yahweh, all alone, standing in a mist that comes from within the earth that he has made. There, in that mist, for no stated reason or cause, he scoops up a handful of wet earth and shapes it into what we would call an earthling. But this earthling is still a mud pie or a clay figurine until (presumably only a moment later) Yahweh blows his own breath, "the wind of life," into the nostrils he has formed. Does Yahweh set his mouth to the earthling's nostrils, or is this a nostril-to-nostril inspiriting? The question is grotesque, and perhaps unnecessary, since Yahweh works up close and either way kisses us, even if Eskimo-fashion. It would be like the lovingly ironic J if her childlike Yahweh breathes from his own nostrils into the child of his art. Howsoever, the sculpture modulates from clay to flesh, and the first creature becomes a living being, yet one whose name, Adam, retains always memories of the red clay dust from which he was formed.

The poet of the Book of Job, much under the influence of my least favorite prophet, the abominable Jeremiah, allegorized this Adamic creation as a moral lesson in humility, reminding us that we sojourn in houses of clay, with dust both as our origin and as our destination. That denigration of the human is alien to J's spirit. Adam is fashioned out of the *adamah,* or red clay, as a tribute to the earth, and so as a tribute to humankind. There is no "Fall" for J, as we are about to see, because for J there is nothing fallen about nature, earthly or human. J is the most monistic of all Western authors, even as Saint Paul is one of the most dualistic. There is for J no split between body and soul, between nature and mind. So far as I can tell, such monism was J's invention, whereas the creation out of clay was not.

J's idea of the human founds itself upon the heroic image of David, though David is of course never mentioned in the Book of J. We are not told by J that Adam is molded in the image of Yahweh, but we can assume that J saw David as godlike or theomorphic, almost as though David truly had been the first Adam, and Adam in Eden a secondary man. Whatever overt humor J intended in the grotesque creation of Adam, that humor is hardly at Adam's expense, but rather at Yahweh's. Adam is not a clay vessel with the breath of Yahweh coursing through it, but a being who has within him the wind of life. J, like the Court Historian's David, is a heroic vitalist or unified being, and her Adam cannot be divided into clay body and divine soul.

Always elliptical, adept at the art of leaving out, J allows us to speculate as to the reverberations of her verbal play with *adam* ("man") and the *adamah* from which he was shaped. The first man's name has no reference to the breath of life, and so the name is more dualistic than the person. Such an irony is a spur not to humility but to a kind of wryness, and is a guide to the story of Eden that follows. In between comes one of the summits of J's originality, the creation of woman, perhaps the most weakly misread of all J's inventions. With no precedents (that we know), J charmingly evades both patriarchal misogyny and feminist resentment while insinuating a kind of Shavian wit not exactly shared either by Yahweh or by Adam.

Eden, later to be described by the exilic prophet Ezekiel as "the garden of God," is in J less a locale than an era, an earliness now forever forsaken. And in J we find, not the garden of God, but a garden appointed for our ancestors, *our* garden, even though we have been expelled from it. Franz Kafka, so frequently the modern writer most in J's spirit, caught the essence of J's sense of Paradise.

> The expulsion from Paradise is in its main significance eternal: Consequently the expulsion from Paradise is final, and life in this world irrevocable, but the eternal nature of the occurrence (or, temporally expressed, the eternal recapitulation of the occurrence) makes it nevertheless possible that not only could we live continuously in Paradise, but that we are continuously there in actual fact, no matter whether we know it here or not.

Paradise is always "there," and our knowing is "here," but our being is split off from our knowing, and so it is possible that we still abide in Eden. Kafka is studying the nostalgias, but so was J. The cost of remaining in Paradise fully was "not knowing good and bad," and here the difficulties of understanding J have been enormous, since so many thousands of exegetes have read J's ironic narrative as a story of sin or crime and its appropriate (or incommensurate) punishment. Everything depends upon those two trees, of life and of knowing good and bad, or are they after all only the one tree? Pragmatically they are, since only the tree of knowing good and bad is involved in the catastrophe, and also is J's own invention. The Tree of Life is prevalent in the literature of the ancient Middle East, and I suspect that J interpolated this traditional tree into her text as an interpretive afterthought. Knowing good and bad seems quite enough; to touch the tree is to be touched, the same day, by death. Yahweh states a limit, more than a taboo of touch or taste. Dividing consciousness is the knowledge of death; I do not hear threat or punishment in this, but rather a statement of the reality principle, or the way things are.

Before death is introduced again, J plays out the lovely fable of the creation of woman, a highly original fable since, as I remarked earlier, we have no other extant account of the creation of woman from the ancient Middle East. The ironies of J's fable encompass Yahweh and Adam, but not at all the still nameless first woman. Misogyny in the West is a long and dismal history of weak misreadings of the comic J, who exalts women throughout her work, and never more than in this deliciously wry story of creation. The lack of a sense of humor in believers and exegetes always has been and remains the largest barrier to the understanding of J.

How does one read the creation of woman? Yahweh reflects that it is not good for man to be alone, and resolves to make a partner to stand beside his creature.

> So Yahweh shaped out of the soil all the creatures of the field
> and birds of the air, bringing them to the man to see how he

would call them. Whatever the man called became the living creature's name. Soon all wild animals had names the man gave them, all birds of the air and creatures of the field, but the man did not find his partner among them. (4)

"Helpmate," our now discredited term for a wife (or a husband), comes directly from the King James version of a partner to stand beside one: "I will make him an help meet for him" (Gen. 2:18). That is an eloquent mistranslation of J, whose Hebrew means "equal to him" or "alongside him," where the "help," far from being subservient or auxiliary, translates a word later used for Yahweh's relationship to us. J's Yahweh seeks a correspondent being for Adam, as earlier Yahweh imparted to Adam a correspondent breeze. Is it Yahweh's joke, or J's, that the quest for that being begins with shaping out of the clay all the animals and birds? The quest is for naming, and part of the joke is that Adam does not name his woman other than as woman when at last he receives her as fit partner. When we consider Adam's task of naming, we often do not remember that what is being named is precisely what is not fit to mend Adam's solitude. J's insight is Nietzschean long before Nietzsche: that which we find words for is that which we cannot hold in our heart.

Yahweh, presumably confounded, resorts to what Keats calls Adam's dream, a dream from which we wake to find it true. The deep sleep, *tardemah*, into which Yahweh puts Adam is J's profound metaphor for the mystery of love, or of what Freud reductively called "object choice." Adam's heavy sleep is not natural, its function being anesthetic, and J slyly hints that man's love for woman is essentially narcissistic, related to the greater mystery of birth. In some sense, what Adam experiences is the only male instance of giving birth. Adam's rib is shaped or built by Yahweh, in one of J's curious wordplays, since the word for "rib" is a structural term inevitably employed in the account of any building operation. But we should stand back here and contrast Yahweh as the artificer of the woman with Yahweh as the much more childlike and haphazard creator of the man. It is not just that J has given six times the space to woman's creation as to man's; it is the difference between making a mud pie and building a much more elaborate and fairer structure. The man provides (involuntarily) the substance with which Yahweh begins this second and greater creation. But that means the woman is created from a living being, and not from clay. Presumably she is animate, and Yahweh need not inspirit her nostrils. Surely J's ironic point is that the second time around, Yahweh has learned better how the job ought to be done.

I do not interpret Yahweh's action in bringing the woman to Adam as that of an attendant at a wedding, or even of a father giving away the bride. J is not in the business, as we will see many times, of endorsing marriage as such, let alone of considering Yahweh the establisher and sanctifier of marriage. J's wryness does not cease at any moment in this sequence. No one has hinted so shrewdly at the limits of sexual love: that it unites in act but not in essence. Parting is played off against clinging, which is revealed as inadequate to overcome parting. We part from mother and father, rather as the woman was parted from Adam. Clinging cannot make us one flesh, and no man since Adam *can* say, "Bone of my bone, flesh of my flesh" (4). Adam and his woman were one flesh, but we only cling, at best.

We are asked to look again at Adam and the woman, because we are moving to the smoothness or slyness of the serpent, a smoothness that is his equivalent of their shameless nakedness. J's remarkable pun here is quite famous, but not always very acutely interpreted.

And look: they are naked [smooth], man and woman, un-touched by shame, not knowing it. (4)

Now the snake was smoother-tongued than any wild creature that Yahweh made. (5)

The Hebrew *'arom* is "naked"; *'arum* is "shrewd, subtle, sly." "Smooth" is the best American vernacular equivalent for the pun, as in "a smooth customer." The man and the woman do not know slyness; the serpent knows nothing else. Our problem, as J's readers, is to disentangle her story of the serpent in Eden from the scandalous prominence it has achieved in Christian theology and in Western imaginative literature. It is an enormous challenge to recover J at this point in particular.

How did the charming serpent of J ever become Satan? The answer seems to go back at least to the first century before the common era, to certain apocalyptic Jewish heretical writings, including the *Testament of Adam*, the *Life of Adam and Eve*, and the curiously mistitled *Apocalypse of Moses*. Behind them is a lost life or apocalypse of Adam, where presumably the Devil and J's serpent first merged, where J's story of disobedience was transmuted to one of lust, and where the tree of the knowledge of good and bad vanished into just any tree at all that could be associated with the serpent who is Satan. Normative rabbis and their Gnostic opponents alike misread J's original story until the opposing readings were subsumed by Saint Augustine's Christian allegorizings. J thinks of the man and the woman as disobedient children, and of the serpent as a smooth imp. Lust is an obsession of dualists, who see soul and body as caught in a wrestling match, but J, as I have shown, was no dualist and so was not much concerned with lust.

That returns us to Eden, and to J's smooth play upon nakedness and slyness. The nakedness of the man and the woman is their childlike astuteness, even as the slyness of the serpent is its nakedness, its quality of being wholly natural, as much at home in Eden as they are. The child's nakedness is virtually identical with the serpent's astuteness, and neither is attached to shame or excessive self-consciousness. Our given endowment, for J, has in it no original shame or original guilt. Solomonic culture, we can infer, was neither a shame culture, like the Homeric, nor a guilt culture, like the Christian. Adam and his still nameless wife have the vitalistic splendor of David, the complete human being, Yahweh's favorite, and such heroic intensity begins unshadowed by guilt or shame. If the serpent's subtle awareness is *its* nakedness, then like the human nakedness, such slyness is the serpent's mode of freedom. The serpent is in Eden because it belongs there; its presence, speech, and discernment do not astonish the woman, and so we are not to think of it as magical or mythological. It is Yahweh's creature, his subtlest, and perhaps we can say now it is Yahweh's most ironical creature.

We have no reason to believe the serpent malevolent. J introduces it by remarking upon its leading quality, not upon its intentions, about which she tells us absolutely nothing. The serpent's quest widens consciousness, through the knowing of good from bad, a discernment Yahweh had capriciously granted to the angels, according to J's contemporary, the author of 2 Samuel. J does not tell us why Yahweh chose not to make the same equivocal gift to the man and the woman, or why the serpent acquired some portion of angelic knowledge. Since the basis for J's style is always ellipsis, we need a close reading to determine what has been left out in such a way as to imply its absence. What is implied here is at once the startling likeness between the Elohim, or angels, and Adam, and the absolute unlikeness between Yahweh and Adam that Yahweh arbitrarily insists upon maintaining. The basis of irony for J is always the clash of incommensurates, a clash that begins in the illusion of commensurateness. That ancient red herring, anthropomorphism, again threatens to divert us from the center of J's imagination: the theomorphic or divine elements in women and in men. J's irony is subtly balanced yet favors the still nameless woman over Adam, Yahweh, and the serpent. Since normative commentary, particularly Christian exegesis, has made the woman the culprit, this point deserves considerable emphasis. Her reply to the serpent curiously modifies Yahweh's admonition by adding "you can't touch." The taboo of touch is entirely her own and is less a mistake than an ironic revision, exposing how childlike her consciousness can be. "You are not to eat it, indeed you can't even touch it," we say to a child, and we enhance the child's sense of deprivation and powerlessness. The contrast between such a sense and Yahweh's impending punishment vastly augments the sympathetic pathos of the first woman.

Is the serpent a liar? No, though he tells a half-truth when he insists, "Death will not touch you" (5). Still, he has no sense of temporality, only of immediacy, and he is not aware that his truth is but partial. Nor does he address himself to the woman alone. J's Hebrew implies that Adam is present, hears what the woman hears, and does not resist her act of handing him the fruit. She is the active child, the more curious or imaginative, while Adam's role is that of the child who imitates. We have, then, two children and a natural creature with some preternatural knowledge, the serpent. J has given us no candidates for culpability, except perhaps Yahweh, already portrayed as a bungler in his original creation of candidates fit for Adam. Setting the tree of knowing good and bad as prohibition and temptation is a parallel blunder, the act of a father all too incommensurate with his children, as his subsequent reactions also indicate. What is it to know good and bad? Again the normative misreading has reduced this issue to the knowledge or consciousness of sexuality, but J has too healthy a view of human sexuality for such a reduction to be relevant or interesting. Good and bad is no less than everything, freedom and the limits of freedom, self-knowledge, angelic, almost godlike. When you know yourself, you know your own nakedness, but the consequent shame has no sexual overtones, difficult as normative tradition has made this to acknowledge. To open one's eyes is to see everything, all at once, and so to see oneself as others might see one, as an object. But who is there to see the man and the woman except for their maker, Yahweh? They have ceased to be children, at least in their own judgment, and have acquired the slyness of the serpent, even as the serpent metaphorically acquires their nakedness in Yahweh's terrible judgment upon him.

What do we, or J, make of Yahweh's judgment upon us? If

like a mother he dresses us far more adequately than we can dress ourselves, still we must note what J subtly passes over in silence: the first killing is done by Yahweh in order to clothe us (Gen. 3:21). The choice is Yahweh's, not ours. Though the intimacy of the scene is remarkable, this mode of presentation is inevitable for J. We are witnessing not the Fall of Man and Woman, disobedience followed by a death sentence with a kind of indefinite reprieve, but a family romance transformed into a family tragedy. What is involved is *not* Fall but a wounding estrangement, an expulsion from home, from a garden where Yahweh, who is both mother and father, likes to walk about while enjoying the cool breezes of the evening. J, as I keep emphasizing, writes in no specific genre, but what we call "children's literature" catches part of J's spirit. What is no part of that spirit is epitomized by Claus Westermann, who for me disputes with Gerhard von Rad the distinction of being the most acute of our modern scholarly exegetes of J: "J is saying much more: what constitutes a crime against God, a sin against God, is what people do in defiance of God and nothing else, not a consciousness of sin nor a bad conscience" (*Genesis: A Commentary*, 1984).

The judgment "a crime against God, a sin against God" is something that I simply cannot hear in J. J does not find crime or sin in the children's tale she tells us. The children know they have been disobedient. When the parent's footsteps are heard, they hide, and see themselves as they now believe they will be seen, sly and naked. When the man says he was afraid because he was naked, do we hear a being capable of sin or crime? And what both the man and the woman say to Yahweh is just, being true if not wholly sufficient. It is not so much that the man blames the woman or the woman the serpent, but that each, childlike, relates the happening as a cause-and-effect phenomenon. We would like to hear the serpent speak once more, in its own defense, but Yahweh forestalls us. Nothing could be more incommensurate than Yahweh's punishments and the childish offenses that provoked them, but such incommensurateness is the center of J's vision, as always.

Yahweh's curses (Gen. 3:14–19) seem to have been revised by J from more ancient doggerels, and their rhetorical bite is proper to their really shocking harshness. The uncanniness of this Yahweh inheres already in his antithetical qualities: a mothering father and a vengeful judge. His invective against the serpent is so excessive that it encouraged two strong misreadings of J, one normative Judaic and Christian, the other Gnostic, the first seeing the poor snake as Satan, the second weirdly exalting him as a liberator. Yahweh's curse against the woman takes on a particular pathos if my speculation as to J's gender is valid. The pain and labor of childbirth, so unique to human mothers, is ironically associated by J with a man's putative sexual mastery over a woman. And Adam's curse, hard labor for bread, is intimately connected by Yahweh with the dust-to-dust cycle of human life and death. There seems little middle ground here; the origin and end of life are the same. Like the other curses, this is powerfully reductive, and most unsympathetic. Setting aside normative moralizings, what has J given us here?

Let us begin by dismissing all Pauline and Augustinian inter-pretations that find here the vision of a Fall, a vision that began in late Judaism in texts like 2 Esdras. J never speaks of a fall from a higher to a lower level of being. The man and the woman suffer terribly in J, *but they are not degraded to a lesser level of being.* J does not see their fate as a "before" and an "after" but as a seriocomic mishap for which they are only barely responsible. "When we were children, we were terribly punished for being children" might be called the essence of J's story. I think that this aspect of J was so well understood by the Jews throughout biblical times that they fundamentally regarded this part of her tale as what we now read as children's literature. That may be why it is never mentioned again anywhere in the entire text of the Hebrew Bible. No prophet, no chronicler, no poet in the Hebrew Bible ever reminds us what Yahweh did in this crisis or how he did it. We were as children in the beginning, and we were made to suffer both for being different from Yahweh and for wanting to be less different from Yahweh. Our suffering, most of all our mortality, ensues from that difference, and surely J enforces the irony that it is Yahweh who insists upon the difference, and so upon the mortality.

When J's Yahweh says that we are dust and must return to it, he would seem to have forgotten that he himself breathed the wind of life into us. J is not writing a moral tale but a children's story that ends unhappily. This is how things got to be the way things are, she is saying, and the way they are is not good, whether for snakes, women, or men.

What J's story hints at, as I read it, is an older Judaism in which the difference between Yahweh and the man and woman was less absolute; in which Adam was a lesser Yahweh, as it were. How fascinating it is that the normative Redactor, a figure like Ezra the Scribe, even if he was not Ezra, let stand one of J's most scandalous moments.

"Look," said Yahweh, "the earthling sees like one of us, knowing good and bad. And now he may blindly reach out his hand, grasp the tree of life as well, eat, and live forever."

(10)

This is a double irony, or a double scandal. What it makes clear is that J does *not* say that our mortality results from our disobedience and consequent expulsion from Eden. *We had been created mortal:* living beings, with clay sides and life's wind moving through us, but not likely to sustain that wind forever. Late, apocalyptic Judaism and early Christianity misread Genesis here, but the rest of the Hebrew Bible does not. Like J, its inaugurator, it knows nothing of immortality. Again I surmise that an archaic Judaism, long preceding J, speculated upon an Adamic immortality, but such a speculation enters J only in Yahweh's extraordinary fear that a knowing Adam might "blindly" eat of the fruit of life's tree and thus become one of the Elohim. The expulsion from Eden takes on a particular poignancy in the context of Yahweh's wariness.

The earthling was driven forward; now, settled there—east of
Eden—the winged sphinxes and the waving sword, both sides
flashing, to watch the way to the Tree of Life. (10)

That Yahweh is terribly in earnest could scarcely be clearer; the
expulsion is not so much to punish childish disobedience as it is
to forestall a blind or unwilled ascension to godhood by human
beings. J implies that there is little difference between knowing,
mature men and women, and the Elohim, or angelic host; and the
little difference is immortality. Kafka is again the best guide to J:
"Why do we lament over the fall of man? We were not driven out
of Paradise because of it, but because of the Tree of Life, that we
might not eat of it."

J's story of Eden, like Kafka's, is anything but normative, as
I have demonstrated. It is not a moral or a theological narrative,
and asserts no historical status. For J's contemporaries, in what I
take to be the final years of Solomon and the early reign of his
inadequate son, Rehoboam, it may have seemed less a straightforward fable of human origins than a sophisticated parable of the
decline of David's kingdom from imperial grandeur to division and
turbulence. For Eden and Adam can one read the heroic age of the
Jews, and David as Yahweh's favorite? The differences from his
creatures upon which Yahweh insists with such terrible ferocity
become also the augmenting incommensurateness between David
and his grandson Rehoboam. Yet the deeper juxtaposition among
humans is not temporal but that between men and women. Hava
(Eve), only just named, abides in our memories of reading J as the
livelier child, and also as the human child more cruelly penalized
by Yahweh.

Cain and Abel

"I have created a man as Yahweh has" (11) is the proud assertion
of Eve when Cain is born to her. What are we to make of her

exuberant exclamation? The story of Cain as J tells it is another of this great author's eloquent enigmas, immense, difficult now to sever from its interpretation in late Judaism or in Christianity. In that exegesis, Cain incarnates evil from the start; some have even said that Sammael was his father, misreading Eve's boast as "I have created a man by Yahweh's angel." J being so subtle, I read Eve's assertion as an ironic, narcissistic mistake on her part, since she would seem to be comparing the making of Cain to her own creation by Yahweh rather than the molding of Adam out of clay. Cain is the first human achievement after the expulsion from Eden, and his crucial quality is not evil but an implied resentment against Yahweh. He, after all, and not Abel, the shepherd, takes up Adam's curse and tills the soil. His offering, fruit of the earth, involves no killing and yet is rejected, though he is the firstborn. J offers us no motive for Yahweh's choice, and is equally laconic as to the provocation for Cain's gratuitous, sudden murder of Abel.

Bitterly alluding to his slain brother as a watcher of sheep, Cain speaks his infamous denial that he is his brother's watchman. Irony is heaped upon irony; Cain must become a nomad now that the soil cries out against its tiller. As his parents were expelled from Eden, Cain is now expelled from the soil, to settle in the windblown land, where he founds a city, the first of all cities necessarily. J, whom I cannot see except as a resident of David's city, of Solomon's urban splendor, perhaps reflects darkly upon what Jerusalem has become under Rehoboam. What is certain is that the urban, for J, is founded upon brotherly murder, a murder provoked by the arbitrariness of Yahweh. Lord Byron's poetic drama *Cain, a Mystery* seems to me very much in the spirit of J's story, since J's Cain too is a tragic rebel, and not a villain.

Giants in the Land

Seth, "another seed," is born to replace Abel, and fathers Enosh, whose name, "sweet mortal," is itself a deliberate contradiction or seems to be one. With a gentle irony, J equates the time of sweet mortality with the age in which Yahweh is called by his name, curiously a "fond calling" (17). Another fond calling ensues as the Elohim lust after the beautiful daughters of men. Such mismatches of mortals with immortals, not acceptable to Yahweh, certainly cause J no horror. Yahweh reminds himself that man is mortal flesh, and insists that the breath of life will watch man only for a set term, the not inconsiderable hundred and twenty years. There is an ironic play here, back to Cain's asking if he is his brother's watcher, when Yahweh thus sets limits for his own watching. But what concerns Yahweh so darkly is a cheerful enough matter for J.

> Now the race of giants: they were in the land then, from the time the sons of heaven entered the rooms of the daughters of men. Hero figures were born to them, men and women of mythic fame. (20)

One does not hear condemnation in J, but a wry appreciation of those mythic men and women, figures whose names have not been scattered, though they are hardly within the Blessing. Yet the impending price is inevitable as Yahweh prepares for the Deluge. J's Yahweh is quite specific in expressing his distaste for all the creatures he has made: humans, beasts, birds. We ought not to glide over J's reserved and witty disengagement from Yahweh's rather outrageous disapproval of natural desire even in beasts and birds! We are about to embark with Noah, but in J there will be comic aspects to this voyage. The righteous Noah, his family, his zoo, all enter, and then Yahweh himself shuts the ark with his own hands.

Noah

We are back in the mode of what we call children's literature, if indeed we have ever left it. The Deluge over, the propitiated Yahweh smells "a soothing scent" (26) and is moved to declare that there will be no more mass destructions of people or of animals. This seems a fit Yahweh for Noah, the first alcoholic, so splendidly celebrated in a poem by G. K. Chesterton in which the most righteous of his generation chants as refrain, "I don't care where the water goes if it doesn't get into the wine." I begin to feel redundant in my insistence that J is a comic writer when we come to the story of Noah and his sons. I have some suspicions that J's exuberance has been censored here, and that Ham did not merely observe his father's pudenda. When Noah "lay uncovered in the middle of his tent," he presumably was enjoying his wife, "tent" being a plausible metaphor for the lady, and there is an uncomfortable edge in the statement that Ham "enjoyed his father's nakedness," almost as though sodomy is suggested. We certainly enjoy the hilariously respectful performance of Shem and Yafat.

> But Shem and Yafat took a cloak, draped it over their shoulders, walked in backward, covered their naked father, faces averted: they never saw their father naked. (28)

These two ingenious young men receive their reward; Ham's son Canaan is cursed, while Shem and Yafat are allied in mastery over Canaan. Historians read this as alluding to an uneasy joint stance of the twelfth-century Hebrews and Philistines against the native Canaanites, but I am inclined to read it as another instance of J's humor. So outrageous is the episode of Noah and his sons that the political allegory must have been just as deliberately rancid. Evidently, Canaan had a somewhat freer mode of sexuality than post-Solomonic Jerusalem overtly manifested, and perhaps J's humorous thrust is that even the Philistines were less sexually depraved than the Canaanites! What seems clear is that J's Noah and the Flood story has little or no spiritual significance for her, unlike P's solemn rendition, which is an account of the First Covenant. Incessant ironist though she was, J seems to have enjoyed Flood, ark, and Noah each for its own sake alone.

The Tower of Babel

A summit of J's art, the Tower of Babel can best be introduced by its legitimate modern heir, Kafka's Great Wall of China. Kafka writes of a scholar who

> maintained that the Great Wall alone would provide for the first time in the history of mankind a secure foundation for a new Tower of Babel. First the wall, therefore, and then the tower. . . . Human nature, essentially changeable, unstable as the dust, can endure no restraint; if it binds itself it soon begins to tear madly at its bonds, until it rends everything asunder, the wall, the bonds, and its very self.

Kafka thus finds in the impulse to build the tower the same force that will destroy the tower. Is that J's judgment also? The question of J's tone, her stance, is again at the center of the problem of interpretation.

All of mankind, united by one language, seeks to keep its name from being scattered, through the building of a tower touching the sky. The purpose is fame rather than rebellion against Yahweh, though to seek fame is necessarily to rebel against Yahweh. All rush to be like the giants in the land and to achieve renown. Yahweh, though he presumably has a perfectly good view of what is going on, descends to enjoy one of his on-the-ground inspections. His reaction is akin to his judgment that Adam and Eve must be expelled from Eden lest they devour the fruit of the Tree of Life. A united humankind seems not much to Yahweh's taste.

> "They are one people, with the same tongue," said Yahweh. "They conceive this between them, and it leads up until no boundary exists to what they will touch. Between us, let's

descend, baffle their tongue until each is scatterbrain to his friend." (29)

1 9 2   Whether Yahweh is speaking to his angels or, more characteristically, to himself, he reveals again that he is, in J, an antithetical imp or sublime mischief-maker, in no way morally or spiritually superior to the builders of Babel, except insofar as his own tongue certainly is not baffled. Mankind builds the tower, but Yahweh invents Babel or bafflement, the confusion of tongues. We seek fame, and Yahweh scatters us, that every name be scattered also, except his own. Babylon or babbling is where Yahweh wishes us to live, except insofar as we become children of Abraham, once Abram has become Abraham.

J mothered Kafka but interprets the parable of Babel rather more darkly even than he does. She sees also that we can endure no restraint, but she does not find in us the force that overthrows the tower even as the same force built it. Her tower is no Great Wall of China, unstable dust aspiring to be a stable foundation for a tower that might jacket heaven. Her tower is a broken tower to begin with, since that which rises against Yahweh must be broken by Yahweh. Incommensurateness is, as always, her rhetoric and her theme alike. We are godlike or theomorphic, or can be, but we cannot be Yahweh, even if we are David. Yahweh *is* irony, and not just the spirit of irony. Perhaps he is the irony of mere maleness, when seen from J's marvelous perspective. We are children always, and so we build the Tower of Babel. J's Yahweh is a child also, a powerful and uncanny male child, and he throws down what we build up. He blesses or he scatters; we are scattered unless, like Abram, we hear and answer a call.

A B R A M

THE HISTORY OF the Jewish people begins with the ancient Hebrews, or Habiru, an unruly lot in the judgment of Bronze Age Egyptian officials, who seem to have been disquieted by these wanderers or semi-nomads, perhaps more a social caste than an ethnic unity. Soon after the start of the second millennium B.C.E., the Habiru began a movement from Mesopotamia westward, until they approached the Mediterranean. One group among them was later headed by a troubled and charismatic seeker, Abram, who as Abraham became the father of Judaism, Christianity, and Islam. It may have been eighteen centuries before the common era that Abram decided to leave Mesopotamia, for reasons that very likely were as spiritual as the Hebrew Bible asserts them to have been. Scholars agree that the lands ruled by the Old Babylonian Dynasty of Hammurabi and his successors were marvelously civilized, but Abram's discomfort with the religious culture drove him out. Yahweh says to Abram, "Bring yourself out of your birthplace" (30), and Abram goes as Yahweh tells him, though such a move at the age of seventy-five is rather drastic. But Yahweh's meaning is stark: "Do not stay to go on praying to other gods."

There is no independent evidence that Abraham ever existed as a historical personage distinct from tradition, yet there must have been some such figure, even if his precise location in time cannot be determined. Religions tend to go back to a single consciousness at their inception, just as stories are written initially by individuals, whatever the morphology of folktales. Yahweh was not invented by the Yahwist, though I argue in this book that J created her own Yahweh. If the Jews are children of Abraham, then their father had a real existence, or perhaps several existences.

J's literary progeny includes Thomas Mann in the beautiful novels *Tales of Jacob* and *Young Joseph*, the first two volumes of the tetralogy *Joseph and His Brothers*. Mann shrewdly notes what might be called the recurrence of an identity among the Hebrew Patriarchs.

> In such wise, and so simply, had Eliezer painted Abraham to Joseph with his words. But unconsciously his tongue forked in speaking and talked of him quite otherwise as well. Always it was Abram, the man from Uru, or more correctly from Harran, of whom the forked tongue spoke—calling him the great-grandfather of Joseph. Both of them, young and old, were quite aware that, unless by moonlight, Abram was not the man, that unquiet subject of Amraphel of Shinar; likewise that no man's great-grandfather lived twenty generations before him! Yet this was a trifling inexactitude compared with others at which they had to wink; for that Abraham of whom the tongue now spoke, changefully and inconsistently, was not he, either, who had lived then and shaken the dust of Shinar from his feet; but rather a different figure perceptible far behind the other, visible through him, as it were, so that the lad's gaze faltered and grew dim in this perspective just as it had in the one called Eliezer—an ever brighter vista, of course, for it is light that shines through.

One Abraham is more than six centuries before young Joseph, while the other is Joseph's great-grandfather; they are two Abrahams, but also one, since the light of Yahweh shines through them, in Mann as in the Yahwist. In *A History of the Jewish People* (ed. H. H. Ben-Sasson, 1976), Abraham Malamat, the distinguished Israeli historian of Hebrew origins, summarizes the same phenomenon in the language of scholarship.

> Attempts to determine a comparatively accurate date for the Patriarchs are themselves doomed to failure, for in fact it is difficult to speak of the so-called "patriarchal period" as a well-defined chronological entity, even where one accepts the biblical tradition as such. It would seem, rather, that imbedded in this narrative cycle are reminiscences of centuries-long historical processes that may hark back to the West Semitic migrations within the Fertile Crescent that made their way ever westwards and reached their apex during the first quarter of the second millennium. These extended time spans were telescoped in the biblical narrative into a mere trigenerational scheme—Abraham, Isaac and Jacob.

It may be true that were it not for the Yahwist, we would know a very different Abraham, but we would still know an Abraham, as his role is inescapable. Moses, despite Freud's assertions, did not invent monotheism; Abraham did, and the promise of Canaan therefore was made to Abraham, and only secondarily to Moses, who in any case was barred from going there. Abraham is therefore the origin, but what manner of man was he? His personality is not as fully developed by the Yahwist (or by Mann) as are those of Jacob and Joseph (how little we know, or care, about the personality of Isaac!), and yet his nature is intense and vivid, and permanently known to us. The center of his consciousness is a certain discontent, an impatience with things as they are. What in particular caused this discontent, though a puzzling matter, is not beyond all conjecture. Rather than idealize Abraham's disaffection from idolatry, we might follow the sober speculations of Ephraim Speiser in his Anchor Bible Genesis: "As a drastic departure from existing norms, the concept of monotheism had to break new ground. . . . with startling suddenness, a call comes to Abraham."

We do not know what impelled J to her abruptness as she began her account of Abram, but the sense of breaking with continuity established the norm for prophetic vocation ever since. Yahweh tells his first proclaimer or prophet that the break is to be triple: with the place of birth, the house of the father, the country or homeland. A triple origin is to be vacated, and not for a visible goal but only for "a land I will bring you to see" (30). "Come out of origins" is an audacious command, and implies, as Nietzsche was to echo, that origin and aim must be kept apart for the sake of life. Of all J's endless originalities, or the originalities of her Yahweh, this is the most startling, and returns us to the most salient characteristic of J's mode: its elliptical tendency, its leaving out. Yahweh does not deign to say *why* he orders Abram to go out and away from his origins; the why is assumed in the style of the injunction. How do we recover what J has so deliberately left out?

Bringing oneself out in response to a call is an enormous act, and transcends mere obedience. No one in J's narrative before Abram is asked to go beyond himself: not Adam, nor Noah. Abram follows the words of Yahweh before he is told the purpose of the call; in some sense he never is told, does not need to be told. He goes out from a highly developed civilization because of his implied discomfort with its culture. Rashi, commenting upon the *lekh lekha*, "bring yourself," read it as "for *your* benefit," because Abram was childless in Ur but in Canaan would be made into a great nation. Much subtler is the Kabbalistic interpretation in the *Zohar*, where Yahweh allegorizes Abram as *ab*, "father," and *ram*, the "height" above him, from which the breath-soul first emanated in the Yahwistic creation of Adam. The allegory thus traces the movement of the breath-soul from Yahweh to the nostrils of Adam, by way of exhorting Abram or the soul to go forth from Yahweh himself to the land or earth that is the Adamic body, a body holy and upright.

Moshe Idel, the great revisionist of post-Scholemian Kabbalistic studies, finds in Kabbalah the survival of a pre-Yahwist Judaism. In the spirit of Idel (and of the *Zohar*), we can find a wholly characteristic irony of repetition in J here. Calling upon Abram to go forth to Canaan repeats the making of Adam into a living being: both acts depend upon the descent of Yahweh's breath-soul, into the body and into the land. The calling of Abram is a second Creation, an urgent new beginning. There remains the profound puzzle, does J see the calling as a movement from idolatry to monotheism, or is such a view entirely the product of the normative tradition that led at last to the rabbinical Judaism of the second century C.E.?

Martin Buber, a great interpreter of the Bible, was not in the normative tradition, and read J's Abram as a seer, the first prophet of Israel: "With Abraham what matters is not his character as God finds it, so to speak, but what he does, and what he becomes." What Abram does is to respond immediately to Yahweh's call; what Abram becomes is Abraham, the father of the Jews, the Christians, and the Muslims, all of whom are the children of Abraham.

J's trope or metaphor for Abram's prophetic call is fatherhood, as Rashi and the *Zohar* both saw and said. And that is J's ultimate humanizing trope: the fatherhood of Yahweh. What Abram inaugurates is the relationship with God the Father, as opposed to the Mesopotamian civilization with its pantheon of essentially equal gods. J was too great an ironist, and too subtle a thinker, to tell us explicitly that the fatherhood of Yahweh was a spiritual advance over the leaderless gods of Babylonia. What we are shown, quite implicitly, is that it was what we (and Freud) would call a psychological advance, a movement away from anxiety into the familial reassurance that is given by the authority of a strong if uncanny father, the God who can be invoked by his proper name.

The name "Abram" itself means "exalted father"; only in P

is "Abram" transformed into "Abraham," or "father of a host of nations." J's metaphor of fatherhood is both simpler and more drastic; Yahweh and Abram both are fathers, not of hosts but of an elite, a few who are chosen. The normative vision of Yahweh as universal father is not in J's spirit at all. But to pursue J's metaphor of fatherhood more fully, we must wait until Jacob is the center of our discussion. For the relation between Abram and Yahweh, I turn back to Thomas Mann's eloquent enigmas in *Young Joseph*.

Mann's Abram does the good deed of one who took "hold upon the manifold and the anguishingly uncertain and converted it into the single, the definite, and the reassuring, of whom everything came, both good and evil—the sudden and frightful as well as the blessed usual, and to whom in any case we had to cling." This concentration of the spiritual world upon the one and only God leads Mann into a boldly ironic formulation.

> . . . in a way Abraham was God's father. He had perceived Him and thought Him into being. The mighty properties which he ascribed to Him were probably God's original possession. Abraham was not their creator. But was he not so after all, in a certain sense, when he recognized them, preached them, and by thinking made them real? The mighty properties of God were indeed something objective, existing outside of Abraham; but at the same time they were also in him and of him. The power of his own soul was at certain moments scarcely distinguishable from them.

I would modify Mann by substituting J for Abraham, in much the same spirit that the sages substituted Moses for J. J is the author of Yahweh, even though she did not invent him, but then Shakespeare did not invent Hamlet. I venture the speculation that J's power as a writer made Judaism, Christianity, and Islam possible, if only because the furious liveliness of her Yahweh presented tradition with an unforgettable and uncanny being. Inevitably the Priestly Author, the Redactor, and the guardians of normative Judaism, Christianity, and Islam muted and evaded J's outrageous Yahweh, but she had given them the vision that had to be scaled down and revised into moralism and belief. Indeed, she had given them more than that, by bestowing upon them the scandal of an all-too-human God who finally resists either moralizing or a removal to the high heavens. To complement her scandalous God, she also gave the normative a fairly scandalous group of matriarchs and patriarchs, passionate women and men not always ruled by scruples, reverence, or the spirit of fairness, let alone the spirit of self-abnegation.

The Abraham of Jewish legend is very different from J's spare portrait. J has no particular affection for her Patriarchs, just as her attitude toward Yahweh is hardly marked by reverence or by awe. One of the miracles of J's subtle tonalities is their unique balance of dispassionateness and ironic engagement. The Abraham of tradition, presumably before J as well as after her, has extraordinary attributes. Even as a baby he proclaims God. He defies the tyrant Nimrod of Babylon, first hunter of men, by destroying the king's idols, and survives Nimrod's attempt to burn him alive in a fiery furnace. There is none of this in J's story of Abram. J begins with Yahweh's call for Abram to go out, and the father of all subsequent followers of Yahweh obeys. At Beth El, Abram first calls upon Yahweh by name (Gen. 12:8), a calling that may be J's dry way of making Thomas Mann's point nearly three thousand years before Mann: at Beth El, Abram fathers Yahweh.

J deals in large rhythms of storytelling, and Abram goes down into Egypt even as Joseph and Jacob and all the children of Israel will go down after him. The descent into the underworld of Egypt and the return into the light of Canaan is the great cycle of J's work, carrying us from the call of Abram through the death and burial of Moses. The first going down into Egypt in J (Gen. 12:10–20) is a peculiar comedy, and scarcely one that favors Abram. In escaping from famine, Abram oddly fears that his wife's beauty will expose him to danger, and ignobly takes on the disguise of being her brother. Sarai loyally complies, with very dubious results, since J's text clearly implies that Abram's wife becomes Pharaoh's concubine, with material gain to her "brother" Abram. It is difficult to contravene the moral judgment against Abram of the normative Jewish sage Nachmanides: "It was a sin." Yet that is not J's judgment; J never makes a judgment, here or elsewhere. It is one of the multitude of extraordinary ironies concerning J that this author upon whom Western religious moralism ultimately must rely is herself the least moralistic of writers, Shakespeare included. We nevertheless should confront the nice question, why does J tell (or retell) so damaging a story about Abram, the fountainhead of her people's religion, or of the religion that became a people?

The supposed E writer tells a similar story about Abram and Sarai in relation to the Philistine king Abimelech in Genesis 20, but characteristically E is prissier, and Abimelech never touches the lady. J inexorably returns to patriarchal cowardice and mendacity in Genesis 26, where Isaac plays a similar trick on Abimelech and his court, but for very little reason, almost as though he is merely imitating his father, by a kind of reflex. Doubtless J used received material (and E, as usual, copied and revised J). But to what purpose, we must wonder, would J have aimed so uncomplimentary an account of Abram? Normative defenses of Abram have been quite desperate and have failed to agree with Nachmanides' judgment of sin only to the extent that they insist no adultery occurred, hardly a reading of J but a mere wish fulfillment. If the inscrutable J gives us any clue to her attitude, then it comes in the repeated emphasis on Abram's enrichment. "On her behalf," "on behalf of Sarai," "on whose behalf . . . ," beats through the episode as an ironic refrain (31–32). On whose behalf indeed? Abram goes out from Egypt "surrounded with livestock, slowed with silver and gold." The father of the religion of Yahweh is as human-all-too-human as Yahweh is, and so far, at least, what J has shown us is that a theomorphic patriarch and an impishly human God are neither of them to be judged, for who is there that could do the judging?

Abram makes a great recovery in J, when he walks with Yahweh upon the road to Sodom and courteously but firmly seeks to argue Yahweh out of his determination to destroy the Cities of the Plain. The sequence that takes Abram from his sojourn in Egypt to the destruction of Sodom is one of the uncanniest transitions in J. We go from Abram's making of the first altar to Yahweh through the separation of Abram and Lot, on to the juxtaposition of degraded Sodom and Yahweh's covenant with Abram. The promise of descendants as numerous as the stars is made to Abram, who "trusted Yahweh, and it was accounted to him as strength" (35). Nothing even in J is weirder than the ceremony that celebrates the covenant that has been cut between Abram and Yahweh.

> So it was: the sun gone, darkness reigns. Now look: a smoking
> kiln and its blazing torch pass between the parted bodies. (36)

This vision is meant to gratify Abram's plea to Yahweh for a confirmation of the divine promise made to him, and yet more than a reassuring sign is involved. For J, a word, whether Yahweh's or Abram's, is also an act and a thing. Yahweh himself is both heat and light, smoking kiln and blazing torch, furnace of affliction and mark of deliverance. The divided sacrifices attest to the astonishing equality of the covenant between Abram and Yahweh, while Abram's subsequent shooing away of the vultures appears to be an apotropaic gesture, a kind of rejecting of superstition while acknowledging its continued force and scariness. Great literary artist that she was, J prepares for the uncanniness of the Exodus prophecy and Abram's own deep sleep and mortal terror by invoking weirdly archaic rituals, gestures that must have long preceded even an older version of Hebrew religion. Solomonic enlightenment and even Davidic vitalism fall away, or are momentarily shrouded by a primitive magic, one that seems primordial yet available both to Abram and to Yahweh.

The cutting of the covenant necessarily opens up the theme of progeny, without which the Blessing lacks even literal meaning. J begins with Sarai's agonized request that her torment of childlessness be set in abeyance through Hagar's surrogacy. The bitter relationship between Hagar and Sarai is masterfully conveyed by J through glances, the destructive power of the rival women's eyes. It is a fine touch when Yahweh's angel (or Yahweh himself, in J's original text) entices Hagar back by resorting to the same image: "Your seed I will sow beyond a man's eyes to count." The entire passage culminates in the apotheosis of the image, when Hagar salutes Yahweh: "You are the all-seeing God. You are the God I lived to see—and lived after seeing" (38). Hagar's well is named "Well of Living Sight," so that the episode becomes a paean to Yahweh's sensitivity as a healer, an emphasis nearly unique in J.

This seriocomic sequence introduces one of J's comic triumphs, the picnic scene at Mamre. Abram, napping in the noon heat, wakes up to find himself staring out of his tent opening at three men, one of whom he recognizes as Yahweh. Normative revision and tradition have worked hard at insisting that Abram entertained three angels, but J's text clearly says that one of these three Elohim was Yahweh himself, come to pay a visit to his elected favorite. Yahweh sits in the shade of the trees with his two companions and enjoys a luncheon of veal, curds, rolls, and milk. Content, he is pleased to utter his outrageous, preternatural prophecy that Sarai will have a son. For once I will venture that J's stance is almost ascertainable; her sympathy, and ours, is with the formidable but aged Sarai, who is well beyond menopause, and who observes with grim accuracy, "Now that I'm used to groaning, I'm to groan with pleasure? My lord is also shriveled."

We have no name (that I know) for J's humor when Sarai laughs and an offended Yahweh proclaims, "Is a thing too surprising for Yahweh?" She is bitterly sensible, and he is quite pompous, but since in fact he is God and no mere godling, Sarai also sensibly becomes frightened enough to say, "No, I wasn't laughing" (41). Where else in Western tradition does God say in effect, despite such denial, "You laughed, all right"? But then, we are about to see J's Yahweh at nearly his most self-contradictory, marching on to Sodom to destroy those who parade their contempt for him, yet pausing to explain it all to Abram, and tolerating a considerable degree of haggling as to whether the destruction is to take place. Since here I suddenly find the reserved J granting considerable dignity and courage to Abram, and remarkable forbearance to Yahweh, I am moved to slow down and worry the matter (which I will examine again in a later section, "The Psychology of Yahweh"). What is Abram doing? Why does Yahweh take it so well? How should we understand J's own attitude here toward Abram and toward Yahweh?

The Sodom sequence opens with a hint of terrible pathos in the image of the "upturned face" of the city that is to be destroyed.

> The figures rose, starting down toward Sodom; from there
> they could see its upturned face. Abram walks with them,
> showing the way. (42)

Presumably that "showing the way" is a courtesy on Abram's part; the host sets his departing guests upon the way, which we presume God and his angels know well enough. But Abram has another motive, and another program: to save lives, to save Sodom. There is only the one way to accomplish this, and that is to argue Yahweh out of his resolve. Abram, knowing (as he says he knows) that he is dust and ashes, nothing in himself, proceeds to act as though he were everything in himself, as though he were commensurate with the incommensurate. Until now, J's Abram has not been a hero, nor even particularly a man of compassion. He rises, not to the test, but against destruction, even supposedly merited destruction. Until now, we have not known enough, in J, to understand why it was Abram who was called, and what it meant that he answered the call, that he came out. What Jacob will show in his reaction to the violence of Simeon and Levi (Gen. 35:30) Abram shows first against the probability of an angelic violence sanctioned by Yahweh.

This is Abram's finest moment in J, and it is worthy of considerable meditation. Abram and Yahweh alike are raised in our esteem and affection when we hear Yahweh declare that he loves Abram and expects "tolerance and justice" to emerge from Abram's teaching and example (42). And just that emerges, from Abram's audacious question: "Can it be—heaven forbid—you, judge of all the earth, will not bring justice?" (43). I do not think the question is answered by the overthrow of Sodom, and clearly Abram does not think so either, nor does J. Yahweh is argued down to ten of the righteous, and Abram has to stop there, as the creator of Adam evidently is about to lose patience. A populace perpetually on fire to bugger every passing stranger is indeed already on fire, and so the angels only confirm a prevailing condition. But J, as we keep seeing, is no moralist, and J's Abram also wisely refrains from moral judgments. Yahweh is there to enforce the only law that J's art accepts: in the clash of incommensurates, a new irony always emerges.

The insouciant inhabitants of Sodom are not commensurate even with Abram, let alone Yahweh, yet they live so as to show contempt for Yahweh. Sin is not one of J's concepts; contempt is. Sodom is not destroyed because of its sin but because of its contempt: for Yahweh, for strangers, for women, for Lot, for all who are not Sodomites. I suggest that for J the fate of Sodom has deep affinities with the destruction of the Tower of Babel. Sodom comes unbound as Babel did, because each had contempt for Yahweh. When Yahweh hears the noise of contempt rising from Sodom, he reacts as if he could be speaking of Babel: "It weighs on me to go down, to see what contempt this disturbance signifies" (42). Disobedience is experienced by J's Yahweh as contempt. As Abram remarks, ignorance and contempt are not the same thing. Abram tests Yahweh's patience when he argues God down from fifty to ten as the number of a saving remnant, but even an impatient Yahweh knows that Abram manifests the opposite of contempt toward him, that opposite being hospitality. When Abram turns back, toward his own place, he knows that he has done everything a man can do to save Sodom, a city that does not want to be saved.

The actual story of Sodom's destruction is one of the most remarkable of J's narratives. No one comes out of it well, including Lot, his daughters, and their unfortunate mother. Moab and Ammon are cheerfully categorized as lands populated by the issue of Lot's incestuous seduction by his daughters, but this is another of J's national jokes, akin to her speculations on the origins of the Edomites, Kenites, and Ishmaelites. But the comic and again somewhat rancid epilogue of Lot and his daughters does not cancel the tonality of the destruction of Sodom.

> Abram arose that morning, hurried to the place he had last faced Yahweh, had stood there with him. Looking out over the upturned faces of Sodom and Gomorrah, over the whole face of the valley, he saw—so it was—a black incense over the earth climbing like smoke from a kiln. (46)

We are intended to remember the fiery kiln of the covenant vision shared by Yahweh and Abram, but the principal image is in the contrast between facing Yahweh and viewing the pathos of the upturned faces of Sodom and Gomorrah. Our sympathies are not with the cities of destruction, but they are also not with Yahweh and his angels. They are with Abram, who has earned them, not by his theomorphic intensity, but by his compassion and by his own courageous venture into the incommensurate.

A Yahweh who is responsible for black incense spreading over the earth returns us yet once more to the mixed nature of J's God, and prepares us for what I take to be a crucial mutilation of J's text in the story of the Binding of Isaac (Gen. 22:1–18). I would argue, following Speiser and John Van Seters, in his *Abraham in*

History and Tradition (1975), that J and not E is the author of the *Akedah* (Binding) story. But the story hardly seems to me what J wrote, or could have written. I suggest that a P version of the *Akedah*, already severely revised, was further censored by the Redactor, who also removed from the J text what must have been accounts of the deaths of Abram and Sarai. Though all this is surmise, it is very curious that the Book of J, as we have it now, gives us no description of the deaths of Abram and Sarai. As I read J, her episode of the Binding of Isaac would begin very differently from the story that has come down to us. Abram battled vigorously for the lives of the sinful inhabitants of Sodom; would he do less for his innocent son Isaac? J had little interest in and even less taste for sacrifice, as we have seen in the tale of Cain and Abel, and of Abram chasing the vultures from the halved animals after the covenant was cut with Yahweh.

I do not find J normative enough to be telling us a story in which Yahweh is putting Abram to the test. The God of the Binding of Isaac is precisely the God who will seek to murder Moses, for no reason or cause, soon after the prophet starts down to make the journey into Egypt. And the Abram of the Binding, as we have it, has been thoroughly cowed by Yahweh, his initial resistance now broken. I think therefore that either P or R added "God put Abraham to the test" (Gen. 22:1), excised Abram's fierce resistance, and also substituted "Elohim" for "Yahweh" in a few places. Later Jewish tradition assigned the idea of the Binding to Mastema, leader of the wicked among the Elohim, or even to the Jobean Satan, who is among the Elohim and who provokes Yahweh into testing the righteous. In J, no angel of Yahweh would call out from heaven, but Yahweh himself would stand alongside Abram and change his mind about the sacrifice. That would eliminate the awkward blemish of the second angelic outcry from heaven, and would restore the direct relationship between Yahweh and Abram. I suggest further that a later tradition, holding that Sarai died of joyful shock when told of Isaac's reprieve, is probably based upon the lost J text. As for Abram, the shock of Sarai's death, added to his own anguish and subsequent joy when Isaac was spared, was probably shown by J as the cause of his death.

Would the sublimity of the *Akedah* be lost in the J version I have sketched? Hardly; nothing that is uncanny or awesome in the text as we have it now would be withdrawn, unless the mindless, total obedience of Abram/Abraham be considered an aesthetic or spiritual value in itself. Kierkegaard's "teleological suspension of the ethical" would be utterly obliterated, but that has more of Kierkegaard than of the Hebrew Bible about it in any case. The outrage of Yahweh's behavior would remain, and is characteristic of J. What is totally uncharacteristic of J, and of her Abram, is the unnatural father of the story as it stands. Rather than cite a normative exegete in defense of this father, I prefer to quote Martin Buber, whose biblical commentary tends to be original and powerful.

> It is part of the basic character of this God that he claims the entirety of the one he has chosen; he takes complete possession of the one to whom he addresses himself. . . . Such taking away is part of his character in many respects. He promises Abraham a son, gives him and demands him back in order to make a gift of him afresh; and for this son he remains a sublime "Terror."

Poor Isaac, the near-victim of Yahweh's possessiveness, is hardly a child in the *Akedah* episode; tradition makes him thirty-seven. But he always remains a child, with a child's justified fear of Yahweh, and he passes from the dominance of Sarai and Abram to that of his wife Rebecca. There is still something childlike in his preference for the rough Esau over the smooth Jacob, and certainly the poignancy of the *Akedah* is increased by the naive nature of Yahweh's apparently intended victim. Isaac's unmerited ordeal centers upon his baffled asking where the sheep is for the sacrifice, and his father's reply that God will see to the sheep. The profoundest irony here, and a likely indication that this story originally was J's, is that the ghastly sacrifice would have taken place on what was to be the site of Solomon's Temple. As a writer with a strong distaste for sacrifice and remarkable detachment toward Yahweh, J implies a very negative judgment upon the cult and its celebrations.

JACOB

BEFORE I BECAME convinced that J was a woman, I tended to believe that Jacob was J's signature, a kind of self-representation, even as Thomas Mann's Joseph is fundamentally a self-portrait. My apprehension of J's Jacob therefore was somewhat troubled, because he is certainly an unlikely hero or candidate for self-identification. Indeed, he is theomorphic precisely because J's Yahweh is so outrageous; Jacob is as cunning as Yahweh, and like Yahweh possesses in abundance the subtle, naked consciousness of the poor snake Yahweh punished so dreadfully. But Jacob's cunning is the defense of a survivor, and while it guarantees the continuation of his long life, it does not protect him from suffering. Most simply, our father Jacob, who became Israel, is a man to whom everything comes hard and belatedly. The charisma of David is invested in Jacob's son Joseph, another favorite of men and of Yahweh. Jacob struggles for every triumph, and risks himself for the Blessing, winning it and yet losing personal happiness in the process.

J's Jacob, like her Abram and her Moses, is an equivocal hero at best. But J has no villains; she has heroines, ironically enough, because Yahweh, her antithetical imp of a God, is a man and not a woman. Her theomorphic protagonists—Abram, Jacob, Moses, even her Davidic Joseph—share some of Yahweh's worst qualities, as well as some of his best. Her heroines—the nameless woman who becomes Eve, Sarai, Rebecca, Rachel, Tamar, Zipporah—are precisely not theomorphic, and are all the more sympathetic for that reason; it is as though they possess only Yahweh's best qualities. And yet her fullest portrait is of Jacob, who clearly is not always regarded by J with deep sympathy. His lifelong agon to receive and secure the Blessing is the source of his fascination for J, and for us.

Jacob's career vies with that of any other figure in Western narrative tradition, if our criteria are essentially aesthetic rather than moral or theological. He battles Esau in the womb over which of them is to have priority of birth, and though bested by his fierce twin, he still emerges combatively, holding on to his brother's heel. We can say that his drive defines the Blessing once and for all: it is for more life. In the name of more life, for himself and his progeny, Jacob dares everything, and is rarely far from danger, loss, and the constant work of mourning, induced by the loss of his beloved Rachel and the long apparent loss of his favorite son, Joseph. He also must know humiliation, since his progress and survival are marked by fraud or tricksterism, by heel-clutching. Yet he holds us fast even when we cannot approve of him. Partly it is his energy of being, partly his heroic persistence, but mostly it is because J persuades us that Jacob, Israel, has the Blessing. But what precisely does the Blessing, more life, mean in the Book of J?

We can be certain that it has little to do with the more familiar Priestly notion, which developed into aspects of normative Judaism and Christianity and so has been with us since. For the P writer, the Blessing is quite simple: "Be fruitful and multiply." There is nothing in it about one's own name and whether or not it will be scattered, as Yahweh scattered the builders of Babel. In J, the Blessing preserves and extends one's name. Jacob wins his new name, Israel, as a Blessing from a nameless one among the Elohim, and Israel becomes the name of a people. When Jacob passes over Reuben, Simeon, and Levi to award the Blessing to Judah, he again changes his people's name. To repeat a joke I once ventured, I would be called a Rube rather than a Jew had Jacob not passed over his firstborn for his fourth son. The Blessing gives more life, awards a time without boundaries, and makes a name into a pragmatic immortality, by way of communal memory. In- deed, the Blessing in J cannot be distinguished from the work of memory. And yet, in J, the Blessing is always partly ironic, and frequently attended by fraud. Usurpation after all is Jacob's mode, as in some sense it will be the way of Jesus. Jacob too is one of the spiritually exuberant who bear away the Blessing by a kind of violence.

Thomas Mann says of his Jacob and Joseph, "The soft unrestraint of the man of feeling was Joseph's heritage from his father." J's Jacob is a man of feeling, of acute sentimentality, a prophet of sensibility, almost of a sort that would be typical in the eighteenth-century European Enlightenment. (May we surmise that the Solomonic Enlightenment had some true affinities with that later movement of thought and feeling? The enlightened irony of J takes as its context a very different social and religious cosmos from the world of Jane Austen, but J's use of irony as a mode of invention and uncovering has some affinities with Austen's procedures.) Jacob, man of feeling, is both a sufferer and a sentimentalist, endlessly intelligent in his quest for the Blessing, and endlessly unable to realize its fruits.

Consideration of J's Jacob as a literary character should commence with his mother, the formidable Rebecca. Unlike Sarai and Rachel, Rebecca has no rivals; she is Isaac's only wife. As J represents her, Rebecca could tolerate no such sharings. She altogether effaces poor Isaac, a figure whom J basically snubs as if of no interest whatsoever—a further indication that J is hardly a patriarchal writer. I have suggested already that the supposed E account of the *Akedah* was bowdlerized from a lost account in which Abram fiercely resists Yahweh's outrageous injunction to sacrifice Isaac. But even if that is so, Isaac remains a merely transitional person in J. He is the first of the mama's boys, whose love for Rebecca is explicitly a consolation for his loss of Sarai

(Gen. 24:67). Rebecca's portrayal shows J's masterful economy at its subtlest. In the great pastoral scene at the well, the qualities abound that Rebecca will manifest in substituting Jacob for Esau, qualities that will endure throughout Jacob's long life and help overdetermine his personality.

Rebecca says very little at the well or directly afterward, but that little is quite enough to confirm that she too is Yahweh's chosen. Excited yet restrained, flattered yet proud, Rebecca contrasts almost immediately with her brother Laban, who so carefully neither approves nor disapproves. Her crucial affirmation comes when she wills to go, accepting her place in the Blessing and the story. A model of self-possession, she exhibits a will that rivals Tamar's, a will unafraid of seeking to usurp the Blessing. Her choice of Jacob over Esau cannot be said to be J's choice, though J disputes no one among her characters. Esau, after all, is something of a changeling, a very odd twin indeed for Jacob! Perhaps Rebecca always resented Esau; one remembers her ironic question to Yahweh as the twins war within her: "Is this what I prayed for?" (56). Jacob presumably is what she prayed for, a son as purposeful and prevenient as herself. Esau, the "ruffian," belongs to the world before Solomon, the cosmos of the hunter. A natural man, he reflects in his pathos J's imaginative sympathy for his vulnerability to both his brother and their mother. He can be and is deceived, and despite his violence he is finally too good-natured to seek revenge. When Jacob is deceived by Laban, he retaliates in his mother's mode, which is that of the trickster.

The crucial incident for J appears to be not Rebecca's deception of Isaac but the proverbial sale of Esau's birthright for a mess of pottage. Powerfully grotesque, the episode touches one of the limits of J's art and raises again the enigmatic question of J's own stance toward her narrative. How designedly comic are we to find this?

> "Look, I'm fit to die," Esau said. "So what use is this blessing to me now?" (56)

Red Esau, who will become the fountainhead of Edom, has always received bad notices in the normative tradition. Rashi, most orthodox of exegetes, is sublimely beside the point: "Esau sold his birthright on the day of Abraham's death; had the latter lived to see Esau despise his birthright, he could not have been said to have died at a ripe old age."

The first perception a common reader receives of J's Esau is that this good-natured outdoorsman is a rougher version of his father, Isaac, and is deficient as to inwardness, despite his indubitably colorful personality. J's entire point is in the sharp contrast or incommensurateness between the acute sensibility of Jacob and the bluffness of Esau. Jacob, the man of pathos, is never pathetic; Esau, profoundly pathetic, is a man of crude but intense ethos, as was Cain before him. J's irony, dangerously subtle, may be that if you are as lively as poor Esau, then you don't need the Blessing or more life. Jacob the struggler needs as much life as he can contrive to get. Esau, like Isaac, is curiously passive and dependent, despite his vigor and animal spirits. In the elaborate and outrageous comedy by which Rebecca and Jacob steal the Blessing away from Esau, we suddenly hear the true voice of feeling in J.

> As Esau heard his father's words he moaned; bitter sobbing
> shook him as he spoke: "Bless me—me too, my father." (62)

A great Hasidic maxim warns us, "The Messiah will not come until the tears of Esau have ceased." The red man of Edom, defrauded of his Blessing, has an unmatched poignancy in the Book of J. When Jacob, after his nocturnal wrestling match at Penuel, next has to confront Esau, twenty years later, the rough brother is again much more sympathetic than the smooth hypocrite. And yet to call J's Jacob that is at once coldly accurate and wildly misleading, since he has just won the new name Israel in an astonishing exhibition of persistence, endurance, even transcendental heroism. We are returned to the perpetual fascination of reading J. Where does the author stand in this incessant clash of incommensurates? One can surmise that Esau, as a figure, was altogether other than the sophisticated J, but something in him is rendered as appealing. That an irony or allegory of Edom is intended by J is palpable in the wordplay, which is so incessant as to constitute a highly deliberate joke. Edom had rebelled against Solomon (whether at the start or end of his reign is not clear), and J seems to rely upon an association of Edom with an image of the unruly and the ungovernable, with what, following Freud, we now would call the return of the repressed. The return of the red man from Edom was to become a prophetic metaphor for the time of troubles preceding a revelation, and so J's Esau became the forerunner of Elijah and of John the Baptist.

In J, Esau is the type of the baffled and the deceived, outwitted by a sly brother and an imperious mother, both of them far more complex beings. Esau is J's study of the nostalgias, of a world simply not available to those who come after Solomon. But J is too knowing to delude herself or us as to any possibility of recovering the perspective of an Esau. We, and J, go off with Jacob, precisely because he carries the Blessing, equivocal possession though it is. When we stand with Jacob at Beth El (Gen. 28), suddenly Yahweh stands alongside us, and a particular place, *makom*, is marked forever as a spot where Yahweh manifested himself. The later rabbinical saying that Yahweh is the place (*makom*) of the world, but the world is not his place, is an insight implicit here in J. What is different, as always in J, is the result of a giant art that relies upon astonishing juxtapositions. Jacob is fleeing from the consequences of his (and Rebecca's) hoax, and in that flight he does receive the first fruit of his usurpation. Yahweh stands next to him and speaks to him, as familiarly as he spoke to Abram.

As we first met Rebecca at a well, we now accompany Jacob to a similar first encounter with Rachel, in another pastoral idyll, even more charming for what it reveals of what is impulsive in Jacob's complex nature. One remembers that J is also Tolstoy's precursor when Jacob suddenly kisses his cousin Rachel and immediately bursts into tears. Surely J intends us to contrast the tears of Jacob with the tears of Esau. Jacob, the man of feeling, of excessive sensibility, is capable of turning on his tears at will, and yet we catch him at the crucial positive moment of his life, in the very act of falling in love with the woman who will be Joseph's mother.

The intricate story of Jacob, Laban, Rachel, and Leah (Gen. 29–31), another of J's comic triumphs, reverses the hoodwinking of Isaac with Jacob now as the deceived, in a striking double irony, since only the authenticity of Jacob's passion for Rachel could have compelled him to ignore all the omens that should have warned him against Laban's duplicity. But Laban, Rebecca's brother, proves no match for Rebecca's son in the next movement of J's ironic conceptual music. One sees that J is nearly as entranced by disguises and deceptions as Shakespeare is; these greatest of writers are allied in their obsession both with wordplay and with coverings. The illusions of rhetoric and of appearance seem to be dialectically allied in the creator of Yahweh and the maker of Hamlet. And there is a Shakespearean zaniness in J's invention of Jacob's most complex trickery of the peeled rods, which leads to the hilarious result that all the properly sturdy animals go to him while only the weaklings adhere to Laban. Sublimely the trickster (rather like J's Yahweh himself), Jacob has now worked himself into the classic dilemma of fleeing Laban, but only toward Esau, who is accompanied by four hundred men. It is another triumph of J's art that Jacob, caught between two possible vengeances, should find in that predicament an opening to a transcendental struggle, to his extraordinary wrestling match with the angel of reality, a nameless one among the Elohim whom the enigmatic J refuses to identify, so that we wonder if this antagonist is Yahweh or the angel of death, or perhaps Yahweh playing the part of the angel of death, a role he will assume again in J in that dreadful night encounter when he seeks to murder his own foremost prophet, the all but blameless Moses.

But before we come to Jacob's own night encounter, we ought to confront Rachel's finest moment in J, her theft and concealment of the *teraphim,* her father's household gods. Doubtless J tells this story for the pure joy of it, as befits this greatest of all narrative writers, but there is to the tale another edge, a touch demonstrating that Rachel is fully the equal of her outrageous husband and her toughly sly father. I discount here the received scholarly opinion that the author of this touch is E rather than J, an opinion in which Speiser concurs. As Speiser says elsewhere, the hand may be E's, yet we hear the voice of J, just as in the *Akedah,* or Binding of Isaac, the faltering hand of E gives us a strange, censored refraction of the mind of J.

Why does Rachel appropriate her father's idols? J's mastery of irony is clearly involved, since nowhere does E seem capable of the grand point of Jacob's being unaware of the theft even as he urges Laban to search everything in the caravan. Speiser is imaginatively apt in suggesting that Laban's insistence that he owns everything in the caravan—goods, wives, children, servants, animals—is founded upon household law dependent upon the *teraphim.* By stealing the idols and so cunningly sitting on them, Rachel guarantees her freedom to go off with Jacob. By playing upon the male awe of a woman's periods, Rachel (and J) frightens off Laban (and the male reader). We are left with the image of freedom as Rachel becomes another in J's line of heroines, commencing with Sarai and Rebecca, to culminate in Tamar.

Jacob's all-night struggle with a nameless divine being (Gen. 32: 24–31) is the central event of his career, and one of the defining moments of the Book of J. In some ways, it may be the most difficult passage in J's work, for reasons that have much more to do with normative traditions of interpretation—Jewish, Christian, secular—than with J. "Wrestling Jacob" is a powerful image, particularly in Protestantism, where the agon is essentially seen as a loving struggle between Jacob and God. But the nameless being who cannot overcome Jacob cannot be Yahweh, at least not Yahweh in all his power and will, and there is absolutely nothing loving about this sublime night encounter, which exalts Jacob to

Israel yet leaves him permanently crippled, and which is fought between a mortal and a supernatural being who fears the break of day, almost as a vampire or a ghoul would. The uncanniest elements in this episode nevertheless concern Jacob more than the angel or demon he holds to a standstill, and so I begin with those.

Has there been anything in Jacob's earlier story that might have prepared us for this moment? The manifestation of Yahweh at Beth El has everything to do with election and nothing to do with conflict. That suggests an answer: all of Jacob's career has been a continual battle to attain the Blessing, from the contest in the womb to determine whether Esau or Jacob would be the firstborn to this crucial encounter at the ford of the Jabbok, the stream whose name suggests both Jacob and the wounding wordplay that associates his name with heel-clutching. Caught between Laban and Esau, Jacob mysteriously but deliberately provokes the issue of survival. To win the new name of Israel is to win also a very different Blessing from the one stolen away from Esau, for this new Blessing, as I read it, is extracted from the angel of death, or if from Yahweh, then from that dark side of Yahweh that later nearly murders Moses before Zipporah heroically intervenes.

Behind J's vision again is an archaic Jewish religion of which we know little, except from hints in postbiblical texts. These writings nominate a good many angels for the role of Jacob's antagonist: Michael, Metatron (an alternate version of Michael, but sometimes also a lesser Yahweh), Gabriel, Uriel, even a guardian angel called Israel, and finally Sammael, angel of death. At least some of these identifications must have been available to J, but she chose to evade all of them and to create a beautifully enigmatic angel of her own. If we read her work closely, we can surmise the powerful ironies of some of her purposes here. Jacob, fearing he will be slain by Esau the next day, leads his people across the Jabbok. Evidently he crosses back by himself and waits in solitude for the angel of his impending death, be it Esau's angel or his own. Jacob's defense is highly aggressive: he waits to ambush his fate, as it were. His purpose is to hold the ford against the apparently nameless one among the Elohim who has been assigned to get across the Jabbok before day breaks. Israel, the new name he seeks to win, seems to have meant "May El (God) persevere" but could mean also "May the angel triumph," which is wholly ironic since Jacob will triumph by persevering against the angel. Sometimes I think that J meant Sammael, but sometimes I reflect that the angel may have been named Israel, and lost his name to Jacob. Either way, and even if the angel was Metatron, the lesser Yahweh, or Michael, what is crucial is to see how deliberate Jacob's ambush is, and how it moves beyond all his previous wiliness by adding a transcendental physical courage to the agonistic spirit that Jacob has always manifested.

Failing to overcome Jacob, his opponent breaks one of the patriarch's thighs at the hip, but to no avail. In desperation, the angel cries out, "Let me go, day is breaking," only to be answered by Jacob's stubborn "I won't let go of you until I have your blessing." Never before in J has the Blessing meant so literally "more life," which makes it all the more extraordinary that the blesser is neither Yahweh nor an earthly father but an angel, and until now presumably a hostile angel. When the angel, unable to get free of Jacob, asks the name of his antagonist, I think the request is authentic rather than ceremonial or formal. There is a note of astonished wariness when the angel acknowledges the difference between the victim he had expected, the next day, and the hero he has encountered throughout the night.

> "Not anymore Jacob, heel-clutcher, will be said in your name; instead, Israel, God-clutcher, because you have held on among gods unnamed as well as men, and you have over-come."

It is both natural and ironic that Jacob courteously begs the name of the angel, and marvelous of J that the reply is altogether ironic, with the Blessing of the new name taking the place of the undivulged name.

"Why is it just this—my name—you must ask?" he answered. Instead, he blessed him there.

This nameless one among the Elohim chooses to remain nameless,
either because he has been defeated or because he has just given
away his own name, Israel, to Jacob. What matters, J implies, is
not so much the identity of the more-than-human that could not
hold on, but the new identity of the human that refused to let go.

> The name of that place Jacob called Deiface: I've seen God
> face to face, yet my flesh holds on.
>
> Now the sun rose over him as he passed through the place
> called Deifus; he was limping on his hip. (73)

The movement from Deifus to Deiface, Penuel to Peniel,
Jacob to Israel, one of the most sublime of J's puns, is near the
center of J's vision here. Jacob, outside the land of the Blessing,
still across the river in Transjordan, fights for and achieves more
life so as to be able to *cross over and survive.* J is telling us that
it does not matter precisely which hostile one among the Elohim
Jacob, henceforth Israel, so obdurately held out against. What
matters is that this lifelong struggler indeed held out. When the
sun rises over him, even as he limps onward on his hip, we are
given an exuberant portrait of J's people, even as they descend
from the Solomonic splendor into the crumbling kingdom of the
dubious Rehoboam. For a sublime moment, the glory of David,
which is to come, bursts forth from David's ancestor, the not very
Davidic Jacob. The triumph is ascribed to Jacob, but the aesthetic
glory is J's alone.

OF ALL J'S HEROINES, Tamar is the most vivid, and the most revelatory of J's identity, both as a woman and as a literary ironist of high civilization and intense sophistication. Since J's heroines are more admirable than her male protagonists, I will go further and observe that Tamar, despite her brief appearance in only a single chapter, Genesis 38, is the most memorable character in the Book of J, in something of the same sense that Barnardine is in Shakespeare's *Measure for Measure,* despite his similarly brief role. Tamar is a triumph of J's elliptical style, in which so little is said overtly, and so much expressed through the reticences of character and situation.

The name Tamar means a palm tree, first made emblematic in the Bible by the palm tree beneath which the prophetess Deborah sits and judges Israel. It is the figure of King David that hovers again in the recesses of J's text, because J assumes that *her* readers and auditors know that Tamar was the ancestor of David. Perhaps J would have appreciated the added irony that for Christian readers Tamar ultimately is the ancestor of Jesus Christ, in a Christian view the Messiah born from the House of David. Tamar indeed is the fountainhead of all who will carry the Blessing after Judah, for only Tamar bears Judah sons who will survive.

Thomas Mann, beautifully expanding upon J in *Joseph and His Brothers,* gives us a Tamar who sits at the feet of Jacob, learns her sense of the Blessing's importance from Jacob as Israel, the father of the tribes, and plots therefore to make a place for herself in the story, so that her name also will not be scattered. J, even subtler and more ironic than the ironist Mann, does not vouchsafe us such an explicit explanation. Mann has a properly novelistic sense of the Blessing: not to be excluded from the narrative. J's version of the Blessing emphasizes aesthetically what it stresses humanistically: more life. For J, as for the author of 2 Samuel, the crucial representative of human vitality is David, at once human-all-too-human and the apotheosis of the most complete and admirable human qualities. Judah, though he carries the Blessing, is hardly a heroic figure for J. David's vitality, she tells us, comes from the heroic tenacity of Tamar. It is not accidental that Tamar is a name only in the Davidic family (the name, in fact, of his tragic daughter, raped by her brother Amnon, avenged by her brother Absalom), or that Judah's wife, the unnamed daughter of the Canaanite Shua, hence called *bat-shua* in the Hebrew, should bring to mind the name of David's queen, Bathsheba. J makes clear that in centering on Tamar she alludes to David, to his personality, career, and legacy.

Tamar's drive to become the bearer of the Blessing is frustrated by the sickliness, the lack of vitality, of Judah's three sons. J, endless punner, may intend a wordplay between Er (possibly meaning "on guard") and *ariri* ("childless"), while Onan (possibly meaning "active") seems to play upon *'on* ("grief"). The third brother, who also doubtless would have retreated from the vital Tamar into death, is called Shelah, which might imply a reluctant emergence from the mother's womb. What is clear is that these fellows are poor stuff to carry the Blessing, and displeasing to Yahweh, whose frequent impishness is reflected in Tamar's shrewd seduction of Judah. What after all was the lady to do? As the widow of the inconsequential Er and the perverse Onan (his name has become synonymous with masturbation, but in J he rather practices what seems coitus interruptus), Tamar had little to expect from the reluctant Shelah, even if Judah had not violated the ancient Hebraic custom of *yibbum,* which obliged the surviving brother of a deceased husband to marry the widow. What is startling, and crucial to J's art, is the boldness and resourcefulness of the wronged Tamar.

Judah's wife dies; the mourning period ends; Judah goes up to Timnath for the sheepshearing, a time of excess, of letting go. As an average sensual male emerging from a set period of abstinence, Judah is scarcely inclined to request that a supposed wayside cult prostitute unveil herself to him. His pledge—the signaturelike seal and scepterlike staff—is Tamar's prophetic defense against the judicial murder that would otherwise await her under patriarchal laws that J is delighted to see outflanked. His fear of being exposed to ridicule is enhanced by his authentic sense of justice, since he is indeed less in the right than Tamar. J is little interested in him anyway, in comparison to Tamar. Wonderfully enigmatic as always, resembling her creator J in this, Tamar handles Judah with consummate tact, sending his pledges to him with the brief remark that these will identify the prospective father. J's mordant observation that Judah was not intimate with her again is a pure irony, since neither he nor Tamar would wish one another again. Yet he has his heirs, vital like their mother, and she has her place in the Blessing's story. What has J taught us of her, and of the qualities she will bring to her descendant David?

J ends Tamar's story with the birth of twin boys, Peretz, whose name means "breach," and Zerah, or "brightness," who thus replace the pallid Er and the unpleasant Onan. The twin-birth is unexpected and clearly alludes to the return of the agonistic spirit, with Zerah recalling Esau, and Peretz the wrestler Jacob, grandfather of these new competitors for the Blessing. Peretz, David's ancestor, breaches his way out first, while Zerah's hand with its crimson thread suggests the repetition of the red man of Edom. Tamar is therefore the second Rebecca, mother of an endless rivalry. J intends us to see Tamar as the prime representative of agonistic continuity in the history of the Blessing, since it is she alone who guarantees the heritage of vitality that runs from wrestling Jacob to the truly heroic and charismatic David, the authentic object of Yahweh's election-love.

The elliptical J gives us no psychological or spiritual portrait of Tamar, no account of her motives or of her will. No other author makes us as much collaborators as J does; we have to sketch Tamar's character and color in her formidable personality. A woman of the people, with no previous connection to the House of Israel, she is presumably Judah's choice for Er precisely because of her vitality. Indomitable, she does not accept defeat, whether from Er, Onan, or Judah. *Her* will becomes the will of Yahweh, and ten generations later leads to David, of all humans the most favored by Yahweh. Pragmatically Tamar is a prophetess, and she usurps the future beyond any prophet's achievement. She is single-minded, fearless, and totally self-confident, and she has absolute insight into Judah. Most crucially, she knows that *she* is the future, and she sets aside societal and male-imposed conventions in order to arrive at her truth, which will turn out to be Yahweh's truth, or David. Her sons are born without stigma, and she too is beyond stigma. Thomas Mann was imaginatively accurate in making her Jacob's disciple, for her struggle is the woman's analogue to Jacob's grand defiance of death at Esau's hands in an all-night contest with death's angel. Of the two agonists, Tamar is the more heroic and battles even greater odds: natural, societal, preternatural. Jacob wins the new name of Israel; even more gloriously, Tamar wins the immortality of her own name, and a central place in the story that she was not born into and so had to usurp for herself.

JOSEPH

THE STORY OF JOSEPH is a romance or wonder tale, doubtless following many ancient models that are nearly all lost to us, at least in the form they reached J. Some scholars have given us more than one Yahwist in part because Joseph's adventures are so much more sustained than those of Abram and Jacob. Why J wrote at some length about Joseph might seem initially something of a puzzle, since the careers of Abram and Jacob, and of Moses after them, are of greater importance for the traditions of the Hebrews. But J, as I have remarked, tends to break down genre restrictions, even as Shakespeare did. And as I suggested earlier, J took the opportunity to meditate obliquely upon David by treating Joseph as his surrogate. J's Abram, Jacob, and Moses bear the Blessing and yet are not charismatic personalities. J's Joseph is, and his charisma suggests the winning quality of David's extraordinary nature.

Unlike David, Joseph has an uncertain historical existence, though more than one Semite served as the chief minister to an Egyptian monarch. For J, Joseph is fable, a figure of romance, and probably his largest interest for her, aside from his Davidic potential, lies in the psychological possibilities afforded by the contrasts between father and son, Jacob and Joseph. Their relationship is the principal instance in the Hebrew Bible of the story of a father and a son, and seems to me J's principal contribution to what we now would call the art of prose fiction. Is there indeed another Western portrait of father and son as fecund as J's vision of Jacob and Joseph? What can we place alongside it, or against it? Shakespeare gives us Bolingbroke and Hal, King Henry IV and King Henry V, while Dostoyevsky perhaps grants us old Karamazov and Alyosha, who more than Ivan or Mitya is the family charismatic. But Hal morally becomes Bolingbroke, despite Falstaff, and old Karamazov and Alyosha represent totally different spiritual worlds. Joseph neither becomes Jacob nor is merely antithetical to him. Their relationship is endless to meditation, as Thomas Mann demonstrates in his retelling in *Joseph and His Brothers,* and as I will attempt to emphasize throughout my commentary upon J's Joseph cycle.

J's Joseph need not be in search of any father, which frees him to manifest the particular consequences of enjoying his father's, and Yahweh's, implicit blessing. The overt Blessing cannot go to Joseph, but goes to the fourth son, Judah, after Reuben, Simeon, and Levi morally disqualify themselves. Joseph, after all, is the eleventh of twelve brothers; he is not even the youngest son, always so useful for the literary purposes of romance. In a way, he is a gentler David, by which I do not just mean that his author may well have been a woman, but also that unlike David, Joseph is anything but warlike, anything but aggressive or hostile. He is a born politician, immensely adroit at getting his way through every means available. His father, Jacob, is always too hard-pressed to be thought a politician; agonists get their way only through struggle, overt or covert, whether by force or by trickery. Joseph is not a contestant and will not wrestle anyone. He is a dreamer and an interpreter of dreams, which means, however paradoxically, that he is a pragmatist and a compromiser with reality. Jacob strives to achieve and keep the Blessing; he is precisely not a charismatic personality, though he makes himself into a very formidable personality indeed. Everything comes easily to

Joseph, who will emerge from every catastrophe more suave and unflustered than ever. Jacob, despite his success, is an unlucky man; Joseph's luck is constant, reliable, and charmingly outrageous.

Though tradition speaks of the Patriarchs as Abram (Abraham), Isaac, and Jacob, Isaac scarcely exists for J, as we have seen, except perhaps as a rather weak personality who acts as a buffer between a powerful grandfather and grandson. It would daunt a novelistic imagination to conceive of Jacob as Abram's son; each is too close to the uncanny, to J's Yahweh. Joseph is not a close acquaintance of Yahweh's; rather, his story is almost free of Yahweh's direct intervention. Israel has to be gotten down into Egypt if there is to be an Exodus, but we never speak of the God of Joseph as we do of the God of Isaac (a God whose name is Fear). Godfearing though he is, Joseph is essentially a wisdom figure rather than a man who walks and talks with God.

Yet Joseph is a representative of wisdom in a purely worldly sense, the wisdom of Solomon, say, and not the wisdom of Samuel. In a curious way, J's Joseph blends the attributes of David and Solomon rather than those of Abram and Jacob. That is to intimate something of the way in which Joseph is neither patriarchal nor prophetic, as Moses is. Rather, Joseph belongs to the world of Davidic heroic humanism and Solomonic urban enlightenment, the world of an ego ideal already much our own, because to some degree that world is one of our origins as regards our notion of an ego. We will never know what kind of a Yahweh J inherited and thus assigned to her Abram, but we can begin to analyze just how J's Yahweh is one of the starting points for our sense of ego. The God of the Book of J has a considerable feeling for his own ego, and that self-investment overdetermines the quests of J's pioneers of the self: Abram, Rebecca, Jacob, Tamar, and Joseph. Joseph, again as David's surrogate, is so large an exemplification of an amplified ego that an excursus upon the Yahwistic ego is properly to be stationed here. The ultimate irony propounded by J turns upon the nature of Yahweh's relation to vitality. The God who will be present when and where he will be present is a God of judgment and justice, but he is also a God who has created a vital universe.

Since the Blessing in J is always the gift of more life, a life that is more mixed than the divine breath or spirit, the Blessing is only secondarily an enhancement of justice. I do not think J ever forgets that Yahweh's most overwhelming Blessing was bestowed upon David, beyond covenant, and was in no way dependent upon David's subsequent behavior. Joseph too cannot lose Yahweh's favor, even though he cannot have the Blessing, since it falls to Judah. The quality of being blessed has clearly more to do with a wholeness of being than with right judgment or moral behavior. David defines wholeness of being, since he is both the ultimate charismatic in the Hebrew Bible and the most comprehensive ego. As such, David incarnates the dynamics of change, and those dynamics belong to Yahweh, whose essence is surprise, even if the wary J is always too alert to be altogether surprised by him. Those who have contempt for Yahweh lack the capacity for change; they are fixed and obsessive, builders of Babel, inhabitants of Sodom, Egyptian slavemasters, backsliding whiners in the Wilderness. Beyond surprise, despisers of wholeness, they have no desire to be helpful to Yahweh. That desire is elitist, and one of its fullest embodiments is the gorgeous career of David, and of Joseph before him. Human caprice, however damned or deprecated by normative tradition, remains the essence of elitism and helps account for what it is that attracts Yahweh to David, and less fully to Joseph.

The question of J's representations of the human ego raises the even more complex matter of J's portrayal of Yahweh, since precisely the same elements of character and personality are involved. J's major personages, Yahweh included, are remarkably like Shakespearean characters, for the good reason that the Yahwist portions of the Geneva Bible deeply influenced Shakespeare's ideas of representation. The perpetually changing consciousness of J's beings is very different from the Homeric state of mind, and prepares the way for a similar dynamism in the Shakespearean personae. What is different in Shakespeare, which is that his characters change by brooding upon what they themselves have said, is a grand originality that Shakespeare developed from hints in Chaucer, and yet even the Wife of Bath and the Pardoner seem less Shakespearean characters than are J's Jacob, Joseph, and Yahweh.

Pascal, Tolstoy, and Thomas Mann all found in the story of Joseph and his brothers a paradigm for their very different spiritual and literary ideals. I am a touch uneasy that Pascal saw in Joseph a foretype of Christ, on the basis that both Joseph and Jesus were their father's particular favorites, and then were sold for silver by their brothers, and in time became lord and savior of those deluded siblings. That is to mistake the relaxed tone in which J writes of Joseph, who becomes a provider but hardly a savior. Tolstoy quite accurately found the Joseph story to be Tolstoyan and ranked it above all Western literature, his own work included. One aspect of J, the Blessing in its exaltation of time, vitality, and change, is altogether Tolstoyan, as is J's sense that the dynamism of the Blessing favors the augmentation of the ego rather than its abnegation before Yahweh. The breathless dynamism of Yahweh, and the consequent sense of human wholeness and vigor, return in the fiction of Tolstoy, whether in the grand meditation upon history of *War and Peace* or in the superb short novel *Hadji Murad,* where the hero is a warrior more in the mode of J than of Homer.

Joseph, of course, is anything but a warrior, so that it is compelling to brood upon why Joseph, rather than Jacob, Moses, or David, won the palm from Tolstoy. One sees why Joseph fascinated Thomas Mann, since Joseph has all the Mannian virtues, irony included. Joseph interested Mann for some of the same reasons he seems to have intrigued Kafka: Joseph is at once the type of the artist and the best and most beloved of sons, who never loses his faith in a familial destiny. I venture that Tolstoy's preference doubled J's own preoccupation with Joseph, which led her to tell his story at some length. It is Joseph's singularity to manifest all the charismatic marks of the Blessing without actually possessing or even desiring the formal Blessing. Judah has the Blessing, yet he interests J considerably less than Tamar does; one cannot conceive of a story of Judah and his brothers. Tolstoy was moved by what moves us in David as in Joseph, which is the overwhelming reality of charisma. J's vision of the charismatic is that its quality lets us envision a time without boundaries, a sense of something evermore about to be, a dream that is no dream but rather a dynamic breaking through into a perpetually fresh vitalism, the true abundance of Yahweh's promise to those he favors.

As J begins her narrative of Joseph (Gen. 37), the young shepherd is presented to us as a tattletale and spoiled brat, hated by his brothers because he is the father's favorite. Jewish legend emphasized Joseph's personal beauty, which reminded the bereaved Jacob of his lost Rachel. The long-sleeved tunic (or "coat of many colors"), the outward mark of Jacob's love, ironically becomes the emblem of the aged patriarch's grief. "Coat of many colors" is the famous and endearing mistranslation of the King James Bible, but alas it is not there in the Hebrew original, where the garment would appear to be one appropriate only to the royal house, like the garment in 2 Samuel 13:18–19, worn by Tamar in the terrible scene where Amnon rapes her. I have speculated that J may have been a princess of the royal house, but there may in any case be another instance here of the many complex crosscurrents passing back and forth between the Book of J and 2 Samuel. Like the tunic of the princess Tamar, Joseph's garment becomes an emblem of violence and cruelty. When the brothers present it to Jacob, they intend it as legal proof that Joseph is dead, and beyond their responsibility.

In another complex irony, J sets the occasion for the brothers' conspiracy at Shechem, not only the spot where Dinah's grief was avenged by the massacre led by Simeon and Levi, but also where Rehoboam was rejected by the northern tribes under Jeroboam, who was crowned there. This is certainly one of J's many deprecations of Jeroboam and his breakaway kingdom of Israel. In J's Joseph saga, Jacob is called Israel, the new name he won in the wrestling match at Penuel, so as to suggest that he is the true Israel, doubtless in contrast to Jeroboam's realm. The selling of Joseph by his brothers (with only Judah reluctant) is thus associated with Jeroboam's disruption of the legacy of David, as if to suggest again a Davidic element in Joseph. Taken down into Egypt, Joseph descends into a cosmos of death, in a movement opposite to the liberation narrative of Moses, so that we can read Jeroboam as the Miltonic "captain back for Egypt," or betrayer of Israel. In another cross-reference to the author of 2 Samuel, J characterizes the young Joseph much as David is described when he first comes to Saul, that is, as a man "with whom Yahweh was" (Gen. 39:2), a lucky man, who brings luck to others. This deft touch would have shown sophisticated contemporary readers and auditors the true intent of J's story of Joseph. Like David, Joseph will give others the aura of being blessed, of sharing in the good fortune of those whom Yahweh favors.

Joseph's rising career in the household of Potiphar is merely preamble to one of J's most delicious episodes, the attempted seduction of the charming son of Israel by Potiphar's lustful wife. Scholars have traced this story to an Egyptian romantic tale, yet it becomes great comic writing in J, comedy for its own sake, as well as another illustration that the Davidic if outrageous Joseph will always survive every scrape and emerge luckier than before. If my surmise is correct that J established the tradition of absorbing the Joseph saga into the patriarchal histories in order to represent David covertly or obliquely, then the virtuous Joseph contrasts sharply with the erotically driven David. In any case, J shrewdly avoids making her Joseph a kind of religious prig. Instead, he declines Potiphar's wife on essentially pragmatic grounds, sensibly observing that everything except the lady has been vouchsafed to him, with an authority equal to Potiphar's except in regard to this temptress.

The contrast Joseph implies here is between himself and

Adam, who was also granted dominion over all that was, with the single exception that destroyed Eden. Joseph, unlike Adam, declines to eat of the Tree of Knowledge, but not just because it would show contempt for Yahweh. As Gerhard von Rad observes, "It is, however, noteworthy that Joseph in addition uses the argument of universal human decency which is unwilling to break a trust." For J, Joseph participates both in David's charismatic prominence and in the afterglow of the Solomonic Enlightenment's last survivors under the ill-starred Rehoboam.

Imprisoned because of the scorned lady's wrath, Joseph immediately rises to power again, bringing Yahweh's favor even to a jail. A short step further and Joseph is in power over all Egypt, to no reader's surprise. When we hear J's voice again, we are well along in the marvelous story of the reunion of Joseph and his brothers, to be followed by the immense pathos of the restoration of Joseph to his father, Israel. Unlike the tale of Noah, where the Redactor doubled throughout the prim P and the ribald J, in the Joseph saga he followed a more exclusionary policy, with frequent omissions of J and substitutions of portions of E for material that we must assume made R uneasy. Thus, we have no certain dreams in the J selections (though the dream of the kine is heavy with J's irony), and no account at all of how Joseph rose to power in Egypt. There are doublets early on, with both J and E versions of how the brothers sent Joseph down to Egypt, but evidently elements in Joseph's governance of Egypt were worrisome to the Redactor, and so were the details of the brothers' first trek to Egypt. Surmise is difficult here, since what survives of J directly before and after the missing portions has little to do with what is gone. In the E account, as used by the Redactor, Pharaoh chooses Joseph because the soothsayer has manifested the divine spirit, while the brothers are rather subdued versions of the roughs they used to be. It would be more in J's mode if Pharaoh were charmed by the charismatic Joseph, and if the brothers arrived as surly as ever, however subdued by need and by awe of Egyptian prosperity and splendor.

The Redactor resorted to J when it came to the brothers'

second descent into Egypt, in Genesis 43, and here I want to slow down and follow the text very carefully, because J's art becomes exquisitely modulated narrative, even for this subtlest of all ironists. Famine becomes yet more intense, until Israel and his son Judah quarrel about the condition set for the brothers' return to Egypt, which is that they bring Benjamin with them. As Benjamin is all of Rachel left to him, the father resists, until Judah in effect promises to forsake the Blessing if he does not bring Benjamin back from Egypt. J covers the way down to Egypt in a phrase and then lingers to enjoy Joseph's penchant for exhibiting a dramatic sensibility akin to his father's. Seeing Benjamin, his younger brother, there among the others, Joseph is deeply moved yet acts to conceal his emotion. The apprehensive brothers are bewildered when they are led into Joseph's own house in order to enjoy a midday meal with Pharaoh's chief minister. Clustering around the steward at the entrance, they anxiously insist upon their innocence in the matter of finding their money returned to their bags on the way home from their first descent into Egypt. In one of J's fine touches, Joseph's steward dryly informs the brothers that their God and their father's God must have reimbursed them, but that he in any case has been paid.

The crucial moment in the banquet scene that follows is Joseph's reaction to his full brother and childhood playmate, Benjamin. Joseph's emotions overcome him, and he is compelled hastily to seek solitude in order to weep. J's wisdom is that one is always a child again, even the grand bureaucrat Joseph. None of J's male personages, Yahweh included, ever surmount their childlike and also childish qualities. The only grown-ups in J are women: Sarai, Rebecca, Rachel, Tamar. Isaac is always a baby, Abram and Judah easily fall into childishness, and the two men of acute sensibility—Jacob and Joseph, father and true son—remain wonderfully spoiled and gifted temperaments, childlike in the extreme, until they die. But the exuberant artistry of J seems to me at its height in the implicit contrast between Jacob/Israel and Joseph throughout the Joseph saga, particularly in its climactic sections, which we now approach. Not even Tolstoy, J's disciple, is a greater master of familial realities than J now demonstrates herself to be.

Why does Joseph play out his elaborate scenario with the increasingly bewildered brothers? In Thomas Mann's *Joseph the Provider*, the last novel of the great tetralogy, the question need not be asked, as Mann is the most playful of dramatic and romantic ironists. J's irony, as we have been seeing throughout, is of a different and more sublime order. It is the irony of ultimates and incommensurates, the irony of Yahweh's love for David. Joseph, favored to some degree as David was favored, is himself an ironist, unlike David. Yahweh's restless dynamism becomes in Joseph an affectionate mischief, or the cunning resourcefulness of his father Jacob, free now to turn itself to play, since everything comes as easily to Joseph as it comes so desperately hard to Jacob. If there is a theology anywhere in J, it involves not Abram or Jacob, or even Moses, but curiously enough, Joseph, who like his creator, J, is a kind of ironic theologian or speculative psychologist. J's greatest literary gift, like Shakespeare's or Montaigne's, or Freud's, may be an original mastery of moral and visionary psychology.

Joseph is totally and refreshingly free of what Nietzsche called the spirit of revenge; there is in him no trace of desire to be avenged upon those who sold him into slavery. As Joseph's career has shown, Yahweh does not allow this favorite to languish long in bondage but raises him always higher, until no one in the House of Jacob is higher in the worldly sense. Joseph is the archetype of all those court Jews to come through the ages, down to Henry Kissinger in the Nixon-Ford era. Yet J's Joseph is also much more than that, because he is her surrogate for the charm of the charismatic David. David was a poet; Joseph is a benign romancer, whose only revenge upon his brothers is to write all of the later scenes of the drama in which he is the hero and they are supporting figures, but not villains. The romance of Joseph has no villains and ends as happily as a romance could end.

It must seem odd, in commenting upon an author who wrote

nearly three thousand years ago, to discover an aesthetic motive in the psychology of a hero, but Joseph's stance as he manipulates his brothers does seem to me primarily aesthetic. Just as Tamar wills to write herself into the story of the Blessing, even so Joseph, who knows that he must yield the Blessing to Judah, compensates himself by writing a benevolent ending to the tale of Jacob and his twelve sons. It is as though Joseph, like his father before him, wishes to make himself absolutely central to the story of Yahweh and the children of Abram. J after all does not allow Yahweh to intervene directly in Joseph's story, as Yahweh did with the Patriarchs, and as he will do with Moses and the people in Egypt and in the Wilderness. We are told that Yahweh's favor is always with Joseph, as it will be with David, but J's Yahweh allows his elite to do their plotting and willing for themselves, and is particularly off the scene in the story of Joseph. Nothing would surprise us more than a sudden personal descent of Yahweh into Joseph's presence. Yahweh walks and argues with Abram, sends his angel to battle Jacob, and buries Moses with his own hands, as earlier he had used those hands to seal Noah and his company into the ark, but we would find it an outrageous violation of decorum if Yahweh were to stand face to face with Joseph and tell him precisely how to stage-manage his self-revelation to his brothers. As I have remarked throughout, I do not believe that J's genre shifts mean we are to decide we are reading two or more Yahwists. Rather, we are dealing with a writer of Shakespearean scope and originality, an author beyond genre, a consciousness so large and ironic that it contains us. We, whoever we are, are more naive, less sophisticated, less intelligent than J or Shakespeare. That is why we cannot write the Yahwistic portions of Genesis and Exodus, or *Hamlet* and *Macbeth*. J, like Shakespeare, is a contingency we cannot escape or evade.

Joseph is the expression of J's creative exuberance because he is *her* David, her best rival to the representation of David by the splendid author of 2 Samuel. Joseph's career, for all his wit, enterprise, genius, has come easily to him; men and women yield to the charismatic prominence of someone whose personality compels one always to say, "Yahweh is with him." Joseph's only agon is the aesthetic enterprise of precisely how and when he will gather his father and brothers in to him so as to become their worldly savior. The enigmatic J gives us not a single hint as to why Joseph has waited to let his father and his brother Benjamin, at the least, know that he is alive and well in Egypt. We must assume that Joseph desires a total triumph of romance so that his story can conclude as marvelously as possible. If there is cruelty in the delay, and there is, it is the selfishness of the child and the aesthete, but again J shows us the limitations of her male heroes, as clearly with Joseph as with Abram, Jacob, and Moses.

Joseph is closest to his father in his self-dramatizing tendencies, as both are expressionists of acute sensibility, persuaders of themselves and of others. Unlike Jacob, Joseph has never had to deceive others, which may be why he has chosen to deceive his ten guilty brothers with such zest and relish. Here as elsewhere we should be wary of literalizing J; when she says of Joseph that Yahweh was with him, she is giving us a complex metaphor for Joseph's persuasiveness. Like J and like Jacob, Joseph is a superb rhetorician, and perhaps one might dare to say that J's Yahweh is the best of all rhetoricians. Joseph is Sigmund Freud's precursor, not so much as dream interpreter but as a favored being who, like a conquistador, goes from success to success. We are won over by Joseph because, like Jacob finally, he yields to the true voice of feeling in himself. The provoker of that voice is Judah, in what is certainly the finest moment in J for Israel's legitimate heir (Gen. 44:18–34). J allows Judah to show that he is not wholly unworthy of the Blessing after all, when he offers himself as a slave in place of Benjamin, after the discovery of the mantic goblet that crafty Joseph has had planted in poor Benjamin's bag, for once deceiving, but toward a good end.

In his strong speech, Judah recapitulates his pledge to Jacob (Gen. 43:9) of accountability for Benjamin's safe return. Since to stand condemned before Israel is to lose the Blessing, Judah rightly knows that he has staked everything on his promise to his father. It is therefore all the more admirable that he now sincerely places the emphasis elsewhere, upon the father's grief that would send Jacob down to Sheol, the Hebraic Hades, if Rachel's other son were lost to him. Judah's speech is most intensely moving, to Joseph and to us, when it touches upon the supposed fate of Joseph himself, torn by beasts and not seen again by his father. Only after Judah refers to the loss of Joseph and the possibility of Jacob's final bereavement does he mention his pledge of self-condemnation. I do not agree with Speiser's view that Joseph is cannily testing the brothers to see whether they have reformed or instead are willing to send a second son of Rachel into Egyptian bondage. Speiser professedly follows von Rad's sensitive suggestion that Joseph is interested not in retribution but in the moral regeneration of his brothers. I do not believe that J, or J's Joseph, is interested in either. Von Rad was a moral theologian, and J was not.

J and her Joseph are both ironists and pragmatists. Does it make any difference whether the brothers have changed or not? And who could believe anyway in the moral regeneration of those butchers of Shechem, Simeon and Levi? Nor can we forget that Judah, the inevitable heir, he who will become Israel and will give his name to the Jews, joined in the plundering at Shechem. The brothers are what they are, but Joseph knows very well that there is no pragmatic harm left in them, and most crucially they are still his brothers. Being Jacob's sons, they must constitute the House of Israel, and each is the founder of one of the tribes. Joseph's game has been a matter of style and not of ethics; it has been a form of Yahwistic play. We may wonder whether it would be over even now, except that the allusions to himself and to his father's mourning undo the passionately restrained Joseph. Like Huck Finn observing his own funeral, Joseph yields to his own sense of pathos. In a marvelous narrative stroke, J has Joseph cry out that all his Egyptians are to leave him, and so clears the room to be alone with his astonished brothers.

In Thomas Mann's revision of Judah's speech, Judah confesses the brothers' guilt over having sold Joseph, but that seems to me one of Mann's rare aesthetic blunders in reworking J. Mann wisely emulates J in passing over Jacob's inevitable reaction to the brothers' crime and long deception, once he has absorbed the shock and joy of learning that his favorite son still lives, and has power over Egypt. There Mann is back in J's spirit, since J was simply not interested in guilt. Her central interest in this story is the relation between Joseph and Jacob rather than that between Joseph and his brothers. The brothers, after all, are not an elite, except for the hapless Judah; they are instead the ancestors of the unruly horde in the Wilderness. Joseph and Jacob are the elite, the natural aristocrats with whom the Davidic-Solomonic J sympathizes most readily. Out of the brothers comes the populace, doubtless as unruly under Rehoboam or Jeroboam as they were under Moses or Joshua, but out of Jacob and Joseph come figures such as J herself.

Alone with his brothers, Joseph greatly reveals himself in the J text, in what I do not consider an anticlimax, as Speiser and others do. There is to be only one proper climax, and J builds toward it with stubborn craft, until the transcendent moment, now in Genesis 46:29–30, when Joseph flings himself weeping upon his father's neck and the immensely dignified Jacob-become-Israel grandly proclaims that at last he can die, having seen face to face that his son is still alive. The scene of Joseph's self-disclosure shrewdly prepares us for that moment, which is anticipated in Joseph's first utterance after declaring his identity: "Is my father still alive?" (100). His anxiety, and ours as readers, is that Jacob will die on hearing the good news, even as Sarai evidently died at discovering the happy outcome of the Binding of Isaac.

We would lack literary tact if we confused Joseph's graceful suggestion that Yahweh sent him to Egypt to prepare the brothers' way before them (Gen. 45:5–8) with a serious theological reflection on J's part. It is a realistic touch that the gracious Joseph cannot forbear reminding his brothers that once they sold him down to

Egypt; no one who is human could well say less. But essentially
Joseph tells them to fret no more about it; his focus, and ours, is
on Israel, who so appropriately says that it is sufficient and that
he will go down to see his son before he, the last of the Patriarchs,
dies. The reunion itself, handled by J with superb and characteristic economy, is both dramatic and self-dramatized as these two
extraordinary actors meet again after so many years. In Mann,
Joseph whispers to his father, "Can you forgive me?" And indeed
Jacob has a great deal to forgive, both in Joseph, who could have
sent word long since, and in the guilty brothers. Only Benjamin,
after all, is quite blameless. But blame is never J's mode, as we
have repeatedly seen. Joseph and Jacob are both overwhelmingly
moved, yet father and son also do not fail to play their parts
wonderfully well. The chief minister of Egypt's ruler calls for his
chariot and honors his father, Israel, by riding up to Goshen to
greet him. Again to his credit, Joseph is overcome by authentic and
tumultuous affection, and becomes a child again, weeping upon his
father's neck for a long time. Of the two master self-dramatizers,
the dignified Israel, once the cunning Jacob, comes off the better performer, maintaining his heroic composure in front of his
people.

That composure is marvelously evident again when Jacob
comes before his son's master, Pharaoh, though the text we now
have (Gen. 47:7–10) appears to be P's rather than J's. But I hear
the irony of J rather than the piety of P when Jacob, in response
to Pharaoh's wonder as to the patriarch's age, solemnly informs
the monarch that though the years of his life add up to one hundred
and thirty, still they have been few and hard, and compare unfavor-
ably with the life-spans of his fathers! In what most scholars agree
is J's text, a very disturbing passage follows, in which Joseph, like
his father, appears a sharp trader indeed, reducing all the farmers
of Egypt to the status of serfs. Scholars argue that J is merely
assigning an important economic function to Joseph, somehow
enhancing his glory, but that is to undervalue J's ironies and

complexities of presentation in regard to her heroes. J means neither to blame nor to praise the formidable Joseph, but it is part of the terrible sadness of postbiblical Jewish history that this passage, like some others in J, has been used for anti-Semitic purposes by certain Christians throughout their generations.

I return gratefully to J's comic powers in the wonderful account of Jacob's blessing of Joseph's two half-Egyptian sons, Ephraim and Manasseh (Gen. 48:10–22). With his death approaching, the almost blind Jacob deliberately reenacts an aspect of the scene in which his blind father blessed him rather than his brother, Esau. True to his mother, Rebecca, Jacob who is Israel slyly crosses his hands, putting his right on the head of Ephraim, the younger, and his left on Manasseh, the firstborn. When Joseph grasps his father's right hand to move it from Ephraim's head to Manasseh's, the dying patriarch stubbornly resists. Aside from the humor of Jacob's lifelong habits persisting to the very end, and J's usual preference for younger sons, we appear to receive another of J's contemporary thrusts against the Northern Kingdom, Jeroboam's Israel, where Ephraim was the dominant tribe or half-tribe. That seems also to be why J has the dying Jacob award Shechem to Joseph as a personal fief, since Jeroboam was crowned there. Perhaps Jacob, no warrior despite Penuel, is raving in his death throes when he asserts that he himself captured Shechem by force of arms, because J surely wishes us to recall how outraged Jacob was when Simeon and Levi decimated Shechem.

What remains in J's Joseph saga is the moving account of Joseph's grief for his dead father and the subsequent journey to Canaan to bury Jacob in the cave of Machpelah, facing on Mamre, where Abram, Sarai, Isaac, Rebecca, and Leah had been buried. It is Joseph rather than the inheritor, Judah, who again weeps upon Jacob's face, for a last time, as he kisses him. After the burial in Canaan, J ends with the return of Joseph and his brothers to Egypt. The scene is set for the story of Moses and the Exodus, but we may well wonder why we do not have a J version of the death of Joseph.

Perhaps there was one and the Redactor excised it in favor of the E story in which the frightened brothers go up to Joseph to beg unnecessarily for mercy now that their father and shield is gone. But I prefer to think that J chose not to write about the death of Joseph, precisely because he was her surrogate for the beloved David, whose life she could or would not make into the subject of her work.

MOSES

OF THE THREE major "sources" of what is now Exodus, J occupies a middle position in regard to the grandeur and significance of Moses, leader and prophet. P is wary of Moses, E exalts him, while J handles the deliverer of the people with the affectionate irony that is distinctive of this author. When J set out to bring together all of her tradition, from Creation through the death of Moses, she had at the center of her vision not Moses or even Abram, let alone Jacob or Joseph, and certainly not Yahweh, but David, as I have emphasized repeatedly. Her standard of measurement is Davidic, though almost by definition she takes David as the subject that is forbidden to her. It is as though David's absence from her writing was a void that his presence could not fill, so far had historical reality departed from the heroic grandfather in the age of his unheroic grandson Rehoboam. David belongs to history, and J does not write history. Her Moses is no more historical than are her Abram, Jacob, and Joseph. This does not necessarily mean that J doubted a historical Moses, or the reality of Egyptian bondage and Mosaic Exodus. Rather, it means that her Moses was as remote as the Patriarchs, unlike David, whose aura lingered even during the time of Judah's decline. J's writing was for her a unity; we read it as a primeval history, a patriarchal saga, a romance of Joseph, and a more or less historical Exodus and subsequent Conquest of Canaan. But for J all these were a single genre, in defiance of the genres of the ancient Middle East. Call them David's foreground, and you have a good sense of J's form and purpose. For her, Yahweh himself matters because he is the God who fell in love with David. As for Moses, he is an uncanny step on the way to David, uncanny because he is so odd a choice for Yahweh to have made, particularly in J's view.

Many modern historians surmise that the actual enslavement of the Israelites in Egypt took place during the reign of Ramses II (c.1304–1237 B.C.E.) and that the Exodus occurred under his successor, Merneptah, possibly in 1220 B.C.E. (I place it somewhat earlier). Since I date J in the generation after Solomon, who died in 922 B.C.E., she was writing of events a full three centuries before her own time, or about as far back as the Cromwellian revolution in relation to current Great Britain. But David's old age was perhaps half a century before J wrote; he was as close to her as Winston Churchill and Franklin Delano Roosevelt are to many among us, a figure of J's earliest childhood, it may be—half historical, half legendary. Moses, being so remote from J, was less important to her than Abram and Jacob, because Yahweh's covenants with them clearly moved her more than the covenant made between Yahweh and the host at Sinai. But that is to get ahead of her story.

> Now Joseph had died, and all his brothers, and all that generation. (105)

> A new king arose over Egypt, not knowing Joseph. (106)

This majestic new beginning reverberates with particular force if J's Joseph indeed was a surrogate for David. A departed glory is another hint at J's contemporary context in the waning days of Rehoboam, who could not preserve what he inherited. The Israelites in Egypt, after Joseph's death, also could not preserve what Joseph had given them, a favored position in a land not their own. Clearly, this reflected no special fault on their part. Possessors of the Blessing, they multiply, and their number and vigor frighten Pharaoh. J's ironic humor enters strongly when the Hebrew midwives tell Pharaoh that they have failed to kill the male babies because the mothers, unlike Egyptian women, are so vigorous that they give birth before the midwife reaches them (Ex. 1:19). This humor, like J's trope of genocide through smooth or shrewd dealing, frames the birth of Moses. I doubt the contention of the learned Martin Noth, in his *History of Pentateuchal Traditions* (1948), that J did not know that the name Moses was of Egyptian origin, meaning "son," since J's characteristic etymological pun in Exodus 2:10, on the Hebrew verb for "to draw out," plays not only on the babe being drawn out of the water but on the work of the midwife assisting the birth of the son. J's remarkably aristocratic fable is weakly misread because of the usual misunderstandings of her tone and stance. An ironic woman who sees through all patriarchal myths keeps being interpreted as a misogynist; the most sophisticated author in the Hebrew Bible is considered naive by scholars and critics light-years less subtle and less literary than the writer they seek to master. What could be more charming, more beautifully self-aware, than a fable of deliverance in which the Egyptian princess is wholly benign, knows Hebrew, and rejects the male violence of her father? And what could be more cunning than J's use of the sister of Moses, who is sent to observe and is thus available to offer the princess the most proper of Hebrew wet nurses, the baby's own mother?

One wonders if any other writer in Western tradition works with an economy at all comparable to J's. In Exodus 2:11 we suddenly confront a mature Moses who has no doubt of his Israelite identity, and is both fierce to avenge his brothers and wary because of his exposed situation. After he escapes Pharaoh, we see Moses again manifesting his strong aggressivity against the shepherds at the well, in defense of the daughters of the priest of

Midian. We have learned already, from his useless revenge against the Egyptian, that Moses is intemperate though wary. Here we see again that he is courageous and, in the naming of his son (Ex. 2:22), wholly dedicated to the fate of his people. But he has qualities in plenty that argue against his suitability to lead a people out of bondage and exile: anger, impatience, and a deep anxiety about his own hold on authority. In personality and character, he could scarcely be further away from the David of 2 Samuel. For J, with her customary uncanniness, that seems to be why Moses receives the prophetic call.

Uncanniness is the peculiar mark of sublimity in the extraordinary dialogue J writes for Yahweh and Moses in Exodus 3. Yahweh's angel or messenger, or Yahweh himself in J's original text, gives the prelude to the dialogue by blazing forth as the fire in the thorn bush, a fire that does not consume, as if to imply that Moses, as messenger, also will not be consumed. That in some sense he *will* be consumed by his prophecy is the legitimate fear implied by Moses throughout his interchanges with Yahweh. This remarkable series of thrusts and parries shows Yahweh overcoming by virtue of more firepower than poor Moses can withstand. Yahweh, who is *in* the fire but is *not* the fire, speaks as fire should, warning his incipient and involuntary prophet not to come too close. Recall that nowhere does Yahweh say to Abram, Jacob, and the beloved David that they are not to approach too near. Indeed, never before has Yahweh spoken of the category of the holy, evidently invented to keep Moses and the mass of Israelites at a distance. J has of course shown us Abram and Jacob at their worst as well as their best, but Yahweh has no desire to fend them off. As will become crucial at Sinai, Yahweh seems to need certain defenses for his own sensibilities even as he resolves to extend his Blessing from one elite family to all of their historical descendants and followers.

When Yahweh announces his saving intentions to Moses, he says, "I come down to lift them out of Egypt's hand" (115). The promise has its ironies for J, since there is always the question whether "coming down" upon Sinai will at all resemble Yahweh's coming down upon Babel, for which she uses the same verb. The descents of Yahweh, even if benign in intention, always seem to have their equivocal and ambivalent aspects in J. Moses somehow senses this when he insists that the people will not listen to him. Minor miracles, such as sticks that become serpents, and hands leprous as snow, cannot persuade the heavy-tongued Moses, who departs only when Yahweh's rhetoric overflows into sheer authority.

> "Who put the mouth in man? Who makes him dumb? And who makes the deaf—or the seeing and the blind? Wasn't it I, Yahweh?" (118)

These are the accents of Yahweh at Mamre, reproving Sarai, and Moses reluctantly obeys, only to be endangered by Yahweh almost immediately. The reluctant prophet sets forth, and Yahweh comes after him to kill him: without cause, without reason. Of all the problematic incidents in J's narrative, the most uncanny, indeed horrifying, is Yahweh's attempt to murder his prophet, Moses (Ex. 4:24–26). Something may have been cut from J's text here, but I am inclined to think not, if only because the Redactor allowed this shocking incident to survive at all. What evidently has been lost is a complex tradition about the origins of circumcision. What remains is one of J's ironic triumphs, one of the passages that first persuaded me that J was a woman, because Zipporah, the wife of Moses, stands up against Yahweh as Moses himself would not have dared to do, even when the question was one of his own survival.

Rashi, desperately seeking to reduce the scandal of Yahweh's unwarranted assault on the prophet, allowed himself the absurd observation that Moses was tarrying at an inn rather than taking his rapid way down into Egypt. But poor Moses was of course making a night encampment, a necessity on his difficult journey.

The enigma is Yahweh's motive, and the answer J implicitly gives us is that there is and can be none. Normative tradition, impatient even with Rashi, came up with the mad explanation that Moses was to be slain precisely because he had failed to circumcise his son! I myself read Zipporah's final remark—"A blood bridegroom marked by this circumcision"—as the Redactor's triumphant editorializing, and so J's own passage becomes instead a weird founding event for the praxis of circumcision.

> On the way, at a night lodging, Yahweh met him—and was ready to kill him. Zipporah took a flinty stone, cutting her son's foreskin; touched it between Moses' legs: "Because you are my blood bridegroom." [Yahweh] withdrew from him.
>
> (120)

Martin Buber, being largely free of the normative tradition, insisted in his *Moses: The Revelation and the Covenant* (1958) that Yahweh had a motive: "He claims the entirety of the one he has chosen." On such a view, Moses has not yet given his full devotion to Yahweh. But complete or daemonic possession transcends even absolute devotion, and so even Buber falls short of J's awesome irony. Perhaps the greatest tribute to that irony was rendered by midrashic legend, which converted the murderous Yahweh into Satan disguised as a serpent that nearly swallows Moses up before Zipporah performs the circumcision on their son.

The most perceptive comments I have seen on this passage are by Herbert Marks, who overtly offers a modified Freudian reading that invokes the emotive ambivalence of the Oedipus complex.

> The identification of the prophet with YHWH is thus dependent on a second identification with the son, which defends against the pressures of historical supersession. Ultimately, this Oedipal son is a figure for the people Israel.

So double and dialectical an identification indeed is in J's spirit, and Marks catches part of the tang of an irony in which Yahweh attacks Moses not for the incompleteness of the identification but so as to emphasize again that total identification is impossible. J's lack of fondness for Moses is part of the story also. For her, Moses precisely is no David, and particularly is not a precursor of the hero who centered Yahweh forever at Jerusalem. The Moses of P, who stammers because he has uncircumcised lips, is a wholly different Moses from J's, who stammers out of dread and bewilderment, and has to be rescued from Yahweh by his wife through their baby son, hardly a dignified salvation for the prophet.

With the introduction of Aaron in Exodus 4:14, Moses acquires a new status in J, as if Aaron's psychological role for Moses is to remove the prophet's overt resistance to his own election by Yahweh. It may be that the presence of Aaron also liberates Moses into his own capacity for cunning. The Pharaoh of J is a subtle fox, but so is her Moses, who begins by requesting not the freedom of his people but rather a vacation for them so that they can go out into the wilderness to worship Yahweh. Since Yahweh is unknown to Pharaoh, the Mosaic request is refused, in another of J's ironies: Pharaoh's ignorance will soon be redressed by Yahweh, who always does see to it that he is known, however eventually. Knowing this, Moses and Aaron do not immediately argue the point with Pharaoh, whose hubris thus becomes overwhelming. As for J's Moses, he is quite underwhelming, as we might say. An object of scorn to Pharaoh, cursed by the overworked Israelites, who are now compelled to make bricks without straw, Moses is reduced to a pathetic stammering: for what, for what, and what of (123). Yahweh disdains comforting the wretched prophet but quite ominously proclaims, "Now you will see what I do for Pharaoh" (124). And the great plagues begin.

J has wonderful fun with the plagues, putting us closer again to children's literature than to wisdom literature. Buber rightly terms this a "fantastic popular narrative" of "wonder to wonder." Brevard Childs, in *The Book of Exodus* (1974), the best scholarly commentary on Exodus, relates the plagues to "the interesting tension in J between the absolute demands of release repeated in the phrase, 'Let my people go,' and the willingness to negotiate." The plagues are signs of interesting tensions indeed, reminding us of the mischief-maker in J's Yahweh, who confounded the builders of Babel. But Pharaoh is himself an interesting tension, evidencing J's Shakespearean ability to represent complex characters by deft, minute strokes. Throughout the plagues and the dialogues between Moses and Pharaoh, J writes in the vein of the romance of Joseph, fabulously and fancifully, and not in the way that represented Abram and Jacob. There the tone was ironical pathos; here it is a purer irony, since now the clash of incommensurates puts J wholly on Yahweh's side. One way of getting a clear sense of J's tone is to compare her plagues with the lurid, harsh visions of the Revelation of Saint John the Divine. The loss is plain in the aesthetic inferiority of the Apocalypse.

In the account of the miracle at the Red Sea (Ex. 14), J's version is strikingly different from P's, which builds on E's. In P, Yahweh orders Moses to raise his staff up over the sea, which divides to create a path between two walls of water. After the Israelite crossing, Moses raises his hand and the waters drown the pursuing Egyptians. Such crude wonders are not J's way. In J, the wilderness festival to honor Yahweh presumably becomes the occasion for flight from Egypt, following the lead of the pillar of cloud by day, the pillar of fire by night. Pharaoh and his troops pursue and overtake the fugitives at the Red Sea. Moses comforts the terrified Israelites, and the cloud ceases to lead, coming between the fugitives and the Egyptian pursuers in so dark a form as to balk their advance. In the darkness, a great Yahwistic wind leaves the seabed bare. J does not describe the crossing of the Israelites but concentrates on the Egyptians, who are driven wild by the pillar of cloud and the pillar of fire, and flee into the seabed (now inundated again), so that all of them are drowned. J's remarkable blend of realism and fantasy emphasizes the terror of both Israelites and Egyptians while giving us Moses at his rare best. Far less famous than P's version of the Red Sea crossing, J's episode is both more aesthetically compelling and more consonant with the uncanniness of Yahweh, and of a Moses who has suddenly and convincingly transcended himself. The voice that spoke first to Moses from the fire now overcomes the Egyptians through the same image.

For the P writer, as for the Deuteronomist and the Redactor, the deliverance at the Red Sea was as crucial as the Creation and the Return from Exile in Babylon. But for J, who had not known exile (though she anticipated it), the deliverance was a less vital story than either of the origins, primeval and patriarchal. The fashioning of Adam and his nameless bride, the going forth of Abram, and Jacob's transformation into Israel at Penuel were for J visions far more central than the events at the Red Sea, at Sinai, and in the Wilderness, let alone the entry into Canaan and the Conquest. Above all else an elitist and an individualist, as we would say, J distrusted traditions centered on the mass of the people rather than on figures such as Sarai and Abram, Rebecca, Jacob and Rachel, Tamar, Joseph, and above all David. The crisis for J's Yahweh does not come in Eden, or with the careers of Abram and Jacob, but arrives at Sinai in confrontation with the unruly host of the Israelites. Perhaps J saw Yahweh's assuagement for Sinai in his election-love for David, even though that led to crises of a more intimate sort for favorite and favorer alike.

Sinai is central for what we call Judaism, and for its heretic child, Christianity, but what we call Judaism was formulated more than a thousand years after J, in the Roman-occupied Palestine of the second century c.e. I find the famous "Sinai theophany," in its original, J version (insofar as it has been preserved in Exodus 19 and 24), to be one of J's most extraordinary ironies, because it plainly shows us a Yahweh who is not only on the verge of going out of control but who keeps warning Moses to tell the people to watch out, because their God knows that he is about to lose all restraint. What drives Yahweh to fury is the nature of the Israelite host, which is portrayed by J as little better or worse than any other mass of refugees enduring privation out in the desolate places. In

J's version of what scholars now call the Wilderness Wandering tradition, the wandering people murmur and grumble, as is natural, and denounce Moses, as is only sensible, for who besides Moses or Yahweh can they denounce, and the Yahweh who dumped a frog in Pharaoh's lap and then destroyed the Egyptian firstborn is not easily available for denunciation. It is one thing for Yahweh to destroy Pharaoh's firstborn, but quite another to slay the baby of the slave girl at her hand mill. Whatever J's Yahweh intends to be ultimately, in pragmatic terms he can scarcely be regarded as a benign personality.

Later writers, being normative revisionists of J, took the side of Moses (and of Yahweh) against the murmuring wanderers, but that is hardly J's stance. Dispassionate or ironic as almost always, she writes with a bemused tolerance for all concerned: the people, Moses, Yahweh. Typical is the very start of the wandering, at Mara, or the bitter waters.

> Moses led Israel from the Sea of Reeds, entering the desert of Shur. They walked three days into the desert without finding water. They arrived at Mara yet couldn't drink there. The water was bitter; Mara, they called the place. The people grumbled about Moses, saying, "What will we drink?" He cried out to Yahweh. Yahweh revealed a tree to him; he threw it into the water, and the water turned sweet. It was there he turned the law concrete, putting them to the test. (152)

J plays upon the bitter people and the bitter water; we become sweet water when we are able to drink it. The people are merely natural, while Yahweh has transformed Moses into someone preternatural, a wizard who cures water. But clearly Moses wins no prizes as a desert guide; if you lead a multitude three days into the desert, they surely have some right to assume that you know where you are going. Taking a multitude to Mara is inept, or else it is a lunatic test, but for Yahweh it is just the way he is. Putting the people to the test at Mara is the mass equivalent of putting Abram to the test at Mount Moriah. Such a procedure tells us more about Yahweh than about the people or their ancestor.

There is a tradition that Yahweh promises manna to the Israelites as a reward for Abram's willingness to sacrifice Isaac, as indicated by Abram's "Here I am." So Yahweh in effect says, "Here I am," when Abram's descendants beg for bread in the Wilderness. I have indicated already that J's Abram was not likely to be so willing, and her Yahweh is curiously grudging on what might be called the manna question. To drop an airlift of food upon a starving multitude *in order to test them* would make us blink were the airlift human, but again J wants us to confront the outrageousness of Yahweh. Forty years of such testing would madden any host, and any God also. The issue, of course, then as now, is who is putting whom to the test, mortals or God? The irony of the question is not mine but J's. I take it that the question of murmuring or grumbling by the hungry in the Wilderness preceded J, even though the normative redactors greatly expanded upon the tradition as preserved by and in J's work. But I think it vital to realize that the irony of the double testing is only J's. Her sympathies are neither with the people nor with Yahweh, except insofar as they are, rather detachedly, with both.

251

> There were further trials. The place was called Massa and Meriba: one name for the quarrels of the people Israel, the other for their testing, saying, "Is Yahweh near—with us—or not?" (155)

Massa is the name for a test, and Meriba for a quarrel. Again the issue is the supposed hardness or skepticism of the Israelites. J's wit has permanent value: can there be a testing, of God or man, without a quarrel? What of the reverse: is every quarrel a testing? The long march of the Israelites consumes the better part of a human life; perhaps a priest or Ezra the Scribe could regard the host as obdurate or ungrateful, but J's more human perspective does not. A journey of four decades is either a myth or a disaster,

particularly since Sinai and the Negev are not exactly North America or Siberia. Moses indeed was prophetic when he attempted, in
vain, to refuse the call. Confronted by the Wilderness Wandering
tradition, the subtle J adopted an irony of literalization. If you
combine the rhetoric of leaving things out with a deadpan literal-
ism, then you arrive at outrage, and the wandering in J is a fine
and deliberate outrage. J's Yahweh, irascible by nature, has endured forty years of quarrel and testing, through his chosen surrogate Moses, and perhaps he can be forgiven for his balky behavior
when the people reach the foot of his holy mountain. Must he
indeed now extend the Blessing to all of these?

Despite the truncation—indeed, the possible mutilation—of
J's account of the Sinai theophany, more than enough remains to
mark it as the crisis or crossing point of her work. For the first
time, her Yahweh is overwhelmingly self-contradictory rather than
dialectical, ironic, or even crafty. The moment of crisis turns upon
Yahweh's confrontation with the Israelite host. Is he to allow
himself to be seen by them? How direct is his self-representation
to be? Mamre and the road to Sodom suddenly seem estranged,
or as though they never were. It is not that Yahweh is presented
less anthropomorphically here, but that J's Moses (to say nothing
of those he leads) is far less theomorphic or Davidic than J's Abram
and Jacob, and certainly less theomorphic or Davidic than J's
Joseph. Confronting his agonistic and theomorphic elite, from
Abram to the implied presence of David, Yahweh is both canny
and uncanny. But Moses is neither godlike nor competitive. J's
Sinai theophany marks the moment of the Blessing's transition
from the elite to the entire Israelite host, and in that transition a
true anxiety of representation breaks forth in J's work for the first
time.

I follow Martin Noth's lead, in the main, as to those passages
in Exodus 19 and 24 that are clearly J's, though my ear accepts
certain moments he considers only probable or at least quite possible. In each case I give my own literally rendered translation, to

be compared to Rosenberg's admirably literate version (156–62), which accepts most of the same verses in a variant order.

> Yahweh said to Moses: "I will come to you in a thick cloud, that the people may hear that I speak with you and that they may trust you forever afterward." Moses then reported the people's words to Yahweh, and Yahweh said to Moses: "Go to the people, warn them to be continent today and tomorrow. Let them wash their clothes. They should be prepared for the third day, for on the third day Yahweh will descend upon Mount Sinai, in the sight of all the people. You shall set limits for the people all around, saying: 'Beware of climbing the mountain or touching the border of it. Whoever touches the mountain shall be put to death; no hand shall touch him, but either he shall be stoned or shot; whether beast or man, he shall not live.' When there is a loud blast of the ram's horn, then they may ascend the mountain." Moses came down from the mountain unto the people and warned them to remain pure, and they washed their clothes. And Moses said to the people: "Prepare for the third day; do not approach a woman." (Ex. 19:9–15)

Yahweh will come at first in a thick cloud, that the people may hear but presumably not see him; nevertheless, on the third day he will come down upon Sinai "in the sight of all the people." Sinai will be taboo, but is this only a taboo of touch? What about seeing Yahweh? I suspect that an ellipsis, wholly characteristic of J's rhetorical strength, intervened here, again characteristically filled in by the E redactors as verses 16 and 17, and then as verse 19; but in verse 18 we clearly hear J's grand tone.

> Now Mount Sinai was all in smoke, for the Lord had come down upon it in fire; the smoke rose like the smoke of a kiln, and all the people trembled violently.

Whether people or mountain (as in King James) trembles hardly matters in this great trope of immanent power. Yahweh, as we know, is finally neither the fire nor in the fire, for the ultimate trope is the *makom:* Yahweh is the place of the world, but the world is not his place, and so Yahweh is also the place of the fire, but the fire is not his place. And so J touches the heights of her own Sublime, though herself troubled by an anxiety of portrayal previously unknown to her, an anxiety of touch and, for the first time, of sight.

> Yahweh came down upon Mount Sinai, on the mountain top; Yahweh called Moses to the mountain top, and Moses went up. Yahweh said to Moses: "Go down, warn the people not to break through to gaze at Yahweh, lest many of them die. And the priests who come near Yahweh must purify themselves, lest Yahweh break forth against them." But Moses said to Yahweh: "The people cannot come up to Mount Sinai, for you warned us when you said: 'Set limits about the mountain and render it holy.'" So Yahweh said to Moses: "Go down and come back with Aaron, but do not allow the priests or the people to break through to come up to Yahweh, lest Yahweh break out against them." And Moses descended to the people and spoke to them. (Ex. 19:20–25)

However much we have grown accustomed to J, she has not prepared us for this. Never before has Yahweh, bent upon covenant, been a potential catastrophe as well as a potential blessing. But then, certainly the difference is in the movement from an elite to a whole people. If, as I suspect, the pragmatic covenant for J was the Davidic or humanistic covenant, then the most salient poetic meaning here was contemporary, whether for Solomon's reign or just after. The true covenant, without anxiety, is agonistic: with Abram, with Jacob, with Joseph, with David, but neither with Moses nor with Solomon, and so never with the mass of the people, whether at Sinai or at J's own moment of writing. J is as elitist as

Shakespeare, or as Freud; none of the three was exactly a writer on the left. Yahweh himself, in J's vision, becomes dangerously confused in the anxious expectation of at once favoring and threatening the host of the people, rather than the individuals, that he has chosen. When Moses reminds Yahweh that Sinai is off limits anyway, Yahweh evidently is too preoccupied and too little taken with Moses even to listen, and merely repeats his warning that he may be uncontrollable, even by himself.

As Exodus now stands, the revisionists take over, and the Commandments are promulgated. I surmise that in J's original text the Commandments, however phrased, came *after* some fragments of J that we still have in what is now Exodus 24.

> Then Yahweh said to Moses: "Come up to Yahweh, with Aaron, Nadab, and Abihu, and seventy elders of Israel, and bow low but from afar. And only Moses shall come near Yahweh. The others shall not come near, and the people shall not come up with him at all."
>
> Then Moses and Aaron, Nadab and Abihu, and seventy elders of Israel went up, and they saw the God of Israel; under his feet there was the likeness of a pavement of sapphire, like the very sky for purity. Yet he did not raise his hand against the leaders of the Israelites; they beheld God, and they ate and drank. (Ex. 24:1–2, 9–11)

This is again J at her uncanniest, the true Western Sublime, and so the truest challenge to a belated Longinian critic like myself. We are back at Mamre in a sense, except that here the seventy-four who constitute an elite (of sorts) eat and drink, as did the Elohim and Yahweh at Mamre, while Yahweh watches enigmatically and (rather wonderfully) is watched. And again J is proudly self-contradictory, or perhaps even dialectical, her irony being beyond my interpretive ken, whereas her Yahweh is so outrageously self-contradictory that I do not know where precisely to begin in reading the phases of this difference.

Rather than entering that labyrinth—of who may or may not see Yahweh, or how, or when—I choose instead to test the one marvelous visual detail against the Second Commandment. Alas, we evidently do not have J's phrasing here, but there is a strength in the diction that may reflect an origin in J.

> You shall not make for yourself a carved image, or any likeness of what is in the heavens above, or on the earth below, or in the waters under the earth.
>
> (Ex. 20:4; my translation)

Surely we are to remember J's Yahweh, who formed the *adam* from the dust of the *adamah* and blew into his sculpted image's nostrils the breath of life. The image is forbidden to us, as our creation. But had it been forbidden to J, at least until now? And even now, does not J make for herself, and so for us, a likeness of what is in the heavens above? The seventy-four eaters and drinkers saw with their own eyes the God of Israel, and they saw another likeness also: "Under his feet there was the likeness of a pavement of sapphire, like the very sky for purity." Why precisely *this* visual image, from this greatest of writers who gives us so very few visual images, as compared with images that are auditory, dynamic, motor urgencies? I take it that J, and not the Hebrew language, inaugurated the extraordinary process of describing any object primarily by telling us not how it looked but *how it was made,* wonderfully and fearfully made. But here J describes what is seen—not so much Yahweh in whole or in part, but what we may call Yahweh's chosen stance.

Stance in writing is also tone, and the tone of this passage is crucial, but perhaps beyond our determination. Martin Buber, an eloquent rhetorician, described it in *Moses* with great vividness but with rather too much interpretive confidence. The seventy-four representatives of Israel are personalized by this theorist of dialogical personalism.

They have presumably wandered through clinging, hanging mist before dawn; and at the very moment they reach their goal, the swaying darkness tears asunder (as I myself happened to witness once) and dissolves except for one cloud already transparent with the hue of the still unrisen sun. The sapphire proximity of the heavens overwhelms the aged shepherds of the Delta, who have never before tasted, who have never been given the slightest idea, of what is shown in the play of early light over the summits of the mountains. And this precisely is perceived by the representatives of the liberated tribes as that which lies under the feet of their enthroned *Melek*.

Always ingenious and here refreshingly naturalistic, Buber nevertheless neglects what he sometimes recognized: J's uncanniness. Buber's motive, as he says, is to combat two opposed yet equally reductive views of biblical theophanies: that they are either supernatural miracles or else impressive fantasies. But had J wanted us to believe that the seventy-four elders of Israel saw only a natural radiance she would have written rather differently. The commentary of Brevard Childs is very precise: "The text is remarkable for its bluntness: 'They saw the God of Israel.' " Childs adds that from the Septuagint on to Maimonides there is a consistent toning down of the statement's directness. Surely the directness is realized yet more acutely if we recall that this is Yahweh's only appearance in the Hebrew Bible where he *says* absolutely nothing. J's emphasis is clear: the seventy-four are on Sinai to eat and drink in Yahweh's presence while they stare at him and he presumably stares right back. But that confronts us with the one visual detail J provides: "Under his feet there was the likeness of a pavement of sapphire, like the very sky for purity." J gives us a great image, which all commentary down to the scholarly present weakly misreads by literalizing it. J, herself a strong misreader of tradition, demands strong interpretations, and so I venture one here. Let us forget all such notions as Yahweh standing so high up that he seems to stand on the sky, or the old fellows' never having seen early light in the mountains before. J is elliptical always; that is crucial to her rhetorical stance. She is too wily to say what you would see if you sat there in awe, eating and drinking while you saw Yahweh. Indeed, we must assume that Yahweh is sitting, but nothing whatsoever is said about a throne, and J, after all, is not Isaiah or Micaiah ben Imlah or Ezekiel or John Milton. As at Mamre, Yahweh sits on the ground, and yet it is as though the sky were beneath his feet. May not this drastic reversal of perspective represent a vertigo of vision on the part of the seventy-four? To see the God of Israel is to see as though the world had been turned upside down. And that Yahweh is indeed seen, contra Buber, we can know through J's monitory comment: "Yet he did not raise his hand against the leaders of the Israelites; they beheld God, and they ate and drank." The sublimity is balanced *not* by a covenant meal, as all the scholars solemnly assert, but by a picnic on Sinai.

That this uncanny festivity contradicts Yahweh's earlier warnings is not J's confusion or something produced by her redactors but is a *dramatic* confusion that J's Yahweh had to manifest if his Blessing was to be extended from outstanding individuals to an entire people. Certainly J emphasizes Yahweh's continued ambivalence toward the host of Israelites and their leadership when we are told, "Yet he did not raise his hand against . . . ," almost as though we might expect some divine violence. I do not suggest that there is anything Coriolanus-like about J's Yahweh, as he hardly resembles Shakespeare's tragic fighting machine. But J's aristocratic bias is felt strongly in Yahweh's revulsion.

I wish desperately that I could intuit what came directly after the Sinai theophany in J's original scrolls, but the Redactor so thoroughly scrambled the final chapters of Exodus that even surmise is very difficult. My inner ear finds J again in the story of the golden calf, though Deuteronomic diction in Exodus 32:7–14 masks the original J material, and 32:25–29 could never have been

J. But the capriciousness of a Yahweh so eager to destroy the Israelites is purest J, and so is the fury of Moses when he breaks the tablets at the foot of the mountain. One of my principal reasons for assigning J to the reign of Rehoboam, Solomon's son, is the clear irony of the golden calf incident, which makes reference to Jeroboam and his breakaway kingdom of Israel, the northern rival to Rehoboam's Judah. Resentful that his subjects continued to go south to Solomon's Temple in Jerusalem, Jeroboam made two golden calves and set up rival shrines at Bethel and Dan, opposite ends of his kingdom. The story, as told in 1 Kings 12:26–33, projects a vision of Yahweh looming above all the kingdom of Israel, since the calves (presumably young bulls) were seen as the platform-throne of Yahweh, just as the sphinxlike cherubim in Solomon's Temple enthroned God. J's thrust is wickedly funny, since Jeroboam's attempt to replace Solomon's Temple is equated with the Israelite host's betrayal of Moses while he is up on the mountain with Yahweh. The formula "These be your gods, O Israel, that brought you up from the land of Egypt," defiantly sounded by Jeroboam, is ascribed by J to the host when Aaron presents them with the golden calf (Ex. 32:4). No one comes out of this episode with much credit, not the mass of Israelites, Aaron, Moses, or Yahweh, by which again I intend no moral judgment, either on J's part or on my own. We have an understandably fickle multitude for whom J feels an aristocratic distaste, and yet she possesses considerable understanding for their perpetual fear of abandonment. Her Aaron is merely a timeserver and faithless trimmer in whom she takes very little interest. The best argument her Moses can produce to divert Yahweh from his murderous rage is that the Egyptians will surely rejoice, and we need scarcely brood on a Yahweh who cannot resist such an argument. When J's Moses smashes the tables of the Law, we observe a gesture of petulance and impatience, and hardly the sublime grandeur of sublimation read into the act by Sigmund Freud. J's irony here is that everyone involved—the people, Aaron, Moses, even Yahweh—mistakes the calves, the platform of God, for godlings in their own right, which is an unfair hit at Jeroboam's expense. Beyond this is a more bitter irony, for the people now carry the Blessing of the Patriarchs, as Moses properly reminds Yahweh, and the Blessing has made no pragmatic difference whatsoever.

The broken tablets are replaced by Yahweh's fresh order to Moses, who at dawn presents himself on top of Sinai, the new stone tablets in his hands. There Yahweh proclaims himself, with terrifying self-knowledge: "Jealous One is my name, Jealous Yahweh" (164). The jealous God might as soon be called the passionate God, replete with zeal, since J here sums up her vision of Yahweh's personality, and we can reflect that indeed he has been very passionate throughout her work. His passion, including his possessiveness, is altogether incommensurate with our own.

What Yahweh dictates to Moses, as J ends her portion of what is now called Exodus, is certainly rather different from the Priestly and Deuteronomist versions of the Ten Commandments. There are more than ten in what is probably J, but J's own phrasing is very difficult to recover here. Martin Noth thought that J "took over the whole from the tradition," but that seems to me not at all J's way. A comparison of J's Commandments, Exodus 34:11–26, with the Priestly version, Exodus 20:1–17, and with Deuteronomy 5:6–21, will produce an inevitable bewilderment. J's emphasis is much more pragmatic than ethical; her Yahweh is passionately concerned with what is his, the firstborn, which must be redeemed, by sacrifice. We are not to appear before him empty-handed. The irony is that J has shown us the triumph of the younger sons throughout, even as Yahweh asserts that the firstborn sons are his own. Perhaps it is because the youngest do not need to be redeemed before Yahweh that they almost invariably inherit the Blessing.

One looks in vain among J's Commandments for the crucial shall nots—swearing falsely, murdering, committing adultery, stealing, bearing false witness, coveting what is your neighbor's— or for the positive injunction to honor one's father and mother.

These matters may have seemed too obvious to the subtle J. An elitist, impassioned Yahweh may have found them too mundane, or bearing too little upon the Blessing of carrying more life onward, into a time without boundaries.   2 6 1

IN AN ESSAY on Numbers, the literary critic Geoffrey Hartman remarks:

> In the Hebrew Bible, human life does not own itself: like every other kind of life, it is God's property, and if the privilege of ownership passes from the Lord, it does not thereby pass into the hands of feudal kings but, rather, of Israel as a people striving to become a nation.

That "human life does not own itself" is a conviction of every writer in the Hebrew Bible with two exceptions, in my judgment, and they are J and the author of 2 Samuel. These great contemporaries, flowers of the Solomonic Enlightenment, survived Solomon's time and wrote under Rehoboam, in an era of falling away. I have been arguing that notion throughout this book, and return to it here at the outset of considering J's share in what we now call Numbers. Genesis and Exodus are frequently harsh, but Numbers is harsher, as befits a work whose Hebrew title, "In the Wilderness," emphasizes the difficulties endured by the Israelites as they wandered a purgatorial forty years in the wastelands of the Sinai.

The God of Numbers is appropriately harsh in all the strands of authorship, which are even more difficult to pick apart than they are in Exodus. But in the portions and episodes that are J's, Yahweh's possessiveness is somewhat countered by the human freedom to strive for more life that is J's obsessive concern, as it was the quest of the marvelously human David of 2 Samuel. Perhaps J would have agreed that human life is not its own possession, but she and her protagonists struggle against that limit. Normative revisionism diluted the freedom of personality that J exalted, with a consequent diminishment not only in the personality of men and women, but a great loss in the personality of Yahweh as well.

Until we reach 10:29–36, everything in Numbers belongs either to the Priestly Author or to the Redactor. It is with the departure from Sinai that J's voice is heard again, in the very human request Moses makes to his reluctant brother-in-law as he desperately seeks a guide through the Wilderness. In returning to J's Moses, we are back with a prophet who knows his limitations all too well, and who moves us not by sublime grandeur but by a sense that he never will overcome altogether his reluctance to lead. Perhaps the life of J's Moses remains his own, apart from Yahweh's fierce possessiveness, only insofar as he never quite forgets his conviction of his own incommensurateness, not just with Yahweh, but with Abram, Jacob, and Joseph, through his failure to achieve their theomorphic status. Most darkly, we sense again in the diffidence of Moses the difference from the heroic David, beloved of Yahweh as Moses is not.

J's voice is unmistakable in Numbers 13, when Moses sends forth spies into Canaan, telling them to bring back the fruit of the land together with the military intelligence that is required. We receive the nice detail that the spies cut down so large a branch of grapes that two of them had to bear it back on a carrying frame, nicely bordered by pomegranates and figs. But with the fruit, the frightened spies bring back a vision of the Nephilim of Genesis 6:4, the giants in the earth or men whose name will not be scattered, fruit of uncanny union between Elohim and mortal women. Only J would have the dark wit to have the spies say, gazing at the Nephilim, that the Israelites looked like grasshoppers to themselves, and that such they must have appeared to the giants.

That night, the entire host weeps in fear, and wishes to choose them "a captain back for Egypt," a great phrase powerfully turned against the English by John Milton when he opposed the Stuart Restoration. Caleb, a solitary hero, stands with Moses against this cowardice, and only he is promised by Yahweh that he will enter Canaan. Moses indeed has to cajole Yahweh once again for the lives of the people, and then fails to persuade a large contrite group of them from going up into the hill country to be slaughtered by the Amalekites. A rabblement of grasshoppers is stamped on, to no purpose, presumably for having forgotten that their lives are not their own and that their acceptance of the Blessing obliges them to behave more courageously.

That J was deeply disillusioned with her nation in the day of Rehoboam and Jeroboam could hardly be clearer, and the implied contrast is between the wanderers in the Wilderness and their descendants in David and his warriors. Since the Calebites, a branch of Judah, held the rich hill country around Hebron in J's day, there may be contemporary force in the allusion that is now lost to us. Something contemporary also seems lost when J enters again in Numbers 16, which is a bitter compendium of revolts against Moses, though the bitterness is not J's. What is J's is a wild story of a Reubenite defiance of Moses, punished by a dreadful swallowing up of the rebels by the earth, so that they go alive down into Sheol, the Hades-like underworld. What Moses calls for, and receives, is an unheard-of negative creation on Yahweh's part, with the ghastly result that the terrified Israelites run screaming away, lest they too be swallowed up by the earth. Nothing in the passage's tone demands that we read this superbly outrageous incident with high seriousness. It is a fabulous tale, and J clearly does not intend that either Moses or Yahweh will look the better for it. You can characterize Numbers, as Hartman does, by way of the dilemma of standing "always in precarious proximity to God," a nearness scarcely to be borne. But J, unlike P and R, does not invariably take God's side in brooding upon human danger. An ironic distancing is always at work, even if we cannot be precisely certain of the limits of that irony.

A beautifully controlled irony is at the center of the Balaam and Balak story, J's finest achievement in the Numbers narrative. The Redactor has so sewn J and E together in this tale (Num. 22–24) that disentanglement is dreadfully difficult, but the great passage of Balaam and his sensible ass is certainly J at her most intensely droll. The story itself, despite its comic colorings in J, has been taken very seriously by subsequent Jewish legend, in which Balaam appears as a Gentile prophet equal to Moses in magical power but wholly malign, the very type of the wicked philosopher. But in J, Balaam is not evil, only a prophet-for-hire who nevertheless fears Yahweh and will not curse those whom Yahweh has blessed.

Balaam's ass, like the serpent in Eden, is a talking animal, but J's smooth serpent began as a talker, whereas the ass is transformed by Yahweh himself. Doubtless Balaam deserves the bad name he has to this day, since Dryden and Pope established him as the eternal type of the political timeserver or public figure available for the highest price. Still, J would have been surprised at the proverbial destiny of her comic interlude. How to read the story without dissolving in laughter ought to baffle anyone's sensibility, yet biblical exegetes sometimes manage to preserve their sobriety. Here is the comment of the distinguished Martin Noth in his study of Numbers.

> At the heart of it lies the idea that an unprejudiced animal
> can see things to which a man in his wilfulness is blind; there
> is certainly also in this respect the presupposition that Yah-
> weh's messenger was in himself "visible" in the usual way.

The mighty Balaam, who seeks to be as dignified as Moses, infuriates Yahweh as he rides off pompously on his she-ass, presumably to at least consider collecting a high honorarium for cursing the Israelites. Balaam is full of Balaam, and can only see Balaam; his sensible ass sees that Yahweh's angel stands in the way with a drawn sword. The ass therefore judiciously swerves from the road into the fields and receives a first beating from Balaam. Next confronting the angel in a fenced lane between vineyards, the ass understandably presses herself against the wall, thus squeezing Balaam's foot against same, provoking a second beating. When the angel then stations himself in so narrow a place that swerving is impossible, the ass does what is best and lies down, carrying the furious Balaam with her. As he beats her with his stick, Yahweh opens her mouth, and she asks Balaam what her offense against him is, that he should beat her three times. The reply emphasizes the prophet's hurt dignity, and so the ass's rejoinder is not less than sublime.

> Now Yahweh opened the ass's mouth. "What did I do to you," she said, "to make you lash out at me on three occasions?" "Because *you* have been riding *me,*" Balaam said to the ass. "If I had a sword in my hand, it would whip you dead this time."
>
> "No! Aren't I your own ass? I'm the ass you've been riding on as long as you've owned me," said the ass to Balaam. "Have I been trying—to this day—to make an ass of you?" And he: "No." (174)

Rosenberg marvelously catches J's tone here, and her scandalous agility in leaping from wordplay to a more hard-edged irony. If the high humor of this passage is to be fully appreciated, we need to remember its appalling context. We are stumbling out of the Wilderness toward Canaan, and we have been immersed in a nightmare of sensory deprivation, dangerous proximity to an uneasy and irascible Yahweh, and all the unruly rebellions, backslidings, murmurings, and laments of a wretched host that can scarcely be blamed for its outrage at learning that the Blessing pragmatically has bestowed the better part of their lives as a wandering in the wastelands. A denunciatory prophet leads this unhappy mob, and though he has his greatness, he is by now half-mad himself, reduced to calling for earth-swallowing-up interventions, impalings, and similar modes of horrible punishment. Confronted by this tormented mass moving toward him, Balak of Moab attempts to hire the celebrated Balaam as counter-prophet against Moses. Who but J, against *that* context, would give us this delicious dialogue of the grand magician and his she-ass? I would not say that comic relief is at all involved here, but as always with J, the irony of clashing incommensurates achieves a wicked triumph. The she-ass is more human and more likable not only than her master, Balaam, but clearly than anyone else, divine or mortal, in Numbers! It is J's Yahweh who has a fondness for talking animals, until they cross him (as the serpent did), and J goes her Yahweh one better by celebrating the she-ass's protest at being beaten for accurate perceptions. There is an implicit contrast between her protest at Balaam's violence and the grumblings of the Israelites at their hardships, and also their inability to protest the vengeful violence of Moses and Yahweh. In some sense the host is also being punished for accurate perceptions, except that the she-ass, after all, has not received the Blessing. She can say, "What did I do to you to make you lash out at me?" The Israelites cannot say that, because they have accepted the awful burden of the Covenant. I do not believe it is my own stance against the normative revisionists of J that makes me prefer Balaam's she-ass to any other speaker in Numbers. She speaks a universal protest against violence and blindness, and her presence reminds us that J does not believe that Yahweh owns us. Balaam owns his she-ass; Yahweh does not own J.

Noth interestingly points out that the Balaam story really has nothing to do with the Conquest of Canaan tradition. Its setting is to the east of the northern end of the Dead Sea, on the border of Israel and Moab, not in the times of David and Solomon, but presumably earlier, perhaps in the days of Samuel and Saul. The story therefore is a surprising departure from J's usual praxis of clearly pointing a contemporary irony or allegory, unless indeed the subtle J is warning Jeroboam, to the north, that he may fall

back into the situation of the pre-Davidic age, when even Moab was a menace. But the setting has a peculiar meaning for J: we are near the region in which Moses will die, granted the Pisgah vision but not the actuality of Canaan. When Balak gives his supposed counter-Moses, Balaam, a Pisgah sight of the Israelites, what Balaam sees is glory (Num 23:14–24). It is another of J's complex ironies that the two prophets hover near one another in the fateful region where Moses tragically ends, still unfulfilled in his quest.

Perhaps it is another irony that the surviving traces of J in Numbers should give us a grim transition to the death of Moses, by way of the orgies shared by some of the Israelites and the daughters of Moab in Numbers 25:1–5. These depravities yoke Israel to the Baal of Peor, and Peor is close by where Yahweh himself will bury Moses in an unmarked grave. The Deuteronomist absorbed J (or JE, as some would prefer) in two crucial passages, 31:14–15 and 23, where Moses hands over command to Joshua, and 34:1b–5a, 6, and 10, where Moses and Yahweh have their final confrontation, face to face in the mode of Abram. Where Balaam stood to view the separateness of Israel, its singularity among nations, Moses stands at the end to see the dimensions of an Israel he himself is not permitted to enter. Any man's life, as Kafka ironically remarked, is not long enough to enter Canaan, even if one has been on the track of Canaan all one's life. What J thought of Yahweh's punishment for Moses we do not know, as that is part of J's text forever torn away by the holy alliance of the Deuteronomist, the Priestly Author, and the Redactor. But J's ironic judgment is implied when we hear Yahweh tell his prophet that he has allowed him to see the land (from afar) with his own eyes but not to cross over. The rhetorical pattern deliberately recalls the promise made to Adam, first giving and then taking away. You are free to eat of every tree in the garden, but not the fruit of the two trees, Knowledge and Life. This is the land I swore to Abram, Isaac, Jacob, and their offspring, but you will not cross there. The same pattern is manifested in the creation of Adam and the death of Moses. Yahweh makes the first man with his own hands, and then he buries his chief prophet, again with his own hands. Our cycle is from clay to clay; everything is given to us, and then what matters most is taken away from us.

Some scholars have traced J into the Book of Joshua, but I do not hear her voice anywhere in that bloody chronicle. Her scrolls, I am convinced, went from Adam to the death of Moses, and then ceased, on principle. Her self-denial was, as I have said so often in these pages, her decision not to write about David, precisely because 2 Samuel's author had done (or was doing) that work so superbly. The Book of J, by a final irony, is buried forever in Torah, a masterpiece of the Redactor's. J would have shrugged off the ambiguity of her writings' fate. If one does not wish to choose forms of worship from poetic tales but wishes to read the tales, one still receives J's authentic blessing, whether one knows it or not.

After Commentary

HAROLD BLOOM

THOUGH EVERYTHING that survives of J is in the Torah, or
Five Books of Moses, mixed with so much else (some of it severely
revised J) that now any recovery of J is highly problematic, it seems
just to remark again that the Torah is very far from J's spirit.
Leviticus of course is wholly a Priestly work, and Deuteronomy is
similarly distant from J, but even Genesis, Exodus, and Numbers
in their redacted, normative form give us a very different vision
than does the Book of J. I am afraid this means that Judaism is
just as far away from the Yahwist as Christianity is. The great
rabbis, say Hillel and Akiba, are in the service of a God who is
very different from J's Yahweh. Like every other religion, Judaism
asserts more continuities in its history than actually exist. We do
not even know what continuity, if any, there was between the
Pharisees and the rabbis of Akiba's day, and though Hillel was
thought of by his disciples as a renewer of Ezra, who may have
redacted the Torah, that is another purely arbitrary or asserted
continuity. What is totally unassailable is the vast gulf between the
Yahweh of the Book of J and the God of Judaism.

We do not know what the faith of the Patriarchs was, or what
Moses believed. The Priestly Author and the Redactor presumably
relied on oral traditions handed down to them, as well as writings
now lost, and yet ultimately what they possessed was J or something like J, perhaps a more unified J than they have left to us.

Oral traditions, as an idea, enchant modern scholars, but I grow increasingly skeptical of such enchantment. I don't envision J, whether a court lady or not, going about as Yeats did with Lady Gregory, in order to listen to Judean peasants recite folktales. What the J text shows to an experienced literary critic are all the powers of an immensely strong writer, comparable in imagination and rhetoric only to the greatest Western authors: Homer, Dante, Chaucer, Shakespeare, Cervantes, Tolstoy. Writing like J's is anything but naive or derivative, anything but a transcription of oral traditions. One recognizes J not by the use of the name Yahweh rather than Elohim, but by vision and wordplay, by irony and humor, by the shock of an originality that cannot be staled by cultural repetitions.

I cannot prove anything about J, not even that she existed, or whether she was a woman, or when she lived, or what was her rank or class, or whether her home was Jerusalem. Obviously, then, I cannot demonstrate, whether to oral partisans or pious souls, that J invented what is most characteristic in her work. But so hugely idiosyncratic a writer, whose work is so deeply different from any other ancient Hebrew texts we possess, is likely to have changed radically everything that she inherited or gathered from others. Her Yahweh, so wildly unlike the God of the rest of Torah, may have been almost entirely her own, just as her Abram, Jacob, Tamar, and Joseph appear to be very much her own. She did not care to make Moses her own, and yet her reluctant and besieged stammerer is considerably more vivid than the grander images of Moses to be found in Torah. However, I have been speaking of her literary characters, which is what I insist upon taking her Yahweh to be. How much of what the later Judaic sages regarded as Torah Judaism is traceable to J, if anything? Or if that is unanswerable, how consonant with normative Judaism is the Book of J?

The Talmudic sages founded their doctrines upon *emunah*, "trust," but does J trust Yahweh? She represents Abram, Jacob, and Moses as trusting him, but trust is hardly the dominant element in the relation of any of those three figures to their uncanny God. Having accepted their call, Abram and Moses hold on as best they can, while the agonistic Jacob fights always to come into the Blessing and then survive in it. Yahweh, however the J Binding of Isaac may have read, threatens to kill Isaac, and most certainly sends a deathly angel against Jacob, and unmistakably attempts to murder Moses. Nor can J's Yahweh be trusted as he rages unpredictably on the approaches to his manifestation upon Sinai. The Talmudic *emunah* clearly has little reference to J's outrageously volatile Yahweh.

And yet J is as strict a monotheist as the sages, and the uncanniness of her Yahweh, even if it inspires little awe or trust or love or fear in her, is the dynamic origin of what in Yahweh most strongly affects the sages. J's Yahweh is present wherever and whenever he chooses to be present; he will be that he will be. Unconditioned and unpredictable, he is the most imaginative of Gods; perhaps he is what we now would call J's imagination, her capacity to write poetic tales that seem to us, as they did to the sages, at once startling and yet inevitable. What the sages called *Gevurah,* the *dynamis,* as Aristotle called potential power, is the peculiar aspect of Yahweh that is manifested in J's tense account of the Sinai theophany. But the rabbinical idea of the power of the name Yahweh is totally at variance with J, to whom the name simply is proper for her God. Just as J's text was effaced, or vanished into R's palimpsest, even so *Adonai* ("Lord") replaced Yahweh when Torah was read aloud. J's curious intimacy in writing of Yahweh could not survive the conversion of Yahweh into a numinous, secret, tabooed name.

However that large difference between J and the Talmudists is to be judged or understood, its significance wanes when placed near J's largest legacy to the rabbis, which undoubtedly is her Davidic exaltation of men and women. I do not know whether J invented the peculiar emphasis that made the creation of Adam and his at first nameless woman the center of Yahweh's enterprise, but it is J's vision of Creation, and not P's, that came to dominate normative Judaism. What we would call an earth-centered vision, naturalistic and humanistic, profoundly monist, is imparted by J to all of later tradition, and my surmise is that this vision might indeed have been J's own invention. It is so consonant with the rest of J's stance that I cannot hold her together without it. Nothing about such a vision was alien to the great rabbis, even if they deduced from it consequences that J might have disdained. J's Yahweh was not their God, but his enigmatic and elliptical nature lingered in their sense of shocked awe, while J's man and woman essentially were theirs also, though seen by them in contexts alien to J.

My argument, then, is that J's God is most certainly not the God of the rabbis, down to this day, but that J's men and women invented the kind of Hebrew humanism that is quite central to normative Judaism. I rely here upon many of the standard accounts of the Talmudic view of the human, but in particular upon Ephraim Urbach's chapter "Man" in his classic study, *The Sages* (1975). When Urbach cites the Bible's monistic view of man, he necessarily begins with moments in J, and then passes to J's influence upon others, without ever seeing that it is J, because he rightly, for his purposes, follows the Hebrew Bible as if all of it, and not just Torah, were a unity, which most certainly it is not, as most certainly Torah is not. But if we brood on the Talmudic Bible-centered monism, as expounded by Urbach, then we will find we are brooding upon J. Man, all of man, is a living soul, where the soul, *nefesh*, is not the *psyche* but all of a unified man. J's *nefesh* primarily means "life" yet just as well means "flesh." J's *ruah*, "breath" or "spirit," is the force that impels the *nefesh*, and thus is another manifestation of *nefesh* as life. Action and movement, Urbach notes, define existence, and clearly we are in J's dynamic world. When Urbach explains that the word for "word" stands also for "substance" or "thing," we are very much in J's sense of the truth, for "the Hebrew tongue" here actually means J:

This unity finds expression in lack of differentiation between the word and the substance in the Hebrew tongue, and the relationship between the word and the substance is like that between *nefesh* and *guf* [the body]. In order to denote the absence of existence, non-being, the Hebrew says: as "naught" [*lo dabhar*, "no word"] = non-existent. For the existent finds expression only in action and movement, and if there is no action or movement, there is nothing [literally "no word"]. The *dabhar*, word, pertains only to that which exists; hence there is no difference between theory and practice, and there is no abstraction. Actuality is the fact of power and action, which are life. Life is conceived as power.

(brackets in original)

I can think of no better description of J's writing and its vision than "Actuality is the fact of power and action, which are life," particularly if one substitutes "Yahweh" for "actuality" as the subject of that sentence. For J, as I have stressed throughout, Yahweh is not to be conceived as holiness or righteousness but as vitality. If God's leading attribute is vitality, then his creature, the human, is most godlike when most vital. A monistic vitalism that refuses to distinguish between flesh and spirit is at the center of J's vision, which is thus at the opposite extreme from either the Gnostic or the Pauline Christian dualism. Though Talmudic Judaism set the holiness and righteousness of Yahweh foremost, it nevertheless retained a scaled-down version of J's vitalizing monism.

Yet it retained more of J than that. The power of Yahweh, his *Gevurah*, the attribute that named him "the almighty" God, is essentially J's apprehension. Presumably it is the *Gevurah* that causes Yahweh to exclude Moses from Canaan, for only Yahweh's overwhelming sense of his own power could have found a "stubbornness" or "disobedience" in that first and most faithful of prophets. Moses dies in Moab at Yahweh's command, perhaps of

Yahweh's kiss, a sucking-out of the breath that was breathed into Adam. J's incessant awareness of Yahweh's uncanny power is so strong a consciousness that Western tradition never quite gets

wholly beyond it, despite every belief, despite every unbelief.

THE REPRESENTATION

OF YAHWEH

IN SOME WAYS no reader needs to be introduced to J, because he or she has been reading J all his or her life, while calling it the Bible, Moses, the Word of God, the truth, or what you will. If we are to read the J writer, then we require decontextualization much more than the framing we normally need with ancient authors. J had a contemporary context that perhaps can be restored, at least in part, and such restoration will help to some degree in learning to interpret J. But J comes to us now enwrapped in a redacted package that we need to pull apart if we are to see what was once there, at our origins. Take the opening of what we can regard as J on our origins.

> Before a plant of the field was in earth, before a grain of the field sprouted—Yahweh had not spilled rain on the earth, nor was there man to work the land—yet from the day Yahweh made earth and sky, a mist from within would rise to moisten the surface. (1)

Directly after this, Yahweh shapes Adam. But what is "this," and who is Yahweh? And when is that "before"? Above all, what is that mist that rises from within the earth so as to allow the red clay to be made into Adam?

Yahweh is J's name for God, a name that has been partly

effaced by normative religion, just as J has been effaced by Moses, not her Moses but the Priestly prophet and lawgiver Moses. J wrote for auditors (and some readers) who shared her cultural sophistication, the urban consciousness of the generation that had grown up, very possibly, in the later years of the reign of Solomon. That audience necessarily took a more intimate interest in the four generations of Saul, David, Solomon, and Rehoboam than it did in everything that had come before. Yahweh's great acts in history had more to do with the remote and legendary past than with the world of J. Nomadism, for J, was something like the Wild West for most of us, a lost tradition. A nomadic ideal rose again under the Prophets, but I do not hear any nostalgia for it in J. Her nostalgia is for the strong kingdom created by David and developed by Solomon, a state founded upon heroic vitalism and enlightened by commercial and cultural diversity and prosperity.

An account of the creation of man and woman certainly seems remote from the concerns of a post-Solomonic Jerusalemite, particularly since those concerns would have had very little to do with the religion of Israel. The proper reply of a grateful creature to Yahweh as creator is *avodah*, the act of "service" or worship. However we learn to characterize the Book of J, especially when we contrast it with the rest of the Pentateuch, we will only do it violence by considering it *avodah*. Whatever J was trying to do for herself, as person or as author, by writing her scrolls, she hardly offered her work as *avodah*. By normative standards, Jewish or Christian, J's portrayal of Yahweh is blasphemy. There is no anxiety of portrayal on J's part where Yahweh is concerned. Rather like a Shakespearean character who runs off the page into our lives, J's Yahweh has the largeness and vividness of a being free of inhibitions, at least at the beginning. As his story progresses, Yahweh changes and develops anxieties, brought on by his fury when any of his creatures manifest what he regards as contempt for him. And as J takes Yahweh out of the primeval period and on through the times of the Patriarchs, we can behold Yahweh becoming more and more uncertain, until we confront a very different being in the Yahweh who chooses Moses, presides over the Exodus, and makes his covenant with the leaders of the people at Sinai. The Yahweh who buries Moses, after letting the prophet see the Canaan he will not be permitted to enter, is a very different figure from the Yahweh who shapes Adam.

As the religion of Israel changed, up to the Babylonian Exile and after the Return, and then on to the time of Alexander the Great, we see a considerable revision of J's Yahweh by those for whom writing was *avodah*, those for whom the cult was all. For such writers, writing was itself a form of sacrifice or worship; it was what even we would call religious writing. Whatever J is, she does not write religion in the great burst into originality that led her to begin with the creation of Adam by Yahweh. The scandal of her work always was and still is a Yahweh at once human-all-too-human and totally incommensurate with the human. I suggest that this was a *deliberate* scandal, though of a high-spirited, comic kind. Scholars assume rather readily that all the ancients invariably were solemn, particularly where God and the gods were concerned. I may be accused of creating my own J, and through her my own impish Yahweh, but I would argue that theologians have created *their* own J—an antiquarian scholar with normative Judaic or Christian beliefs in a transcendental Yahweh, just and orderly, a kind of heavenly university president. Divine bureaucrats do not squat on the ground under terebinth trees and devour roast veal so as to strengthen themselves to walk down the road and destroy a sinful city or two. Believers—whether Jewish, Christian, or Muslim—prefer an invisible Yahweh above the clouds, a kind of troublesome but remote gaseous vapor, or failing that, a tyrant suitably enthroned. J's lively Yahweh commences as a mischief-maker and develops into an intensely nervous leader of an unruly rabble of Wilderness wanderers. The scholarly name for this disparity between J's Yahweh and the normative, cleaned-up Yahweh is "anthropomorphism," a notion that created first Jewish theology and then the Christian theology that came after it. Since the normative and scholarly adjective that generally modifies so-called anthropomorphism is "crude," I am moved to say again that the normative and the scholarly are crude, while J is sophisticated. Her idea of Yahweh is imaginative, even Shakespearean, while the normative reductions of her Yahweh are quite primitive.

Since we are humans and not trees, we are compelled to be anthropomorphic rather than dendromorphic. The god of a tree will share in the image of a tree; our God will share in the image of a human. J's imagination was uninhibited; the religious version of imagination is always stunted by anxieties of representation. A superb early instance of normative procedure comes in Deuteronomy 4:12–18, where we are told that the host at Sinai heard Yahweh's voice but saw nothing, even though J clearly says that the elders, at their picnic on Sinai, saw Yahweh face to face. As the revision of J proceeded (in my judgment) from E through D and on to P, ending in the R palimpsest that we have now, the human attributes of Yahweh consistently diminish. And yet he remains in R what he always is for J, a person and a personality, the most extraordinary of all personalities. It is in Jewish theology, from the Alexandrian Philo through Maimonides, that the anthropomorphic, so called, vanishes all but utterly, a process carried still further in Christian and Muslim theology.

One can speculate that the history of Western theology is haunted throughout by the unassimilable personality of J's Yahweh; that haunting may be the force that still drives theology along. Yet the impetus to theologize Yahweh has also had the paradoxical effect of remythologizing Judaism, Christianity, and Islam. As God is rendered more abstract, the whole realm of demonology opens up as a substitute for the lost color of personality. A fine early example served as one of my own starting points of preoccupation with the scandal of how J has been weakly misread by normative conventions. A Pharisaic writer in about 100 B.C.E. composed the Book of Jubilees, also called the Little Genesis, though it includes the Exodus and is far more prolix than Genesis and Exodus. Jubilees indeed is a normative travesty of Genesis and Exodus, far more severely, say, than Chronicles is a normative reduction of 2 Samuel. But though he himself is a boring writer, what is wonderfully illuminating about the author of Jubilees is that he totally eradicates J's text. Had he set out deliberately to remove everything individual about J's share in the Torah, he could have done no more exquisite a job. Gone altogether is Yahweh's shaping of the red clay into Adam and then breathing his own breath into the earthling. Gone as well is Yahweh at Mamre, where only angels appear to Abram and Sarai, and so there is no subsequent haggling between Yahweh and Abram on the road to Sodom. Not Yahweh but Mastema, satanic prince of the angels, brings about the trial of Abram in the Binding of Isaac. Jacob and Esau do not wrestle in the womb, and there is no night wrestling at Penuel between Jacob and a nameless angel. Joseph lacks all mischief and consequently all charm, and the agony of Jacob and subsequent grandeur of the reunion are lost to us. Most revealingly, the uncanniest act in J, Yahweh's attempt to murder poor Moses on the prophet's way down into Egypt, is ascribed to Mastema. And wholly absent is J's most enigmatic vision, the Sinai theophany, an absence that allows the safe removal of J's too lively Yahweh back to a sedate dwelling in the high heavens.

If the Pharisee who wrote the Book of Jubilees was a believer in Yahwism, then clearly the Yahwist herself was something else, and that something else is my subject in this book. She was a writer, above all else—an assertion that few biblical scholars will accept. Should that seem anachronistic, I would simply point to the astonishing strength of the writing. Why does someone of immense literary power write, whether now or three thousand years ago? Doubtless there are hosts of reasons, but I think essentially it comes down to the Blessing: more life, into a time without boundaries. But authors did not have names until the times of the writing prophets, someone may object. David, in some of the Psalms, had a name, as did Solomon, in some of the Proverbs, and perhaps in her own day, in Judean court circles, J had a name also. That name is lost to us, but the Book of J is not. To call it theology, history, epic, saga, document, prophecy, or even religious writing strikes me as just plain wrong. It is a series of extraordinary stories, the stories of how the people of David became a people, and the stories of how Yahweh created the Blessing of life and then extended it to many, at some cost to himself, and thus prepared for the Blessing given to David and Solomon. But if you want to call it the story of Yahweh, you certainly can; yet you would be wrong to call it the history of Yahwism.

Though Judaism, Christianity, and Islam are descendants of Yahwism, they are all belated versions of that archaic faith, the origins of which, insofar as they lie beyond J, are not available to us. Judaism essentially is the religion founded by the great rabbis of the second century of the common era; it asserts its continuity with the tradition that goes from early Yahwism through the Prophets and then on eventually to the Pharisees, but that assertion is almost as arbitrary as similar Christian assertions. Since my own principal assertion in this book is that the Yahwist herself is not *a* Yahwist but a tale-teller taking Yahweh as her protagonist and Yahwism as her matter, my reader may begin to feel a certain bewilderment or even fury at not being told exactly what Yahwism was, anyway. But like the scholars of early Yahwism, I do not know, though I am very willing to make surmises. Whatever Yahwism was, I follow J in refusing to believe that Moses was its founder, and again like J, I choose instead the archaic figure of Abram, who became Abraham. Religions do need founders, even as strong literary works need authors. Just as "oral traditions" do not compose works of aesthetic shape and value, even so oral traditions do not found cults of worship or modes of divine service. Bernhard W. Anderson, an excellent biblical scholar, introduces his translation of Martin Noth's indispensable *History of Pentateuchal Traditions* by insisting, "It is still true that, as the first Prophet of Israel, Moses was in some sense the founder of Israel's religion and the fountainhead of Israelite tradition." But J clearly did not think so. Here I am happy to cite Gerhard von Rad yet again, because my experience of reading J's text is very close to his assessment in *Old Testament Theology* (vol. 1, 1962).

> In an examination of the narrative strands in J, it is amazing to find how really slight is the role which the narrator has assigned to Moses in all these manifold events. . . . What then, in J's view, was Moses? He was no worker of miracles, no founder of a religion, and no military leader. He was an inspired shepherd whom Yahweh used to make his will known to men.

At that, von Rad gives J's Moses much the best of it. He is not particularly inspired, though he is certainly used, and even ill-used, by Yahweh. Reluctant at first, and then doggedly stubborn, Moses plods along in J, loyally trying to make up in zeal what he lacks in zest. I take it that her rather low opinion of Moses is what inspired the zestful J to begin so far back. J's greatest originality surely was in linking a vision of primeval origins to the patriarchal story, and then combining the result with the tales of Joseph and an account of Moses, the Exodus, and the wanderings in the Wilderness. Yahwism, or the human response to Yahweh, begins for J with Adam, passes to Noah, and culminates in Abram. Whether J believed in the historicity of her Abram I cannot know, but then her ironic handling of Moses may mean that she doubts even the first prophet's historicity. I suspect that real history, the reign of mere fact, began for J with the transition from Saul to David. Her Yahwism, if it can be called that, began with David, but of course she knew that Yahweh was both the given and the giver long before David. A lifelong monarchist, as I read her, a distruster of priests and people alike, she had more faith in David than in Yahweh. Her Yahweh moves her at the rare moments when he is Davidic. What she could accept, in the days before David and Solomon, was the kingship of Yahweh rather than the images of Yahweh as a solitary warrior.

I find support for this reading of J in *Canaanite Myth and*

Hebrew Epic (1973) by Frank Moore Cross, though Cross would hardly have endorsed my irony that J preferred David even to Yahweh. Cross traces in J's work what he calls "the Judaean Royal Theology," but what he describes as the ideological work of J and the Court Historian of 2 Samuel again does not seem to me so much a theology as a monarchist idea of order. Yahweh is not the center; David and Solomon are. The unconditional pledge concerning Solomon and his descendants, made by Yahweh through Nathan to David in 2 Samuel 7:12–16, deeply colors all of J's versions of the patriarchal covenants. Those versions invariably suggest the dimensions of David's domains at their greatest extent, from the Nile to the Euphrates, and embracing much of what is now Lebanon and Syria, if only as vassals. Even the transition from David's military state to Solomon's commercial empire is emphasized subtly by J, particularly in the indubitably ironic formula that foretells a blessing for every other people through the promise made to Abram (Gen. 12:3). Christian theologians and Bible scholars delight in this passage, since it is one of the foundations of Christianity, but J slyly ironizes the meaning of "more life" in this context. This is not the Blessing, as it were, Davidic and heroic, but only a blessing, Solomonic prosperity and civilization. J is hardly unaware that the individuality of the Israelites was much diminished in the passage from David, who held on to tribal traditions, to Solomon, whose "wisdom" necessarily entailed becoming yet another Oriental despot. And always ahead in J's text are the falling shadows of Rehoboam and what will come after, the division of the kingdom into Israel and Judah.

If a description of *the* Yahwist as not being a fervent believer in Yahwism seems altogether too paradoxical, one ought to remember that J's fundamental scheme is paradox, even as J's rhetoric relies upon the wordplay of false etymologies and puns. Nothing in J is quite what it seems to be, and since Yahweh is for J just the name for reality, Yahweh also cannot ever be what he seems to be. It is J who introduces into the Western consciousness our permanent distrust of appearances. Notoriously not a visual author, J makes dynamism and movement count for more than the external world as we see it. No other great writer cares less than J does to tell us how persons, places, and things look. Since J's Yahweh is not invisible but speaks face to face with Adam, Eve, Abram, Jacob, Moses, and a large group of elders on Sinai, we certainly would wish J to describe Yahweh to us. But then, J does not tell us what anyone looks like. J's art, and not the Hebrew language, invented the most characteristic element in the Hebrew Bible, which is a preference for time over space, hearing over seeing, the word over the visual image. I do not find much connection between J's modes of representation and the Yahwistic prohibition of graven images, beyond my occasional wonder as to whether J's temperament may have produced the first intimation of what became a national religious peculiarity, and afterward a traditional aesthetic limitation, which from a literary viewpoint was much more a strength than a limitation or inhibition.

To prefer the word over the image is to be wary of representing one's passion, the image of one's desire. J chose never to represent David directly, but nearly all her work centers upon the representation of Yahweh. For J, representation is always a matter of so imitating reality (or Yahweh) that the mimesis establishes the precise degree of commensurateness or incommensurateness in the struggle between any two figures. Probing psychological elements in the stories of how Yahweh deals with Abram or Jacob or Moses is the heart of J's activity as a writer. The extraordinary vividness of J's art depends upon its ability to convey restless interactions between persons, persons and groups, individuals and Yahweh, groups and Yahweh. Even covenants must be subsumed under that phrase, "restless interactions," for there are scarcely any limits to J's dynamics of irony.

Covenants, as J well knew, were the particular devices by which the ancient Israelites first became a people. As J clearly demonstrates, the Israelites were not a people that became a religion but rather a religion that became a people. The formula of a religion becoming a people catches up the context of J's work, for the movement from Samuel to Saul to David to Solomon is essentially the story of the kingship of Yahweh passing to the Davidic royal house. Yahwism, in J, is not the service of the transcendental but instead a storytelling in which the Blessing diffuses itself until it becomes the possession of an entire people wandering in the Wilderness of Sinai. Cross shrewdly presents his own formula for J's achievement: "Kingship in Israel became rooted in creation and fixed in eternity." This is the basis for J's fivefold repetition of Yahweh's Blessing, made three times to Abram and once each to Isaac and Jacob: Genesis 12:3, 18:18, 22:18, 26:4, and 28:14. If all the families of the earth are to find a blessing in Israel, if Yahweh is to bless those who bless Israel and curse those who curse Israel, then one sees why the last major sequence that J wrote is the Balaam story in Numbers. One sees also why J's imaginative transposition of the glory of David and Solomon back into the mythic era of the Patriarchs became the literary basis for biblical prophecy from Isaiah on, and why J, rather than the author of 2 Samuel, became the precursor of the visions of the Messiah, both of the House of Joseph and the House of David, and at last of the Gospel of Mark's visions of Jesus as the fulfillment of his ancestor David's renown.

An imperial Yahwism is not to be regarded as a Yahwism without Yahweh, but it does work to distance Yahweh, to return him to the origins. J begins as one must begin, wholly with a solitary Yahweh, and certainly shows us an active Yahweh down to the moment when, with his own hands, he buries Moses. The Conquest of Canaan, and the subsequent age of the Judges, did not belong to J's subject. For J, her work and the Books of Samuel were enough: she would have been happy to see the national Bible culminate just there. With the advent of David, Yahweh leaves the stage and is present only as the anxious, fatherly, exasperated love, behind the scenes, that will guarantee the good fortune of David and his house, perhaps forever. J's Yahweh, in Genesis and Exodus alike, is seen implicitly as waiting for David without quite knowing that he waits. That J knows more than her Yahweh does, at least in this one respect, is a dramatic irony that is decisive in determining J's tone and stance in regard to Yahweh. This may be why her Yahweh begins as a creative imp and remains so playful and childlike until his anxious theophany upon Sinai. The truly theomorphic man, David, is stationed between the outer limit of J's subject as a writer and her own historical moment as a human being. J looks back through the sophisticated splendors of the Solomonic period, and what she sees is the heroic vitalism of David. She never ceases to keep her eyes on that charismatic glory, but what she hears, and makes us hear, is the story of the realities of the remote past that were transformed forever when they were seen as the necessary prelude to David.

Of the views of theological scholars on the nontheological J, von Rad's seem to me much the most accurate, since they stress how much we rely upon J for our authentic information as to the nature of Yahweh: "We have to realise that in fact we owe all the information that we have about the early ages in Israel solely to the work of the Jahwist who preserved and rearranged it." For "preserved and rearranged" I would substitute "imagined or reimagined," because J certainly created Yahweh though she did not invent him. I am very dubious, as I have said throughout, whether there is an E source. Whoever gave us E was conscious of J, and Exodus 3:14, always assigned to E, seems to me as much revised from J as the Binding of Isaac was, if I am correct. The God who says to Moses, "I will be [when and where] I will be," present or absent as a pure consequence of will, is a very J version of God, punning elaborately upon his name, Yahweh, and the verb of being, *ehyeh*. The essence of J's Yahweh is *ehyeh asher ehyeh*, or the power that is perpetual potential.

If J is as late as some scholars have argued, if indeed, as I myself suggest, she outlived Solomon, then it is of some importance that we seek to surmise what visions of Yahweh she had taken as her own starting point. What archaic Yahweh did she reimagine? The question is quite unanswerable, since all we have is J. Only she can take us back beyond herself, and here we run right up against her refusal to answer our preconceptions. J is not

a religious writer, unlike D or P or R. Yahweh is taken for granted by J. She assumes that you know who and what he is, and so she is quite matter-of-fact about Yahweh, equally so when he is present and intervening, and when he is absent and events go on with no apparent reliance upon him. This characteristic J shared with the Court Historian, and perhaps she learned it from him, or perhaps here, as elsewhere, these two great writers exchanged influences. I resort to von Rad again for a scholarly statement on this Solomonic Enlightenment in which J and the Court Historian shared, but I will then suggest a literary critical modification of von Rad's emphases. Here is von Rad on the Yahwistic secularization (to call it that for a moment).

> This reality—we should say Nature and History—became secularised, and was, as it were, overnight released from the sacral orders sheltering it. In consequence, the figures in the stories now move in a completely demythologised and secular world. Unquestionably, we have here to do with the traces of an Enlightenment on a broad basis, an emancipation of the spirit and a stepping out from antiquated ideas. It did not mean, however, any abandonment of belief in Jahweh, nor was it a veering to an attenuated rationalised piety. Jahweh too had taken this road: out in this desacralised, secular world as well he allowed men to find him.

If J "believed in Yahweh," it only meant that she trusted in the Covenant, which for her, as for the Court Historian, meant the covenant with the House of David. I swerve from von Rad when I observe that the distinction between sacred and secular writing is always a sociopolitical and never a literary judgment. J is so strong a writer that you say something only about yourself when you call J's work religious or secular. It seems to me no more religious than Shakespeare, and rather less so than Tolstoy. That the era of David and Solomon was a great literary period we know: the Psalms, the Song of Songs, 2 Samuel, the Book of J—we are on the sublime heights of Hebrew imagination. If Yahweh took an enlightened path, then J set him upon it. Man, as von Rad says, is at the center, from J's Creation story onward: "This newly-awakened appreciation of the human, this focusing of attention upon man, this interest in the psychological and the cultivation of rhetoric, give us every right to speak of a Solomonic humanism."

It might be better to speak of J's Yahweh and the Court Historian's David as instances of a Solomonic vitalism, or of a Davidic Blessing. I would be very hesitant to speak of Yahwistic humanism; the uncanny is too steady an element in J's representation of Yahweh. What von Rad phrases splendidly is J's concept of what he calls the theomorphic.

> Actually, Israel conceived even Jahweh himself as having human form. But the way of putting it which we use runs in precisely the wrong direction according to Old Testament ideas, for, according to the ideas of Jahwism, it cannot be said that Israel regarded God anthropomorphically, but the reverse, that she considered man as theomorphic.

It is at the center of her work that J sets the theomorphic David, unspoken but invariable. But her Yahweh is both more and less than anthropomorphic: he is wild and free, an almost unconditioned impulse. There is a glint in J's eye whenever we receive a portrait of Yahweh, for his restless dynamism will not consent to be confined. Of all J's beings, Jacob is the most theomorphic, because he is the most vital in his restlessness, his desperate quest for the Blessing. Not that Jacob much resembles (or is much loved by) the incommensurate Yahweh; one could never say of Jacob what J says of Jacob's son Joseph, in William Tyndale's wonderful phrasing: "The Lorde was with Joseph, and he was a luckie felowe." To be a lucky fellow is to be a charismatic, imbued with a strong touch of Yahweh's own passionate vitality. Vitality can be defined as the prime characteristic of J's Yahweh, since all life whatsoever has been brought into being by him. He stands beyond sexuality, as he stands beyond men and women, because he created human sexuality when he created both a man and a woman. His *dynamis* is not therefore to be confused with sexual love, and J casually takes it for granted that Yahweh is not a sexual being. He has no gender; he is pure will, as well as willfulness, which may be why he is open to the charge of what a Catholic reader might want to contend was a kind of haggling. There are survivals in J of an archaic Yahweh, about whom we know less than nothing. Presumably he was a solitary warrior-god, though surrounded sometimes by a pesky collection of angels, who seem not to have been particularly pleased by the creation of humankind. J's Yahweh is neither the archaic Yahweh, concerning whom I will venture some speculations shortly, nor the more familiar God of rabbinical doctrine. J's Yahweh is not endowed with such rabbinical attributes as holiness, purity, and goodness, though he does have some relationship to truth and justice, that is to say, his truth and justice, which are not necessarily our own. His leading attribute is zeal or zest, so that the zestful and zealous David is clearly the most theomorphic of humans.

"Man" is one of the ancient rabbinical names for God, though discarded when it seemed to verge upon the doctrines of the *minim*, or Gnostic heretics. J's incommensurate Yahweh's more human qualities may be an ironic echo of archaic Judaism, and return me yet once more to the vexed issue of J's anthropomorphism. The great scholar of Kabbalah, Moshe Idel, who yet will seem the antithetical completion of Gershom Scholem, has pioneered in applying the elaborate conceptual structures of the Kabbalah to earlier Jewish material, in the Talmud or in Midrash, in order to reconstruct coherent images of beliefs otherwise not available to us. I do not wish to apply Kabbalist concepts to J, but Idel's work has convinced me that archaic Yahwism, before J, was wildly anthropomorphic. The Priestly Author says that man is made in the image of God, meaning, I think, that man is a kind of aesthetic representation of God, a small-scale, rather dim figurine compared to the gigantic, light-blazing reality of what is being imitated. J is far too subtle to make any such assertion. Her Yahweh presumably imitates his own form in molding Adam, but we do not know that. We can assume that J's auditors considered that Yahweh once had made the Elohim, who evidently were sexual beings, but we do not know whether those contemporaries of J assumed that Adam and the woman were more beautiful than the Elohim, as is attested both in rabbinical and in Gnostic traditions. Probably that is J's implication, so that we are to understand that Yahweh or Man is fashioning Adam or man. What we can see for certain is how radically P departed from J in the Creation that now forms the first chapter of Genesis. P gives us a cosmological harvest festival, a great autumnal redemption that has in it overtones both of the miracle at the Red Sea and the Return from Exile in Babylon. It is appropriate, then, that the Egyptian and Babylonian waters recede in the Creation, and that the dry land be emblematic of the land of Israel. J, who did not take the crossing of the Red Sea too seriously, and who lived long before the Babylonian Exile, sets her landscape in the dry wilderness and gives us a first spring in which Yahweh's will-to-life rises as a mist, allowing a garden to be planted. P's sublime Creation is a cosmos; J's gentle irony is content with an oasis.

Yahweh in J is not a gentle being, and his deliberate ironies tend to be ferocious. They transcend Kafkan irony, though they are precisely Kafka's source. Founded as they are upon the play of incommensurates, Yahweh's ironies move toward two limits, the first at our creation, where Yahweh implicitly says to us, "Be like me; breathe with my breath," and the second at the Sinai theophany: "Don't you dare to be too like me." Later Judaism evaded these ironies, but Protestantism, as I understand it, is always caught between them. Since the scandal of J is her Yahweh, we need a clear characterization of Yahweh, an analysis of him as a literary character. Introduced to us as a solitary, he creates without stated motive, presumably so as to acquire both more context and more companionship. But he insists always upon legislating both context and companionship; that seems a crucial meaning of J's story of the Tower of Babel. J does not condemn the builders of Babel. Their motives belong to all of us; they wish to bring themselves together, so as to arrive at fame, to keep their name from being scattered. In effect, they wish to give themselves the Blessing of more life, but it is not theirs to give. It is not so much that it belongs to Yahweh; it *is* Yahweh. They wish therefore, quite pragmatically, to be Yahweh. Speaking presumably to the other Elohim, his angels, or perhaps even to himself, Yahweh decides to descend, to make one of his familiar terrestrial inspections, and once there makes mischief, baffling language into languages, confusion, ruin, scattering. We have been given J's largest insight into the psychology of Yahweh: he sets limits, boundaries, contexts for his creatures, and he does not allow presumptuous violations of limits, whether by Adam and Eve, Cain, the builders of Babel, or even the Patriarchs and Moses, let alone Pharaoh and the Egyptians.

Yahweh's touchiness about limits indicates at once a lively pride and an anxiety about his creatures. More crucially, it shows an endless exuberance of energy, the vital zest and zeal I have remarked already. The largest difference between J's Yahweh and the more normative versions of God that come after J is that this original Yahweh is just too much for us; he is nonstop and knows no rest. In J's version of the Commandments, there is no Sabbath. Her Yahweh is presence, is the will to change, is origination and originality. His leading quality is not holiness, or justice, or love, or righteousness, but the sheer energy and force of becoming, of breaking into fresh being. What we encounter in him, however, is not an abstract becoming or being but an outrageous personality, a person who is more than a person yet never less than a person. He is not holier than we are, as far as J is concerned; she has not the slightest interest in holiness. He is in every sense livelier than we are, because he is not to be distinguished from living more abundantly, living more like David, who had exhausted every human possibility yet went on in fullness of being, open to more experience, more love, more grief, more guilt and suffering, more dancing in exuberance before the Ark of Yahweh.

THE PSYCHOLOGY

OF YAHWEH

SCHOLARS TEND to agree that the Israelites dominated Canaan only from about the twelfth century before the common era. Even then the land teemed with an extraordinary variety of peoples: Canaanites, Amorites, Hittites, Philistines, and many others. The heroic David, throughout his career, was surrounded by non-Israelite freebooters and mercenaries, and the cosmopolitan Solomon opened his empire to commercial and social relations with all neighboring peoples, and some remote. J does not seem to me any more patriotic or nationalistic than she was devout. Her disdain for Rehoboam and for Jeroboam seems about equal. Where, then, beyond those to David and Solomon, are her loyalties? No one—not Yahweh, Moses, Aaron, the priests, the people—seems to emerge from the Wilderness of Sinai with her complete esteem. Though evidently a monarchist, J manifests what could be called a politics of disdain. Can we surmise any ideological or moral design in her work?

I return to what various authorities have judged to be J's greatest originality: the scope of the Book of J. It begins with the creation of Adam and passes through Eden to Cain and on to Noah and the Deluge. Then come the great cycles of Abram, Sarai, Isaac and Rebecca, of Jacob and Rachel, of Joseph, of Moses, Pharaoh and the Exodus, and of the wandering in the Wilderness until the blessing of Balaam and the death of Moses. The one binding figure in this great variety is Yahweh, a unique God who remains the precursor of what is called God by Judaism, Christianity, Islam, and even the secularists of the Western world. J's principal character is God, but her Yahweh remains too original a representation for tradition to assimilate, down to our moment. That representation is intimate but neither loving nor awed. Whatever J was trying to do for herself, as a writer and as a person, she chose to do it through a portrait of Yahweh. Had she written directly of David and Solomon, Yahweh would have been peripheral to her subject. She chose otherwise, and whatever her work does and means can only be interpreted by asking what her Yahweh does and what he means. Why is it so hard to describe him, particularly since he is at once the most idiosyncratic and the most universal of J's figures?

J is not a wisdom teacher, and education hardly seems to be her purpose in writing. Nor is she wholly a student of the nostalgias; she chose not to write of David. Celebration of the past, even of the origins, is not her design. Scholars, biblical and otherwise, always warn against anachronistic interpretations, but there are none possible of J, or of Shakespeare. Writers whose powers of representation are overwhelming do overwhelm us, they contain us, we scramble to catch up to them. Shakespeare changed us by changing representation itself; twenty-five hundred years before him, J did the same. Until Shakespeare, no writer equaled J in portraying the psychology of men and women. Where no one has yet equaled J is in depicting the psychology of God. What is the personality and character of J's Yahweh? How does the psyche of Yahweh differ from that of Shakespearean man? And since Freud inherited Shakespearean psychology, how does Yahweh compare to Freudian man? I return us to Yahweh on the road to Sodom so as to see him in close relation to Abram, and to move out from that relation to the contrast with dramatic representation in Shakespeare and psychic cartography in Freud.

From the standpoint of normative Judaism, Christianity, and Islam, J is the most blasphemous writer that ever lived, far surpassing the beleaguered Salman Rushdie. So little anxious is J about blasphemy that we generally are too startled to realize how uncompromisingly uncanny her Yahweh is. Her Yahweh is always getting out of hand, more even than her equally Shakespearean Jacob. Since Shakespeare and Tyndale, the principal translator of the English Bible, wrote the same idiom, and since Shakespeare learned so much from J via Tyndale's lasting effect upon the Pentateuch in the Geneva Bible, we are likely to get the hallucinatory feeling sometimes that J was influenced by Shakespeare. I do not think that J was much interested in any distinction between fable and history (nor was Shakespeare), but it is worth remarking often that Yahweh's crisis of nerve in J, the Sinai theophany, is caused by the passage from the fabulous to the supposedly historical. Here I want to emphasize another passage, where Yahweh refuses a crisis.

When Yahweh, two angels, and Abram walk down the road to Sodom together, J gives us Yahweh speaking to himself in a revelatory monologue, which we need not take literally.

> "Do I hide from Abram what I will do? Abram will emerge
> a great nation, populous, until all nations of the earth see
> themselves blessed in him. I have known him within; he will
> fill his children, his household, with desire to follow Yah-
> weh's way. Tolerance and justice will emerge—to allow what
> Yahweh says to be fulfilled." (42)

There are two troubling possibilities as to the ironic relationship between an archaic Yahwism and J's stance toward Yahweh. One would see J, an ironic opponent of Yahwism, as sometimes satirizing lost cultic attitudes toward Yahweh. The other, which I find more persuasive, beholds in J a more sophisticated distancing from Yahwism, an attitude too aristocratic and worldly for belief or disbelief. I recur to my biographical fiction of J, which I again insist comes after my interpretation of J, and is dependent upon that interpretation, rather than determining my exegesis. A great lady of the Davidic house, living under Rehoboam, is separated from popular Yahwism by the half-century of Solomonic Enlightenment, with its eclectic and syncretic tolerance for many versions of belief. J writes of Yahweh in a way at once intimate and estranged, as though he is her familiar and yet she is always prepared to be surprised by him, which means that unlike ourselves, she never is altogether surprised. Walking on toward Sodom, the well-fed and rested Yahweh (having had his midday meal at Mamre in the shade of the terebinth trees) reflects that it is, after all, Abram whom he has known within. "Known within" in Rosenberg's translation renders the verb usually translated as "known" in the Authorized Version, whenever it is used in the context of sexual experience. Here it refers to having been chosen for the Blessing, singled out or picked among so many as the unique bearer of Yahweh's election. If Abram has been acknowledged, ought Yahweh not to give his favorite a sense of Yahwistic "tolerance and justice"? The idiom could be rendered also as something like "righteousness and justice," but there is an apt, ironic coloring in Rosenberg's choice of "tolerance" in the context of the impending destruction of Sodom, where "tolerance" could also be rendered as "charity." It may be justice, in a very harsh mode, we want to murmur, but can this be tolerance? What, according to J, is Yahweh's motive for destroying Sodom?

A noise or outcry has been augmented from the Cities of the Plain, Sodom and Gomorrah, conveying to the hearing of Yahweh the outrage of their contempt for his way. Yahweh himself is bitterly ironic: "As their contempt grows heavy, it rises" and weighs on him to descend. Disturbed by the clamor, Yahweh has been brought down, in more than one mode, and if his inspection finds offense, he will pull the cities down also. His angels descend toward Sodom at his words, but Abram stands to one side, confronting Yahweh, and then draws close for the most remarkable dialogue in J, indeed in the whole of the Hebrew Bible. But before I examine that dialogue closely, in more detail than in my Commentary, I must anticipate the subtle J by reflecting upon the "contempt" that Sodom and Gomorrah have shown for Yahweh.

Essentially the sin of the doomed towns is inhospitality, now as then a betrayal of the nomadic ideal. Jewish legend, some of it in earlier versions doubtless available to J, emphasized the wealth and greed of Sodom and Gomorrah as the cause of their savagery to strangers, who were exploited, robbed, starved, and indeed forcibly sodomized. J takes all this as known by her audience but gives us an instance anyway, when the mob gathers around Lot's house and demands that the wayfarers come forth to receive Sodom's customary salutations. It is of some importance for us to realize that this particular activity, or local custom of doing an unkindness to strangers, is not in itself more than part of the sin of Sodom and Gomorrah. Doubtless it is the most vivid part, but the cruel inhospitality is the larger outrage, of which homosexual rape is only the symbol or synecdoche. Tolerating the violence of Sodom would be a lunatic mode of tolerance, by any standard.

Why, then, does J's Abram confront Yahweh to plead that the offending cities not be destroyed? After all, J's Abram is not P's Abraham, "father of a multitude," sage and holy, though he is impressive enough, particularly because of this resistance on the road to Sodom. Yet nothing J has portrayed earlier in her Abram prepares us for his audacity in his magnificent and humane haggling with Yahweh. Abram in Egypt, exploiting his "sister" Sarai's relation to Pharaoh, is rather reprehensible, and his reaction to Sarai's cruelty to Hagar is simply craven. Before both Pharaoh and Sarai, Abram acts as though he, bearer of the Blessing, is scarcely commensurate with the earthly monarch and the wife he confronts. Standing before Yahweh, knowing himself to be only dust and ashes compared to his creator, Abram nevertheless behaves as if he were everything in himself rather than nothing in himself. He speaks with the highest respect to and for the incommensurate, and yet he is remarkably aggressive. We have just seen him entertaining Yahweh and the angels, as hospitable as Sodom is inhospitable, and we have heard Yahweh resolving to bestow upon Abram the dignity of letting the patriarch know what will happen to ungracious Sodom. But Abram has not heard him, and so the point must be Abram's immediate awareness of Yahweh's compliment to him. He speaks to Yahweh explicitly as the man of the Blessing, the unique man whom Yahweh has acknowledged and inwardly known. That returns us to the personality of Yahweh, the deep question of his motivation. What moves him to extend the Blessing, what moves him to augment Creation, what indeed moved him to create, anyway? Why were the angels not sufficient company for him?

J, as I continuously insist, is an author who tells stories, and not a theologian. Yahweh's holiness is of little interest to her, but his zeal or exuberance is Yahweh, to J. In P, and throughout the Hebrew Bible except for J, Yahweh's holiness and his zeal are not to be distinguished. Again I come back to a contention I make throughout this book: to read J we need to clear away what her revisionists did to her Yahweh. Her uninhibited anthropomorphism, to call it that, mingles differences in degree and in kind, so that our distinction of such differences is worn away. Yahweh, in J, looks like a man because he is the creator of man, but he is not a man. Yet like men and women, Yahweh is a person and possesses a personality, an uncanny personality, in his case. One index to his personality is his own words, acts, truths. Another is the theomorphic qualities in his favored beings: Abram, Jacob, the Davidic Joseph, Tamar, but not Moses. Vitalism, the drive for more life, is always the mark of J's Yahweh. The haggling at Sodom between Yahweh and Abram turns itself around that center: ought the creator of life to destroy it when it has come to show contempt for him?

Martin Buber, in his essay "Abraham the Seer" (1939), accurately says that on the road to Sodom, Abram "utters the boldest speech of man in all Scripture, more bold than anything said by Job in his dispute with God, greater than any, because it is the word of the intercessor who is moved by the purpose of his intercession to lose even the awe of God." The purpose of Abram's intercession is to augment life by reminding Yahweh just who Yahweh is, or is supposed to be. Of Yahweh's "Divine Demonism," Buber remarks in his *Moses,* "It was proper to withstand Him, since after all He does not require anything else of me than myself." I do not know that I would speak of J's Yahweh as a "divine demon," but at least Buber catches what the biblical scholars seem deaf to, or are too pious to hear, the daemonic element in J's Yahweh. Abram certainly apprehends it, and moves to withstand it, for the sake of life, which means for Yahweh's own sake. Perhaps that is J's deepest imaginative stance and purpose in portraying Yahweh: Yahweh sometimes must be struggled with, for his own sake, since in struggling for the Blessing, one affirms the life of Yahweh. That sounds more normative than I think it is, but if life itself is the only good, if Yahwism is a daemonic vitalism, then Shakespeare's Falstaff or Chaucer's Wife of Bath is more in J's spirit than is the prophet Jeremiah or the Jesus of the Gospels, except perhaps for the Jesus of the Gospel of Mark.

Yahweh resolves to pull down Sodom because its inhospitality diminishes life and so shows contempt for the creator of life. Abram's perspective is necessarily different: for him Yahweh seems in danger of forgetting his promise to Noah after the Flood, and in danger of forgetting also how fragile life can be, how difficult human birth can become. Abram's desire is for justice, in the very precise sense of demanding that Yahweh be accurate in seeing the difference between the innocent and the contemptuous. Such a demand is made against the uncanny element in Yahweh himself, who is asked to be canny, to be *heimlich* or familial, rather than *unheimlich,* in the Freudian meaning of "the uncanny." Hence J gives us the sublime but rather menacing comedy of the wary Abram haggling with the unwary Yahweh, arguing him down from fifty innocent to forty-five to forty to thirty to twenty to ten as the number for whose sake the inhospitable cities will not be destroyed. Always pressing further, repeatedly urging Yahweh not to lose patience with him, watching carefully the doubtless mounting impatience of the zealous God, Abram ventures to "speak further—for the last time." And after Yahweh proclaims, "I will

not pull down on behalf of these ten," J makes wonderfully clear
that incommensurateness has reached its limit.

> Now Yahweh, having finished speaking to Abram, went on. 3 0 3
> Abram turned back, toward his place. (43)

"His place" is both literal and a return to the commensurate, and
Yahweh indeed makes clear that he has "finished speaking." Yet
we have hardly finished reading the phases of this difference
between Yahweh and Abram.

Let us begin again by reflecting on the uniqueness of the
representation of Yahweh, since no other biblical author has anything like it. In a Shakespearean aside, Yahweh has struggled with
himself, resolving that he must communicate his likely judgment
to Abram because Abram merits it, having been known or singled
out for the Blessing. To let Abram know is to recognize his dignity,
to enhance his life. Yahweh has extended himself before, by creating, and by a kind of covenant with Noah. He now realizes that
this covenant, with Abram, is different, since it has not only the
preservation of life as its intent but the burgeoning of life. That
is so close to the center of Yahweh's own restless dynamism that
the creator and the creature, Yahweh and Abram, seem enveloped
by a common aura as they bargain for the lives of Sodom on the
road to its destruction. Clearly Yahweh undergoes a change in his
aside as to whether he will tell Abram, and even more clearly
Abram changes remarkably in courage, compassion, and dignity as
he argues for mercy. The ethics of these changes interest me rather
less than does J's representation of change itself. I return therefore
to the center of my own argument in this book: how does J's
Yahweh appear if we read him against Shakespearean representations of character, and how does the psychology of God in J
compare to the psychology of man in Freud? This is the sign of
J's permanent originality in the creation of character, for no other
writer has given us so uncannily persuasive a portrait of God.

Shakespeare's greatest originality was in representing his characters in the act of changing by first overhearing themselves speak, whether to themselves or to others, and then pondering their own words, and moving on the basis of the pondering to a will to change, and then to change itself. J's Yahweh and Abram are not Shakespearean characters in that full sense; though Yahweh speaks to himself, he scarcely listens to his own speaking or ponders it, and he certainly has no will to change. But he does change, if by no means necessarily for the better. Perhaps Jacob wears him out a bit, and his patience diminishes steadily throughout Exodus until he loses it on the approaches to Sinai. By the time he leads the host in wandering through the Wilderness, he is a thoroughly violent and irascible personality, given to dreadful outbursts against the mob to whom he has been extending the Blessing. His trouble, I outrageously venture, is that he is not Shakespearean enough. I would contrast him to Shakespeare's Lear, who is purged by the passage from fury through madness to compassion and reunion with his daughter Cordelia. J's Yahweh is necessarily an even more formidable and daemonic paternal personality than Lear, who I think is modeled implicitly on the Yahweh of the Geneva Bible, Shakespeare's Bible. Lear's fury at the actual ingratitude of Goneril and Regan, and the supposed failure of filial love in Cordelia, evokes the shocking anger of J's Yahweh in Numbers 14, where he threatens to destroy the entire people in the Wilderness, insisting even when he yields to Moses' pleas for mercy that only Caleb, Joshua, and the little children will survive to enter the land. Since J's Moses himself is included in this interdict, presumably because Yahweh finds even Moses too stubborn or unfaithful, we seem justified in regarding J's Yahweh as a giant version of Shakespeare's Lear, a Lear who cannot be softened into a renovated consciousness.

And yet we need always to recall that the Yahweh who pulls down Sodom is also the Yahweh who emboldens Abram to protest, precisely when he acknowledges Abram. This is also the Yahweh who allows himself to be seen by poor Hagar after she is cast out.

Though he casts out Cain, Yahweh also protects Cain by his saving mark. We have, J makes clear, no standards of measurement that will work for this most incommensurate of all personalities, who combines in one overwhelming ambiance the complex natures of a Lear, a Hamlet, a Prospero, even a Falstaff. Martin Buber remarks in his fierce *Moses* that "where Yahweh is, there the whole of divine demonism can be found as well." We are close to the center of J's Yahweh again, and so to one of the origins of Shakespeare's representations of daemonic intensity in his tragedies. But here I want to turn to another of J's legatees, to Freud rather than to Shakespeare. In "The Uncanny" (1919), Freud reminds us that the uncanny or daemonic "is in reality nothing new or foreign, but something familiar and old-established in the mind that has been estranged only by the process of repression," that is, the process of unconscious but purposeful forgetting. J's Yahweh troubles us most because he too is nothing new or foreign but something familiar and old-established in our mind that we have forgotten, purposefully though unknowingly. In Freudian terms, then, who is Yahweh, or rather, since Freud did not believe in Yahweh, what does the daemonic force or uncanniness of J's Yahweh tell us about our own repression, our own estrangement from a reality that nevertheless keeps pulling us back and away from our own narcissism?

Freud's overt views on Yahweh, in his *Moses and Monotheism,* are rather weak and uninteresting, but that is not Freud's true vision of Yahweh. J's uncanny Yahweh erupts into late Freud as the Superego of *Civilization and Its Discontents.* The Freudian Superego just about *is* J's Yahweh, and causes our unconscious sense of guilt, a "guilt" that is neither remorse nor the consciousness of wrongdoing. Rather, Freudian guilt is a Yahwistic irony: it comes from the unfulfilled wish to murder our father and creator, Yahweh. We do not know this guilt as an emotion; we know it as depression, anxiety, the failure of desire, the castration complex, as all of negativity taken together. And precisely here, in one of the greatest of ironies, Freud is J's descendant and is haunted by

J's Yahweh in the figure of the Superego. The Punch and Judy Show element in Freud's scenario of the relations between Superego and hapless Ego is precisely like J's dark comedy of the relations between Yahweh and the hapless Israelites in the Wilderness. Yahweh and the Superego keep demanding that Israelites and Ego surrender all their aggressivity, and with each fresh surrender the wretched Israelites and Ego are berated still more strenuously, whacked harder for harboring unconscious aggressivity toward the creator and father. Poor Ego never will enter the Promised Land, because the personality of Yahweh is one with the daemonic intensity of the Superego.

Throughout this book, I have asked the reader to work back through three stages of varnish, plastered on by the rabbis, the Christian prelates, and the scholars, stages that converted J into Torah, Torah into Hebrew Bible, and Hebrew Bible into Old Testament. To read J, you need to clear away three sealings-off, three very formidable layerings of redaction. But if you will do the work, then as Kierkegaard says, you will give birth to your own father. Yahweh and Superego are after all versions of yourself, even if the authorities have taught you to believe otherwise. To say it another way, J's Yahweh and Freud's Superego are grand characters, as Lear is a grand character. Learning to read J ultimately will teach you how much authority has taught you already, and how little authority knows.

THE BLESSING:

EXILES, BOUNDARIES,

JEALOUSIES

A PERVASIVE EMPHASIS in the Book of J is that exile is an ironic reduction or displacement of the Blessing, a substitution of wandering in a space without boundaries for coming home to a time without boundaries. Rehoboam, to J, must have seemed a wholly ironic exile from what ought to have been the United Monarchy of David and Solomon, an exile within the confined boundaries of little Judah. And yet there is, as always, a whole range of ironies in the elliptical and profound Book of J, more ironies, I am certain, than any single exegete can uncover. Is there not a critique in J of those who hold the Blessing, and yet also a critique of the Blessing itself? Is anyone except Yahweh himself strong enough for a life without limits? Can such an existence be desirable, except for a David? Was it a sorrow even for him?

Here are J's three great tropes of exile.

The earthling was driven forward; now, settled there—east of Eden—the winged sphinxes and the waving sword, both sides flashing, to watch the way to the Tree of Life. (10)

"You may work the ground but it won't yield to you, its strength held within. Homeless you will be on the land, blown in the wind."

"My sentence is stronger than my life," Cain said to Yahweh.
"Look: today you drove me from the face of the earth—you
turned your face from me. I return nowhere, homeless as the
blowing wind. All who find me may kill me." (14)

From there Yahweh scattered them over the whole face of
earth; the city there came unbound. (29)

The expulsion from Eden, the dispossession of Cain, the fall of the
Tower of Babel: these are three metaphors in J for the passage from
Solomon to Rehoboam, with the subsequent coming apart of the
United Monarchy and the sad reduction of the City of David to the
center of the small hill kingdom of Judah. Implicit in these tropes
of exile is what can be called the stuff of prophecy to come: the
fall of Israel and the later fall of Judah. But think of the five-
movement shape of the Book of J.

1. The Primeval History; or, Eden and After
2. The Patriarchs: Abram and Jacob
3. Joseph and His Brothers
4. Moses and the Exodus
5. In the Wilderness

The design is palpable, ending not with the Conquest of Canaan
or with the Judges, let alone with Saul, David, and Solomon, but
with the entire people wandering, and not permitted to enter Canaan. Images of exile in the primeval history culminate in the
Wilderness and in the death of Moses, still outside the land, and
allowed only a longing prospect of the promise fulfilled. The Blessing can be realized only in Canaan; indeed, in one sense the
Blessing *is* Canaan. All of the Blessing is equivocal, J intimates,
but this is a more than Solomonic wisdom. J's Yahweh, at Sinai
and later in the Wilderness, is concerned to fix boundaries between
himself and the Israelites, lest they trespass and be destroyed by
him. Without boundaries separating them from the incommensu-

rate, they cannot survive. Yet Yahweh's Blessing intends to award a temporal freedom from the bounded. Can the Adamic dust sustain the Blessing? To be Davidic or theomorphic is J's ideal, but evidently her irony reaches even the ideal, and a seriocomic exuberance always shadows the Blessing.

Wisdom in Israel, Gerhard von Rad's true subject, seemed to him the particular product of what he termed the Solomonic Enlightenment. If my surmise as to J's date is accurate, then she knew Proverbs 10–29, generally dated to the reign of Solomon. Yet she never seems to me a wisdom writer, despite her portrait of the wise Joseph. Her Joseph is wise because he is charming; for J the dull are unwise, and she scarcely bothers with dullards. To qualify for the Blessing, you need not necessarily charm Yahweh, as David and Joseph do, but you must not be dull. Jacob is clearly light-years livelier than Esau, and even Judah is considerably more interesting than are those passed-over brothers, Reuben, Simeon, and Levi. Of Abram we can at least remark that he increases in our interest as his cycle goes along. J's Moses is a curiously flat, hesitant, even estranged personality, but then he himself does not bear the Blessing. Perhaps J gives us so equivocal a sense of the Blessing only because David is never her explicit subject. For J, David is not there for the sake of the Blessing but rather the Blessing is there for David. And that, I surmise, explains the role of the Blessing in J's primeval history and in the patriarchal and Joseph sagas. Yahweh is questing for David, trying out the Blessing on those who can sustain it best.

How well does J's Abram sustain it? The crucial text, if we had it, would be J's original Binding of Isaac, but what we have, the so-called E version, has no trace of J's language, and features an Abram who will not do for Isaac what he ventured for the sake of Sodom. We have no vision of Abram in exile akin to those we have of Jacob, Joseph, and Moses, and will have of David when he is cast out by Saul. I suspect that J's imagination might have risked doing more with Abram in Egypt except that the Blessing extended to Abram is different in kind from those conferred upon

Adam and Noah: more life, in this third Blessing, cannot relate only to progeny, since the entire point of Abram is not what he is but what he will become, a particular people. This provided the elliptical J with an enormous problem in representation; Abram, in himself, does not convey the literary force of the Blessing of Yahweh. We do not behold in him a great agonist, as Jacob will be, or a charismatic like Joseph or David. Nor do we see much of leadership in him, not even as much as J's Moses will manifest. It may be that exile or falling away is a necessary metaphor for J's imagination, which is to say, for J's Yahweh.

If we return to J's three figurations of exile—the winged sphinxes or cherubim with their waving sword; the homeless Cain, wandering in the blowing wind; the scattered builders of Babel unbound in confusion—we find therein three extraordinary images, each of them illuminating the Blessing through their startling negativity. J intends the expulsion from Eden to remind her auditors of the two cherubim in Solomon's Temple, very formidable gold-plated wooden sculptures with animal bodies (and so four legs), human heads, and birds' wings. Under the shadows of those wings was the golden Ark, containing the supposed tablets of Moses. Since the cherubim in that Holy of Holies constituted the throne of Yahweh, the implication is that Yahweh is also enthroned upon the cherubim who guard the way back into Eden. Exile is thus subtly associated with the invisibility of Yahweh, and also with the golden calves set up by the breakaway usurper Jeroboam at Bethel and Dan. There is an obvious critique here of Jeroboam, but a subtler irony is being ventured against Solomon, whose Temple imitates the expulsion from Eden and so is as much a withdrawal from the Blessing as is the secession of the north under Jeroboam. J's metaphor of the expulsion from Eden thus indicts, not Adam, but Jeroboam and Rehoboam, and most profoundly Solomon.

The exile of Cain, on these models, seems to me J's warning against the brother-murder of wars between Judah and Israel following Jeroboam's secession, and the third Yahwistic figuration of exile, the scattering of Babel, previsions an even darker fate for the Israelites, in consequence of the unbinding of the United Monarchy. The ultimate exile is confusion, the scattering even of boundaries, the loss that is namelessness. All this, in my view, returns us to J's central if equivocal concept of the Blessing. Yahweh, who himself is *olam,* or time without boundaries, pure duration, cannot give his own attribute as a gift without involving the favored one in all the dilemmas of incommensurateness. To fall out of the Blessing is to be driven into exile, but to be wholly within the Blessing is to run the risks of having too few boundaries set between oneself and Yahweh. It seems to me that J's heroines bear the Blessing better than her male protagonists, except for the extraordinary father-son combination of Jacob and Joseph. Davidic as J's Joseph is, her women are more clearly heroic, and certainly more vitalistic. They are also craftier than the men, except for the cunning heel Jacob, and they are certainly more jealous, which brings us yet once more to Yahweh's qualities and to the nature of his Blessing.

When J's Yahweh refers to himself as "jealous," he means burning with zeal, the zeal of the divine warrior, the truest mark of his vitality, his daemonic force. This zeal is the heart of the Blessing, and its pathos or felt intensity is conveyed as desire, possession, power, the converse of which comes close to sexual jealousy. In possessing the one to whom his favor has been extended, J's Yahweh has trouble maintaining boundaries. Indeed, he has a lively anguish of contamination, the divine version of an anxiety of influence. This explains his equal revulsion from other gods and godlings, and more interestingly from representation of himself, with presumed exceptions for the Ark, the Tent of Meeting, and the cherubim in the garden and in the Holy of Holies. To represent Yahweh is to compromise his relentless dynamism. For J's Yahweh, as for the pathbreaking David, as for J, everything that matters most is perpetually new. And it is J's women, more than her men, who live at the edge of life, rushing onward, never in a static present but always in an incessant temporality that generates both hope and anxious expectation. There is a grand hardness in J's women, in Sarai, Rebecca, Rachel, Tamar, and Zipporah, a hardness that perhaps J found in herself, or in Solomon's mother, Bathsheba. They are jealous of and for life even as they grasp at the Blessing, lest it slip away from them. If J *was* a great lady at the court, a *Gevurah*, then she would have appreciated that the *Gevurah* or hardness of Yahweh, his dynamic power, was also the trait she had chosen to represent him by, rather than his holiness or his righteousness.

What unites J's women is a *Gevurah*, a hardness in which they surpass most of J's men. "Hardness" may be too indelicate a term here; the American "toughness" might suffice. Elliptical and economical as always, J goes beyond herself in the art of giving us vivid breakthrough of representation, catching up the personalities and characters of these fierce matriarchs. Adam's nameless wife, later to be Hava or Eve, is as much a child as Adam, but Hava's descendants are wise women, deeply conversant with the harshness even of more life, with the equivocal elements in the Blessing of Yahweh. I think of Sarai's bitterness when she first says that Yahweh has held her back from having children, and so drives herself to suggest that Abram beget a child upon her Egyptian maid, Hagar, who becomes the mother of Ishmael. "I have been hurt on behalf of you," Sarai says to Abram (37), and drives the pregnant Hagar away with jealous cruelties. Yahweh's angel, or Yahweh himself in unredacted J, sends Hagar back to Sarai's cold eyes, showing that Yahweh, unlike ourselves, does not like Sarai the less for her jealousy. Yet it is Yahweh who is affronted by Sarai's derision when he promises her a child also. Her theomorphic quality is not to bear contempt, any more than Yahweh will tolerate it. When we last hear her in J as we now have it, a triumphant laugh is her proper farewell to us: "But I gave birth to a son—not to wisdom—for his old age" (48).

Rebecca, an even tougher being, establishes her *Gevurah* in the outrageous scene she devises for the hoodwinking of Isaac in order to secure the Blessing for her favorite, the shrewd Jacob, rather than Isaac's provider of game, the natural man Esau. Grimly funny as the scene is, its audacity at usurping a Blessing that must take place with Yahweh's approval would be quite astonishing were it not for Rebecca's toughness. Her reaction to Jacob's fear of a paternal curse is a quite cool taking of any such curse upon herself, and we are meant to notice that Isaac speaks of giving Esau his very own blessing, while Rebecca blasphemously adds the approval of Yahweh. Contrast her boldness not with her weak husband but even with the slyness of her son Jacob, and one begins to understand something in J's spirit that is wholly other from the spirit of any other biblical writer whatsoever. Rebecca is not only Jacob or Israel's mother; she is the source, the fountain of Israel's will. Her caprice, her preference for her younger and smoother twin son, is sacred to her, and she hammers her will upon history. When Jacob stands against the deathly nameless angel of Yahweh at Penuel, he stands stubbornly in the place of his mother's immovable will. It is Rebecca's *Gevurah,* manifested in her preferred son, that struggles with one of the Elohim even as it has struggled against men, and it is Rebecca's *Gevurah* that prevails.

Rachel, because of her tragic early death in giving birth to Benjamin, might seem an odd entrant in this pageant of toughness, but she very nearly matches her mother-in-law's intensity of will. I can begin to see in J's matriarchs the origins of the Protestant will whose heroines dominate British and American fiction: Clarissa Harlowe, Austen's protagonists, Hester Prynne, the moral visionaries among the women of George Eliot and Henry James, Lawrence's Brangwen sisters. Rachel, stubbornly faithful to Jacob's love even when he, the master trickster, is tricked by Laban into marriage with Leah, holds to her own will, to her own desire. Yet we remember her most vividly for her own impishness, her own outrageousness, the theft of her father's household gods or figurine idols, the *teraphim.* As Speiser remarked, we see a very resolute woman taking the law into her own hands in order to guarantee her husband's share in her inheritance. The wonderfully weird humor of Rachel's sitting upon the idols, and telling her father that she cannot rise because a woman's period is upon her, is wholly characteristic of J, Chaucerian to her core, and also deftly blasphemous when we recall the normative recoil from menstruation, a recoil that came early enough in cultic tradition so that J fiercely mocks it here.

Strong as the earlier matriarchs are, J gives us new heights of the will's intensity in Tamar's entire project, and in Zipporah's desperate and successful defiance of Yahweh. As I have meditated upon Tamar at some length in my Commentary, here I prefer a final overview of what was surely one of J's favorite personages. We would like to know how Judah initially chose Tamar for the sickly Er, his firstborn, but J does not tell us. Thomas Mann, in J's wake, imagines Tamar as working through Jacob to sway Judah to the choice, and since Tamar as much as Jacob is a struggler for the Blessing, that seems persuasive enough to me. Tamar triumphs, on her own terms; she forces her way into the story and becomes the ancestor of David. Yet it is characteristic of J that the cost, for a questing woman, should be so high. When Judah accepts Tamar as the mother of the twin sons who will be born to her, he also resolves never to be intimate with her again. She has achieved her vision and has become the mother of the Blessing, but without a husband, since her father-in-law has begotten his own grandchildren, as it were. Judah can scarcely bear the Blessing; Tamar has the might to do so, in pride of will but in lifelong loneliness. It is not that she, or Jacob, in any way desires the other, but rather that she has chosen pragmatically to be without a husband. Mothering the future, this fountain of David's monarchy has seen to it that except for her twin sons, she will live and die alone in the present.

J's Moses, even at his rare best, never stands up to Yahweh as does his wife, Zipporah, in the frightening bridegroom-of-blood episode. Sometimes I associate Zipporah with the other bitterly laconic biblical woman, Job's nameless wife. As the afflicted Job sits upon the ashes of his existence and scratches his inflammations with a potsherd, his wife cries out to him, "Do you still retain your integrity? Curse God and die!" Zipporah, who comes earlier, surpasses Job's wife in bitter eloquence even as she smears the blood from their infant son's foreskin between the legs of Moses: "Because you are my blood bridegroom." Spoken to a barely conscious, perhaps dying man, this has grand force, since it is intended actually for Yahweh, who is abashed enough by it to withdraw from his murderous and mysterious attack upon his own faithful prophet. Few moments in J, or elsewhere in the Hebrew Bible, match the strength of Zipporah's still bitter but triumphant modification of her remark after Yahweh has departed: "A blood bridegroom marked by this circumcision," which may be a redaction of J. To have acquired a bridegroom of blood as your share in the Blessing is to have to bear a hardness that the prophetic bridegroom himself is unable to bear. The zealous Yahweh has evoked the powerful defensive zeal of Zipporah, but for which the capricious and daemonic God would have murdered his own prophet.

Exiles, boundaries, jealousies, are curiously intermingled in the psychic space created by J's Yahweh whenever he extends the Blessing. The host at Sinai is the largest instance of this intermingling in the Book of J, since the ultimate cost of the Sinai theophany is the forty-year wandering in the Wilderness. The Exodus, for almost all who took part, was not a pragmatic liberation from exile but a new exile, an ultimate dying in nomadism. Whatever the Blessing was to be for the children of the host, for the people themselves it became a martyrdom. Forlorn of his self-protective boundaries, the zealous Yahweh became still more the zealous (or jealous) God. J, perhaps contemplating Jerusalem under the dwindling Rehoboam, leaves us with an ironic vision of the Blessing as Yahweh, with his own hands, buries his prophet Moses in an unmarked grave, outside the boundaries of the land. Pragmatically, Moses dies an exile, still in the service of his fiercely jealous God.

CONCLUSION:

THE GREATNESS OF J

BY COMMON CONSENT, the Yahwist is one of the small group of Western authors we identify with the Sublime, with literary greatness as such. J's peers are Homer, Dante, Chaucer, Shakespeare, Cervantes, Milton, Tolstoy, Proust, and only a few others. Recovering J, which is the purpose of this book, is obviously a more difficult project than is the direct confrontation with Homer or Shakespeare, since their texts are not so literally enfolded or embedded in revisionist censorings and usurpations. And yet I would assert that the difference between confronting J's greatness and Shakespeare's is more a difference of degree than one of kind. Shakespeare's text is, more or less, much more readily available to us than J's is, but Shakespeare's originality remains as veiled from us as J's, and for startlingly similar reasons. We have been so influenced by J and her revisionists, and by Shakespeare, that we are contained by their texts more than we contain them. Our ways of representing ourselves to others are founded upon J's and Shakespeare's way of representing character and personality. Since J's prime character is Yahweh, we ought to reflect that the West's major literary character is God, whose author was J. That peculiar mark of J's originality and greatness was my starting point in the long process that led to this volume, and so quite properly it must be my conclusion as well.

Being the author of the author, or writing God, would be an

impossible burden for even the strongest of our writers in this century, and sheer tact has kept them from it, with an exception or two like the intrepid James Merrill, in his remarkable *The Changing Light at Sandover.* Blake and Victor Hugo in the nineteenth century were equally courageous (or tactless), but Milton's disaster in *Paradise Lost,* where God's failure as a literary character is the only blemish on an otherwise sublime work, seems to have warned others away. J lived three thousand years ago, and her freedom in portraying Yahweh seems to have no shadows in her work. It certainly has shadowed others, and should remain a scandal and a blasphemy today. J's Yahweh is a person in a far more radical sense even than the Jesus of the Synoptic Gospels. The mysterious personality of Jesus, which has charmed the centuries, is not marked by the terrifying extravagances that burst forth in the career of J's Yahweh. We do not see Jesus suddenly becoming murderous toward a favorite disciple, but that distance from J's Yahweh may be the point of the most fascinating version of Jesus, in the Gospel of Mark, the only Gospel that is in the spirit of the Yahwist, a tendency pointed out to me by Barry Qualls. The Yahweh of J, rather than the Priestly Author's or the Redactor's normative Yahweh, seems to be the acknowledged father of Jesus in Mark.

I have written throughout this volume in the conviction that J was a dramatic ironist, interested in her story and in her personages, rather than a historian or theologian. If scholars wish to protest that aesthetic achievement is only a by-product for a biblical author, I would begin by noting that J hardly wrote or could have written *as* a biblical author. There was no Bible at all until some six centuries after J, and the Bible as we know it, whether as text or interpretation, came into being after yet another six centuries, among the canon-making rabbis of the second century C.E. Most of what was available to J in Hebrew doubtless is lost to us, but what we have, embedded in J's text or preserved elsewhere, like the magnificent War Song of Deborah and Barak in Judges 5, is sufficient to show that what we call the aesthetic impulse preceded J in Hebrew literature. It is considerably more anachronistic to regard J as a historian or a theologian than as a prose poet. She is a narrator on the grandest scale who combines, for the first time in Hebrew or indeed in any language, every genre available to her in ancient Near Eastern literature, in which I believe she was deeply read and schooled, as would befit a high sophisticate who may have lived through the cultural splendors of Solomon's literary era. If I suggest further that Solomon's was a literary culture rather than a religious one, I again am involved in nothing like anachronism. Syncretic and eclectic, Solomon's time already had elements that were to develop further in the Hellenistic Jewry of Alexandria a thousand years later, or in the literary culture, Jewish and Gentile, of our own age. J's imagination, urban and speculative, is not bound by any constraints of cult.

Confronting J, or Shakespeare, directly in order to describe their greatness is a dire activity, and not now much in critical fashion. Historicizing J, more than minimally, seems to me as vain as historicizing Shakespeare, whether in modes old or New. The strongest writers have the knack of overrewarding even a lazy or casual reading, indeed any reading whatsoever. Shakespeare's originality, his lasting strangeness, is singularly difficult to recover, and so is J's. We owe Shakespeare so much that we have a tendency to believe either that he held a mirror up to human nature or that he *was* human nature. He has become human nature, because to a remarkable extent he reformed it, shaped it anew, though that hardly could have been his intention. J's intention, so far as I can know, was to tell or retell the story of her people and their God, from her own perspective and with her own seriocomic irony. Shakespeare wrote so powerfully that he has become a universal author, domesticated in languages and cultures even he could not have imagined. J, though in a guise fixed by her revisionists, has become an even more universal author, and has served moral, spiritual, and institutional purposes beyond even her ironic capacity to imagine or sustain.

Universal authors, whether they are creatively or weakly

misread, are those few who have an imbuing power, the power of
J's Yahweh: dynamic, unbinding even as it binds, unbounding
even as it sets boundaries, redeeming time rather than space,
inspiring the auditory more than the visual freedom of the reader.
The Bible is true, in one way or another, to most who read it
regularly; it confirms or even defines extraliterary belief. J, like
Shakespeare, works between truth and meaning, just as belief
does, but neither J nor Shakespeare seems to me a believer,
whether in Yahweh or in Yahweh and Christ, at least not a believer
as most people believe. J and Shakespeare, being poets upon the
heights of the Sublime, do not waste their energies by choosing
forms of worship from poetic tales. They work rather to represent
reality, but in the urgent mode of compelling a perpetually fresh
reality to appear. The British scholar A. D. Nuttall wonderfully
says of Shakespeare that he alone allows us to see aspects of reality
that we could not see without him. Reality appears, rather than
remains latent, because Shakespeare summons it; he does not
imitate a reality already manifest. Clearly J compelled reality, or
Yahweh, to appear, in the uncanniest form in all Western tradition
since. J's Yahweh and her theomorphic men and women are far
closer to Shakespearean characters than are the gods and humans
of Homer. We listen to J relating the long agon of Jacob, from the
womb until burial, and we come to know Jacob as I do not think
we can come to know even Odysseus. The contrast between J's
Jacob and Odysseus is akin to the similarly fecund contrast between 2 Samuel's David and Achilles. Jacob and Odysseus present
many parallels, in personality and in experience, both being heroes
of craftiness and stratagem, resourcefully wily, and both striving
toward an end to strife. The difference is between Yahweh and
Zeus, which is the largest element also in the difference between
David and Achilles, both of them charismatic leaders, heroic warriors, poets, men whose name never will be scattered.

In calling J a prose poet, I mean something like a prose
Shakespeare, because J's narratives have a Shakespearean exuberance of invention, and her language brims with ceaseless wordplay,

as does Shakespeare's. I do not mean that J wrote prose epic or saga. We need to be like wise children in reading or listening to J, because her mode, and not just in the primeval history of humankind, is like a more sophisticated kind of children's literature than any we now possess. Her Yahweh is a wise child's Yahweh, and her Joseph is the ultimately wise child. Kafka intuitively apprehended the essence of J's art, and of all Western authors he resembles her most when she is in her uncanniest vein. Here is one of his parables concerning Abraham.

> Abraham's spiritual poverty and the inertia of this poverty are an asset, they make concentration easier for him, or, even more, they are concentration already—by this, however, he loses the advantage that lies in applying the powers of concentration.

These are ironies in J's spirit. Abram's poverty, or imaginative need, is the malaise that causes him to be sent forth by Yahweh. It is also the childlike quality in him, for a child shares in Abram's ache of poverty, in the inertia that is a concentration already, since we cannot distinguish between imaginative need and imagination. J's poetic, like Kafka's, centers on disarming us, making us like children, helping us to lose the supposed advantage that lies in applying our powers of concentration. This is a poetic of surprise, fit for a cosmos created and perpetually visited by J's Yahweh. Perhaps J and Shakespeare resemble one another most in the endless newness of their imaginative worlds. Despite Yahweh's curiosity and his power, his creatures are made free to invent and reinvent themselves constantly, and that is the law of being for Shakespeare's protagonists also. In Freud, you are always overdetermined; your character is your fate, and your character is fully formed in your infancy. In Homer, you are also overdetermined: even Zeus is subjected to fate. J's Yahweh is subjected to nobody, not even to Yahweh. He is an imp who declines to overdetermine anyone or anything. That is the splendor of his Blessing:

more life means that everything is possible, because the dynamism of Yahweh is one with all that is potential. Jacob is born a heel, clutching at Esau's heel, and he remains a heel and goes on clutching in desperation. And yet Jacob rises to the agon when Yahweh sends a nameless angel against him, and wrestles as an uncanny hero, not a heel. Jacob wrestles as Israel, and so becomes Israel, because Jacob prevails. Everything will keep coming hard to him; he will suffer terrible loss and grief, but he will triumph, not because Yahweh determines it, but because the writer J chants the song of perpetual human becoming and overcoming, the chant of dynamic Yahwism, the exuberance of being. Call it puckishness even, because there is something of J's Yahweh in Shakespeare's sprite, Puck, and something more of him in Shakespeare's rare sprite, Ariel. Perhaps that is the characterization I have been seeking throughout this book: there is more of Ariel than of Prospero in J's Yahweh.

J has a Shakespearean vivacity of invention, and I never forget that Dr. Samuel Johnson, the best of all critics, taught us that the essence of poetry is invention. Victor Hugo remarked that after God, Shakespeare had invented most. J invented God, though I would not want to argue that J altogether matches Shakespeare as an inventor. It is not that Shakespeare's range is greater or that his characters are more profound, their personalities more vivid, or even that Hamlet, Shakespeare's David, is a more comprehensive imagining than any single figure in the Yahwist's work. There is always Yahweh himself to set against Hamlet. J, like Homer, is just a touch short of Shakespeare because Shakespeare's men and women change by overhearing themselves, pondering what they overhear, and then resolving to change. J's characters have will, and they change, but they do not have the will to change, unless you want to give that as one of the meanings, or consequences, of sharing in the Blessing.

J's great advantage over Shakespeare, her one advantage, is the Blessing. Even the wisest and most passionate of Shakespearean beings—Hamlet, Rosalind, Falstaff, Cleopatra—cannot be said to have the Blessing, which does not exist in Shakespeare, except perhaps in the Forest of Arden, where the superb Rosalind has her being, but which will not always be her habitat. We see Shakespeare's most favored figures, whether tragic or comic, at their apogee, but not advancing toward more life in a time without boundaries. J and Shakespeare share in a vitalism, Solomonic and Elizabethan, that may ensue from the floodtime of two nations, ancient and Renaissance, but only the poet of and at the origin has a clear sense of the Blessing. "Exuberance is Beauty," William Blake's motto, sums up J and Shakespeare alike. Neither was a moralist, or God-intoxicated. I find them deeply consonant with one another.

Translator's Appendixes

DAVID ROSENBERG

Appendix A
Notes on the Translation

I. A POET'S PROSE

When I began this work, the first certainty to learn was that J would not use a phrase, not a single word, without playing upon it, sometimes in the same sentence, sometimes in the next. Every word was a fresh one, because the nature of the play, shading from light to grave, was unpredictable. A translation requires that every English word also be chosen with an ear to its tone and weight—and with a healthy skepticism toward simplification. This poet of narrative makes every sentence of description or dialogue sound as if nothing had been described or said before.

In Hebrew J's sentences, like lines of verse, are strung together in stanzas rather than paragraphs. Since the conventional biblical chapter divisions are arbitrary, made by later editors, I gave J a chapter sequence that more naturally follows the breaks in her narrative. Whether she or her editors are responsible for discontinuities, we can only imagine.

More than translation, a reconstruction of the Book of J should risk sensitivity to the original narrative voice. While piecing together chapters and fragments of authoritative J, I imagined the structural density of the original Hebrew, which echoes clearly in many parts of the existing text. I've hoped to restore a measure of its rhythmic gravity.

·　　·　　·

Jewish tradition provided the figure of Moses as leader-writer. Along with David and Solomon, who are author-figures for other biblical books, he embodies the kind of hero we don't have in Western history: a national leader who is also a great poet. In postbiblical Jewish culture, bereft of a nation (until our time), the model of a leader-figure in itself was difficult to imagine, especially one who is a potent artist. Yet in this century we have seen great poets of the Hebrew language, and a lament by Bialik, a mythic story by Agnon, or a sonnet-psalm by Leah Goldberg is comprehensible beside the biblical canon. And that is how the voice of J crystallized for me: it was not until I read the modern Hebrew poets that I could imagine the biblical authors as living men and women.

J's stories are told or retold in scenes: as if the author were there when they were happening, as if she were a witness. This poet was not concerned with a conventional storyteller's pose, the marshaling of points of view, but with the *stance* of the poet: the witness who pares away a needless virtuosity of conventions observed. The intense drama makes the action resonant with poetry: we hear the poet present as she weighs each word and sounds it against the others.

The play of word with—and within—word produces a basic poetics of diction and rhyme. It is a diction based on Hebrew phrasing that can only be translated into English if it is recreated. The King James translation embodies the standard for English diction but substitutes much of J's ironic stance—the way she shades meaning—with a less modulated grandeur. Later translations, especially recent ones, give up both grandeur and irony in one fell swoop of reduction.

Likewise, the rhyme in J is shaded, an off-rhyming in Hebrew, primarily assonance and consonance. To parallel it in English requires an ear for ironic repetitions as well, since a greater range of variations on word roots is possible in Hebrew. Repetitive devices and a sophisticated sense of parallelism characterize J's writing. In his biblical scholarship, Martin Buber dug deep into the use of what he called "word-motifs": "The repetition need not be merely of the word itself but also of the word-root; in fact, the very difference of words can often intensify the dynamic action of the repetition. I call it 'dynamic' because between combinations of sounds related to one another in this manner a kind of movement takes place: if one imagines the entire text deployed before him, one can sense waves moving back and forth between the words."

At a certain point, describing my work to a poet-colleague, I was asked how old I thought the J writer at the time of writing. I was stunned by the question—or rather, by my not having faced it. I had focused on the major taboo nonreligious readers would have to overcome: to imagine the writer as a human being in the first place. So I confronted her age, found her with enough experience of life and history to be just over forty, with a still vital appetite for life. I realized I was only identifying myself, yet the imaginative health in restoring authorship can nourish a tradition limping with taboos.

Jewish biblical commentary is deep and imaginative because it does require an author. In fact, it requires quite a leap to imagine an author like Moses, one who could have written the entire Torah. By contrast, much biblical scholarship can rarely imagine an author of a fragment, and when it does it is unable to imagine him or her as human rather than as a voice of historical accretions.

In Jewish tradition still under the spell of superstition, the taboo against spelling even the word "God" is a sign of great love—an awesome tenderness felt for the creator-father, at its best; at its worst, rote fear. Postbiblical Jewish writers turned to the realm of imaginative commentary—midrash and aggadah—where they might again recreate scenes and conversations with God, as the Bible's writers had.

Modern biblical scholarship arose in European universities, yet in religion departments from Geneva to Oxford, Jews were prohibited. The professors of Bible were of Christian belief or education. The nineteenth-century German scholars who developed the Documentary theories known as Higher Biblical Criticism were charmed by their Christian superiority into primitive misunderstandings of the Hebrew. For myself as a Jew, the discovery of a unified sensibility and imagination in the J writer reveals hidden strength in our heritage, as does midrash and kabbalah. For a reader unwilling to accept the superhuman author Moses, the humanity of J, her art, offers a fresh, modern midrash.

The scholarly sources I followed for extracting the J text are the standard authorities in the field, as refined most recently by Martin Noth and superseded by the insights of Harold Bloom. Overall, I followed a conservative approach to the last hundred years of J scholarship. In some cases, even when I thought I could sense the way J was revised by later hands, I resisted the temptation to improve on the scholars. Yet in other cases, such as Joseph's dream, I did look through the opaque text scholars have labeled E, to rescue pieces of J.

There are many biblical stories in which passages of J are clear while others are clearly edited and revised by R or E (or by yet another redactor scholars call JE) until J's heightened language has been irreparably distorted. I have had to pass over these portions of J's narrative, even though we can reliably ascribe the irony still resonant in the scenes to J. The general outline of the stories can be easily followed in the popular British translation by James Moffatt, where all suspected J texts are printed in italics. Published in 1922, this translation makes no attempt, however, to reproduce the refined prose of J, nor does it reflect recent advances in textual scholarship.

Occasionally, Bloom's interpretation involves speculation about passages of J that appeared adulterated or too uncertainly J's voice for me to translate, unless I applied more poetic license than I wished to. Yet I stand by Bloom's intuition, usually grounded in several scholarly authorities, and supported by the tonal nuances in the Hebrew. Traces of the latter are still conveyed in the King James Version but are often diluted beyond recognition in the modern translations. For the Hebrew, I used Israeli editions of the standard Masoretic text, readily available in Jewish bookstores.

II. ON TRANSLATION

I would like to point out aspects of the translation that indicate my concern for accurate verbal texture. I wanted to avoid the false simplicity that modern translations deliver with smooth clichés, awkward idioms, and undistinguished sound. In almost every case, the simplifiers exchange poetic irony for terse sentiment.

My basic approach to J's diction is typified in the translation of conjunctions (*veh*) and syntax modifiers (*v'yhi* and *hinneh*), which in Hebrew determine the sentence structure. What is translated as "and" and "behold" in the older renderings, and as subordinate narrative clauses in the modern versions (beginning "when," "if," "then," etc.), I have translated as "so" or "so it was," "now" or "now look," "watch" or "listen"—among other variants that allow a structure of shifting tenses, from past to present to past, and create the atmosphere for it. The Hebrew tense is often indistinct, and in the same way the uniform conjunction *veh* often suggests different meanings, depending on context. I wanted to reproduce this contextual richness. Scholarship has often noted the shifts in narrative point of view, particularly from third person to first person.

Not all the "he says" and "she says" and "God spoke untos" were intended for translation; they are not part of a primitive style but sometimes merely a form of punctuation: quotation marks or stage directions. Often the pronoun is willfully indistinct, like the tense. For a moment we are unsure who is speaking. Yet this too allows the author playful ambiguities, and I did not ignore these modulations as do conventional translations.

Further attention is required to J's near-rhyming texture of sound, an alliteration I reproduced in English with consonance and assonance. In most cases, I resisted changes to poetic ambiguity in the Hebrew. And finally, I adopted a chapter structure that allows J's entire text to be read through fluidly, like a novel in a multiplicity of scenes.

What follows are more specific notations of the English style, chapter by chapter. For the corresponding chapter and verse of the Hebrew Bible, consult Appendix B: Biblical Sources.

"Now look," in chapter 1, reflects the Hebrew, where it's crucial that the playful connection between earth and creature be sustained in the play of language. As the creature shaped of earth becomes a man, the poet brings the reader closer, asks us to look upon the scene: the cliché "behold" can't carry the required resonance, and to ignore this drama of the Hebrew narrative—as translations often do—would remove poetry from the text.

In chapter 2, the verb "settled" allows a resonance with later usage, unlike a dulling "put" or "placed." And in chapter 3, "touch," "desire," "watch," and "tend" are among key words the poet will develop further. Where the translation appears to depart from a literal word-for-word slavery, it is for the sake of accuracy: to convey syntactical and contextual nuances in the Hebrew text.

In chapter 4, "partner" and "side" are key words, intimately played upon. The final paragraph puts us up close again, and as we look we hear the recurring "touch" and "know," which echo through to the following chapter.

It is one thing to project psychology onto the snake in chapter 5, in terms like the King James Version's "subtle"; the Hebrew text, on the other hand, sets up a subtle resonance that "smooth-tongued" only begins: "smooth" itself will return in many different contexts, ultimately establishing the character of the snake, which will crawl on its smooth belly. Here too, the repeated juxtaposition of "fall" and "open" is crucial, as is the alliteration of "lovely" and "lively." "Grasp" will become a word intimately played upon. And in the next-to-last paragraph, the man's presence is revealed in dramatic proximity by the quick sketch of inevitable natural processes: looking, thinking, eating, and sharing.

"Smooth-skinned" is a further revelation in chapter 6, as are trees to hide behind. And in chapter 7, "bound" becomes a key word, to develop later into "boundary."

In chapter 8, "having children" is what we do. The Hebrew plays on the sound of Eve's name, associating it by assonance with giving life. Hava's sexual sentence requires some ironic expression of the small pleasures that inhere there. "Eager" and "desire" echo forward, as "give" and "grasp" already echo backward. "Bent" is a key word toward later transformations, starting with a bending to earth. And in chapter 9, "Hava" is closer to the Hebrew than "Eve." "Skins," by picking up the consonance of "smooth," underlies its resonance.

chapter 10, the key words of the immediately preceding paragraphs are played upon in the first paragraph. Suddenly, the Tree of Life is mystical—exclusive province of those godlike beings to whom Yahweh is speaking. And in chapter 11, "conceived" is double-edged, for the further small comforts that naming one's child in the flesh now gives. Yahweh confirms the irony of "conceive" in the final paragraph of chapter 12, as it works in the mind and in the flesh.

In chapter 13, the resonance of "turn" and "watch," previously established, projects forward. And in chapter 14, "soil," "bitter," "face," "voice," and "word" are among the words reflecting the intense play in the Hebrew. Even the ground to which we return, speaks. The new wind that blows is not the spirit in man's nostrils: Yahweh's shaping preservation of Cain's life is darker than it was for his father, whose death was to be unmarked.

In chapter 15, Irad, the first child born in a city, gives his name to the Hebrew for city, *ir*. In chapter 18, there is an echo of Hava's response to the Tree of Life. And in chapter 20, "enter" begins a series of permutations. Variations on the heart's weather begin in chapter 21.

In chapter 30, "bring," "fame," and "blessing" are picked

up from the previous chapter. And in chapter 33, "holding" and "letting go" prefigure the destruction of Sodom in chapter 46.

In chapter 34, "broad," "count," and "contempt" rebound forward; "seed" and "dust," forward and back. "Pass" begins to take on new shadings in chapter 35. And in chapter 36, "part" undergoes further modulation, as does "contempt."

At chapter 37, the uses of "hand" will multiply—immediately in Sodom, and much later when Joseph will also be a servant accused of handling his master's wife. In chapter 38, the assonance produces Ishmael, as sound often works in naming. *Ish* in Hebrew is a man.

Regarding the figure "split sides" in chapter 41, the several contexts for its usage here prevent its popular meaning from obscuring the depths and mysteries of its origins. To begin with, Yahweh "closed the flesh of the side" of Adam, and "returned Hava to the side of the man." But one can think far back in English, to *Cymbeline*, for instance: "O, can my sides hold, to think . . ." (act 1, scene 6); and a bit later, in Milton's "L'Allegro": "Sport, that wrinkled Care derides, / And Laughter, holding both his sides." The figure also mirrors the uncanniness in the passage, from "in the time a life ripens" to "sides split." ("Is a thing too surprising for Yahweh?") Conclusively, out of "sides split" comes the assonance for the naming of I-saac.

(My test for the appropriateness of a figure in English is to consider Dickinson's ear: I try to hear it as she would, so that an idiom must have aged at least a century. Dickinson's ear for a combined religious and secular context is closest to J's for me.)

On the figure "count on it," immediately following "split sides," there are many modulations of "count" throughout the text, from the uncountable stars before Abram down to Sarai's spirited irony with what *she* heard from Yahweh: "Now I can count on giving birth . . . ?" "Ripen" is also undergoing shadings in pitch and resonance here.

In chapter 44, Lot's very human fear, in the end, is tested by the "grasping" of his arm, as well as "his wife's, the hands of his two daughters." But it is Yahweh who revitalizes the figure by "reaching out to him." The play of language in Hebrew is different yet more lively than translations have suggested. Here, and in a few other rare instances, I have departed from the literal Hebrew in order to be true to the text. In one such instance, in chapter 45, I have had to recreate a name in English, Smallah—based on the meaning of the Hebrew word. Since the Hebrew name for this town is also mythical, what counts is the place of resonance in the naming itself. A later town, similarly mythical—"Deifus" in chapter 73—also frames Jacob-Israel against the sun.

In chapter 47, "side," "seed," and Lot's "having her" echo distantly back to Hava's drama. And in chapter 48, "conceive" and "ripe" are paralleled, to reappear later. "Mothered," in chapter 49, recalls Hava's naming. And "veil," in chapter 50, will touch upon marriage as well as justice and revelation, in later chapters.

In chapter 64, "Yahweh stood beside him." In chapters to follow, the overdone "Yahweh is with you" becomes more accurate by being supplemented with "beside," "behind," and "attends." So, further in this chapter, "Yahweh stands by this spot." In J, Yahweh stands and walks comfortably on earth.

The kind of "vision" J prefers is found in chapter 66, the "finely formed" Rachel. And the kind of disarming revelation the author prefers: Leah, of the "exquisite eyes" (and little else worth noting). Later, in chapter 89, the "handsome vision" of Joseph will echo back.

The alliteration in the naming of Joseph parallels the punning in Hebrew, in chapter 70. The idiom "warm heart" and its many variations allow for more vital play in English—to culminate in Pharaoh's hard heart and Moses' singed one—than the less resonant clichés, such as "find favor in your eyes," of the standard translations.

In chapter 73, Israel has "held on" in resisting heavenly

attack. "Yet my flesh holds on" then parallels the naming puns (Peniel/Penuel) of the town already unknown in ancient Israel. Already echoing Jacob's thigh, Dinah's guard "was broken" in chapter 75. His heart "touched," Shechem "had fallen in love"— but Jacob then hears "how he had fallen upon his daughter." In turn, Jacob will "fall upon" his brother Esau's neck, and Joseph on his father Jacob's. "Desire" and "open hearts" further deepen the irony of Jacob's fate among the Canaanites.

"Holy lady" is a deliberate idiom of the townsfolk in chapter 85. And in chapter 86, "linger" recapitulates Tamar's disguise.

In chapter 88, "tend," while reminding us of the world's first human, is a key root for the Joseph story—as is "hand," which prefigures the story of Exodus from Egypt. Later, as Yahweh vows, "I will attend you," in chapter 177, the appointment of Joshua re-echoes the tending in the Joseph story as well as the early "Yahweh lifts the man, brings him to rest in the garden of Eden, to tend it and watch." In a minor key, a variation remembers Yahweh's "tenderness," as well as Lot's appeal, "If this servant has warmed your heart, evoked your tender pity—you have kept me alive . . ."

Noticeably by chapter 90, the punctuation and diction become more mannered, subtle, as the story of Joseph in Egypt advances. The sophistication of the society at King Solomon's court in Israel found an echo in J's expression of Egypt, culminating in chapter 106 in the lively characterization of Pharaohs: "A new king arose over Egypt, not knowing Joseph . . ." The use of "inmates" in chapter 90, for instance, presages a contemporaneous vocabulary; likewise the function of "matured" as a verb. The diction and syntax are colored by irony in the sentence beginning, "Not a fault . . ."

A crucial element of the Joseph story can be found in chapter 95, where "veiled" echoes back to Tamar. Further variations in the alliteration and meaning of key words abound in the later chapters.

In chapter 174, we might find one of several possible traces of the author's personality. If, in the several layers of irony, the ass's mouth is opened to speak for the hidden narrator, it is clear who is riding whom.

Appendix B
Biblical Sources

Chapter number in the Book of J is followed by the corresponding chapter/verse citation in the Hebrew Bible.